The future of asylum in the European Union

Flora A. N. J. Goudappel · Helena S. Raulus
Editors

The future of asylum in the European Union

Problems, proposals and human rights

T·M·C·Asser press

Springer

Flora A. N. J. Goudappel
Erasmus School of Law
Erasmus University Rotterdam
Burgemeester Oudlaan 50
3062 PA Rotterdam
The Netherlands
e-mail: goudappel@frg.eur.nl

Helena S. Raulus
Erasmus School of Law
Erasmus University Rotterdam
Burgemeester Oudlaan 50
3062 PA Rotterdam
The Netherlands
e-mail: raulus@frg.eur.nl

ISBN 978-90-6704-801-9 e-ISBN 978-90-6704-802-6
DOI 10.1007/978-90-6704-802-6

Published by T.M.C. Asser Press, The Hague, The Netherlands www.asserpress.nl
Produced and distributed for T.M.C. Asser Press by Springer-Verlag Berlin Heidelberg

Cover design: eStudio Calamar, Berlin/Figueres

Printed on acid-free paper

Springer is part of Springer Science+Business Media (www.springer.com)

Preface

Asylum law in Europe is currently undergoing great changes. A bit more than a decade ago, with the adoption of the Treaty of Amsterdam, the Community gained competence to adopt measures in asylum, in connection with the Area of Freedom, Security and Justice policies.[1] This has resulted in the building of the Common European Asylum System (CEAS) by the Union.

The goal of the CEAS could be described as creating a European-wide fair, efficient and flexible asylum system. The current framework of CEAS is based on the following main aspects: allocating responsibility for asylum seekers to an appropriate Member State[2]; and creating common standards for processing asylum-seekers,[3] their reception conditions[4] and their qualification as a refugee in the Member States.[5] To continue the development of the CEAS further, the Commission opened a public consultation in the Green Paper in 2007.[6] As a result the Asylum and Immigration Pact was adopted by the Council of Ministers which

---

[1] Article 63 EC Treaty. Now the Union has competence to adopt measures on asylum under Article 78 TFEU, the powers have changed considerably here. Previously the Community could only adopt minimum harmonisation measures, whereas now the Union can adopt uniform measures.

[2] Council Regulation (EC) No 343/2003 establishing the criteria and mechanisms for determining the Member State responsible for examining an asylum application lodged in one of the Member States by a third-country national, OJ 2003/L50/p. 1 ff., the so-called Dublin Regulation .

[3] Council Directive 2005/85/EC on minimum standards on procedures in Member States for granting and withdrawing refugee status, OJ 2005/L326/p. 13 ff.

[4] Council Directive 2003/9 laying down minimum standards for the reception of asylum seekers, OJ 2003/L31/p. 18 ff.

[5] Council Directive 2004/83/EC on minimum standards for the qualification and status of third-country nationals or stateless persons as refugees or as persons who otherwise need international protection and the content of the protection granted, OJ 2004/L304/p. 12 ff.

[6] Green Paper on the future Common European Asylum System, Brussels, 6 June 2007, COM(2007) 301 final.

encourages the construction of "Europe of Asylum"[7] leading to setting up the European Asylum Office, solidarity between Member States on processing asylum applications and creation of a single asylum procedure. By using these means in particular it should be possible to achieve the aims set out in the Green Paper, inter alia, "to establish a level playing field, a system which guarantees to persons genuinely in need of protection access to a high level of protection under equivalent conditions in all Member States while at the same time dealing fairly and efficiently with those found not to be in need of protection."[8]

The EU developments must take into account that asylum law has its underpinnings in international human rights law. All the Member States of the Union are parties to the 1951 Convention relating to the status of refugees and to its 1967 Protocol.[9] Furthermore, the European Convention on Human Rights (ECHR)[10] and, in particular, the jurisprudence of the European Court of Human Rights (ECtHR), has been influential in shaping the standards for the protection of asylum seekers and refugees in Europe.

The Member States are currently debating and new measures are being proposed on how to achieve the bold aims of the renewed CEAS. These aims include creating a single asylum procedure and making sure that the international obligations are respected and potentially also strengthened by the Union. To join in this conversation, the Erasmus School of Law organized a conference "The future of asylum in the European Union. Proposals, problems and interaction with international human rights standards" in April 2009. Scholars and practitioners from many different Member States were invited to discuss the implications of recent developments in EU asylum law and the participants were asked to contribute their views in this book. Even though this book is published two years after the Conference, the building of the Common Asylum System is still discussed in the Union structures and the main discussion points from the Conference are still applicable. The rebuilding of the CEAS is in no means an easy task. These questions for the Conference and the following publication could also be framed using the words of the opening speaker of the Conference, the Dutch State Secretary for Aliens' Affairs at the time, Ms. Nehabat Albayrak:

> ... I would like to give you several questions for further consideration during this conference. First of all: what more can we do to harmonise the European asylum policy, for it to become a reality? Which concrete obstacles have to be overcome? How can we realise that we actually protect the people for whom the asylum policy is intended? Given the large number of well-informed specialists, I would even stimulate you to also think about the long term. How should we proceed [after the Stockholm Programme, after 2014]?

---

[7] The European Pact on Immigration and Asylum, Commitment 4.

[8] Green Paper, *supra* n. 6, p. 2.

[9] Resolution 2198 (XXI) adopted by the United Nations General Assembly, available from http://untreaty.un.org/cod/avl/ha/prsr/prsr.html. There are altogether 144 States parties to this Convention.

[10] Council of Europe, Convention for the Protection of Human Rights and Fundamental Freedoms, available from http://conventions.coe.int/treaty/en/treaties/html/005.htm.

In the organisation of the Conference and process of editing of the book we, the editors, would like to thank following persons. Our student assistants, Caroline Peters and Eva Hendriks, for the original Conference organisation, gathering background materials and for general support. Our other student assistant, Alex Verhoeff, for the painstaking work on changing and bringing the footnotes together.

Rotterdam, April 2011

Dr. Flora A. N. J. Goudappel
Dr. Helena S. Raulus

Contents

1 **Introduction—The Future of Asylum in the European Union? Proposals, Problems and Interaction with International Human Rights Standards** 1
Flora A. N. J. Goudappel and Helena S. Raulus

2 **Conference on Recent Developments in European and International Asylum Policy and Law** 15
Nebahat Albayrak

3 **Border Control: Not a Transparent Reality** 21
René Bruin

4 **The EU Qualification Directive and Refugees *Sur Place*** 43
Sylvie Da Lomba

5 **The Goals of the Common European Asylum System** 65
W. van Hövell

6 **Mutual Recognition in European Immigration Policy: Harmonised Protection or Co-ordinated Exclusion?** 73
John O'Dowd

7 **A Few Remarks to Evaluate the Dublin System and the Asylum Acquis** 111
Juha Raitio

8 **Conditions and Criteria for Determining Asylum** 125
Alessandra Ricci Ascoli

9 The Future of Asylum in Europe? A View from the European Council on Refugees and Exiles 135
Bjarte Vandvik

10 Conditions and Criteria for Determining Asylum 139
Jens Vedsted-Hansen

Annex 1 157

Annex 2 169

Annex 3 187

Index 215

Chapter 1
Introduction

The Future of Asylum in the European Union? Proposals, Problems and Interaction with International Human Rights Standards

Flora A. N. J. Goudappel and Helena S. Raulus

Contents

1.1 State Sovereignty and Asylum Law 1
1.2 Building of Common European Asylum System: from Mutual Trust to Minimum Harmonisation 2
1.3 From Minimum Standards to Uniformity: New TFEU Provisions and European Asylum Support Office 8
1.4 The External Borders and Return Operations 10
1.5 Conclusions 12

1.1 State Sovereignty and Asylum Law

The general principle in immigration is that a State is sovereign to decide who is allowed to enter and stay in its territory. Asylum law is an exception to this, here sovereignty is curtailed under international obligations: all the Member States of the Union are parties to the 1951 Convention relating to the Status of Refugees and

F. A. N. J. Goudappel
Erasmus University Rotterdam, Rotterdam, The Netherlands
e-mail: Goudappel@frg.eur.nl

H. S. Raulus (✉)
Erasmus School of Law, Rotterdam, The Netherlands
e-mail: Raulus@frg.eur.nl

F. A. N. J. Goudappel and H. S. Raulus (eds.), *The future of asylum in the European Union*, DOI: 10.1007/978-90-6704-802-6_1,

the attached 1967 Protocol,[1] and under this regime, the Member States have undertaken the obligation to grant protection for persons who are persecuted in their home States. The category of persons who are entitled to this protection is limited though; according to the 1951 Geneva Refugee Convention only persons facing persecution or having a well-founded fear of persecution in the State of nationality or habitual residence and who due to this fear are unwilling or unable to return to that State, must be given this protection.[2] This protection principle is enforced by Article 33 of the Convention which contains the non-refoulement principle. Under this provision the participating States have undertaken the obligation not to return a refugee to the territories where his or her life or liberty would be threatened.

However, the Member States have retained their sovereignty in interpretation and application of the Convention obligations. They still decide who is allowed to enter and stay in their territory as a refugee by applying independently the notion of well-founded fear of persecution. According to the statistics available from the Eurostat, States have very differing views on how to apply the Convention and whether they grant protection for persons coming from the crisis zones.[3] To a limited extent, the United Nations High Commission for Refugees (UNHCR), the UN Refugee Agency, can oversee that the Convention obligations are respected and, for example, it has published guidelines on the criteria to be used when States are trying to establish whether to grant a person a refugee status.[4] Similarly, the European Convention on Human Rights (ECHR) as interpreted by the European Court of Human Rights (ECtHR) places obligations on the Member States on who is entitled to asylum.[5]

1.2 Building of Common European Asylum System: from Mutual Trust to Minimum Harmonisation

This main premise that the Member States are sovereign to decide on the interpretation and application of the Refugee Convention is also reflected in the development of the Common European Asylum System (CEAS). The first

---

[1] Resolution 2198 (XXI) adopted by the United Nations General Assembly, available from http://www.unhcr.org/3b66c2aa10.html (accessed 14 August 2011). Altogether 144 States are parties to the Convention, and the Protocol. 141 States are parties to the both, three States being only parties to the Convention or to the Protocol separately, source: http://www.unhcr.org/3b73b0d63.html (accessed 14 September 2011).

[2] Article A(2) of the Convention.

[3] For 2010 statistics on the EU Member States, see for example http://epp.eurostat.ec.europa.eu/cache/ITY_OFFPUB/KS-QA-10-042/EN/KS-QA-10-042-EN.PDF (accessed 14 August 2011).

[4] The UNCHR Handbook on Procedures and Criteria for Determining Refugee Status under the 1951 Convention and the 1967 Protocol relating to the Status of Refugees, http://www.unhcr.org/publ/PUBL/3d58e13b4.pdf (accessed 14 August 2011). The Handbook was first adopted in 1979 and re-edited in 1992. See Chap. 8, Ascoli, for further discussion.

[5] Under Article 3 prohibition of torture and inhumane treatment, the ECtHR case law on asylum is raised for discussion in many papers in this book. See, for instance, Chap. 3, Bruin, Chap. 6, O'Dowd and Chap. 10, Vedsted-Hansen for different aspects of the ECHR. See also below discussion on the recent ECtHR case law on the Dublin system.

instrument adopted in asylum law was the Dublin Convention,[6] which was subsequently turned into the Dublin II Regulation,[7] on determining which Member State has the responsibility for processing asylum seekers in the Union.[8] The aim of the Dublin system is to prevent multiple asylum applications by an asylum seeker in various Member States, in other words, prevent asylum shopping in the Union area.[9] Therefore, under the Dublin criteria a single Member State is allocated responsibility for processing asylum seekers entering into the EU.[10] In the Stockholm Programme, which sets the new priorities for the Area of Freedom, Security and Justice, the Dublin system is still referred as "the cornerstone" of the common asylum system.[11]

The Dublin system is based on the mutual trust principle: the national authorities of the Member State where an asylum seeker submits the application are required to transfer the asylum seeker back to the Member State responsible under the rules.[12] The Regulation sets out for the national authorities or courts the obligation to decide whether the asylum seeker is to be processed in that or another Member State and following that, if another Member State is deemed responsible, the procedures for the transfer.[13] A Member State may accept the responsibility for the asylum seeker even if it was not responsible under the Regulation,[14] however, this is only specifically allowed for humanitarian reasons, that is, for family reunification or cultural reasons.[15]

Importantly, mutual trust does not take any account of the divergences between the national systems. There is no explicit exception granted on the basis of divergences between the national systems, and the executing authorities or courts are not required to review the law or decision-making processes of the State responsible under the Regulation. As a result, the national authorities or courts making the decisions on whether to transfer an asylum seeker are not required to consider whether the return has implications for the status of the asylum seeker

---

[6] The Dublin Convention, Convention determining the State responsible for examining applications for asylum lodged in one of the Member States of the European Communities, signed in 1990, OJ 1997/C254/pp. 1–12.

[7] Council Regulation (EC) No 343/2003 establishing the criteria and mechanisms for determining the Member State responsible for examining an asylum application lodged in one of the Member States by a third-country national, OJ 2007/L50/pp. 1–10.

[8] The Dublin system is also applied in Norway, Iceland and Switzerland.

[9] See Dublin II Regulation, Summaries of EU Legislation, http://europa.eu/legislation_summaries/justice_freedom_security/free_movement_of_persons_asylum_immigration/l33153_en.htm (accessed 14 August 2011).

[10] See also Chap. 7, Raitio.

[11] European Council, "The Stockholm Programme—An Open and Secure Europe Serving and Protecting Citizens", OJ 2010/C115/pp. 1–38.

[12] Article 3(1) and Article 17 of the Regulation.

[13] See Articles 17 and 18 of the Regulation.

[14] Article 3(2) of the Regulation.

[15] Article 15 of the Regulation.

on the basis of procedural, substantive or even human rights protection considerations.

This has resulted in a situation that the potential asylum seekers might not be recognised as such in the Member State where they are to be returned. As mentioned earlier, States, including the Member States of the Union, interpret the 1951 Convention in a diverging manner. However, at the same time, each Member State has undertaken the obligation to respect the non-refoulement principle of those persons they consider as qualifying as refugees. Questions have arisen in national courts on the application of the Dublin system that if the Member State where the asylum seeker applied for asylum considered a person as entitled to protection as a refugee, but the Member State responsible under the Dublin system did not, would this constitute a breach of non-refoulement and therefore a breach of the 1951 Refugee Convention? In that case the asylum seeker would be in the eyes of the Member State authorities returned back to the State of persecution. The UK courts in the early cases decided that this would be a breach of non-refoulement and refused to make the transfer unless the asylum seekers were safe from refoulement in the Member States responsible under the Dublin system as well.[16] This approach has also received recognition in obiter from the ECtHR.[17] Initially, one of the problems of the Dublin system was the reluctance of the national courts and authorities to effect the transfers to other Member States.[18] In order for the Dublin system to function properly, the national courts need to trust that the asylum seekers' claims will be duly processed by the other Member State authorities.

The lack of procedural harmonisation may also create hesitation for national authorities or courts obliged to transferring asylum seekers. The conditions and procedural rights guaranteed for the asylum seekers while they are waiting for the asylum decision vary considerably between the Member States. While the international obligations here are not as clear what asylum seekers can expect from their host States, for instance, the UNHCR Handbook is not binding on the States, some indications are available from the ECtHR.[19]

---

[16] *R v. Secretary of State for the Home Department, ex parte Adan and R v. Secretary of State for the Home Department ex parte Aitseguer, House of Lords, [2001] 2 WLR 143 169*, per Lord Slynn of Hadley, at pp. 144–145, "It seems to me that the Secretary of State may not send back an applicant if the Secretary of State considers that the other state's interpretation would lead to an individual being sent back by that state to a state where he has established a fear of persecution which the Secretary of State finds to be covered by the Convention."

[17] *T.I v. the UK*, European Court of Human Rights, Application No. 43844/98, p. 15, "The Court finds that the removal in this case to an intermediary country, which is also a Contracting State, does not affect the responsibility of the United Kingdom to ensure that the applicant is not, as a result of its decision expel, exposed to treatment contrary to Article 3 of the Convention. Nor can the United Kingdom rely automatically in that context on the arrangements made in the Dublin Convention concerning the attribution of responsibility between European countries for deciding asylum claims." See also Chap. 3 by Bruin, who discusses these cases.

[18] See Chap. 7, Raitio.

[19] See Chap. 10, Vedsted-Hansen.

To support the Dublin system, the Community adopted at the following stage the common minimum harmonisation Directives on processing asylum seekers,[20] their reception conditions[21] and their qualification as a refugee in the Member States.[22] These level the playing field and provide some indications for the common standards. However, as pointed out by the contributions to this book, all these are minimum harmonisation measures leaving a wide margin of flexibility for the Member States and there are many provisions where the Member States may choose to lower the standards of protection. For instance, Vedsted-Hansen discusses the optional clauses under these Directives[23] and da Lomba discusses the particular problem of refugees *sur place* under the Qualification Directive in her contribution.[24] There are even doubts expressed whether these provisions fully comply with the standards required under international law.[25]

Although it can be argued that the Qualification Directive sets out equally vague conditions for a person to be recognised as a refugee[26] as the 1951 Convention and therefore, the divergences remain between national systems interpreting the provisions, there are some advances here. First, the Directive also grants subsidiary protection for persons who are in a real risk of suffering serious harm.[27] Second, being a Union law measure, the European Court of Justice is involved in the interpretation of the Directive. National courts can ask preliminary rulings from the Court of Justice on how to interpret the provisions of this and any other Directive in asylum law.[28] The Court of Justice gave already in *Elgafaji*[29] instructions for national courts on how the concept of subsidiary protection is to be

---

[20] Council Directive 2005/85/EC on minimum standards on procedures in Member States for granting and withdrawing refugee status, OJ 2005/L326/p. 13 ff.

[21] Council Directive 2003/9 laying down minimum standards for the reception of asylum seekers, OJ 2003/L31/p. 18 ff.

[22] Council Directive 2004/83/EC on minimum standards for the qualification and status of third country nationals or stateless persons as refugees or as persons who otherwise need international protection and the content of the protection granted, OJ 2004/L304/p. 12 ff.

[23] See Chap. 10.

[24] See Chap. 4.

[25] See Chap. 10, Vedsted-Hansen and Chap. 4, Da Lomba.

[26] Article 1(c) defines a refugee as "a third country national who, owing to a well-founded fear of being persecuted for reasons of race, religion, nationality, political opinion or membership of a particular social group, is outside the country of nationality and is unable or, owing to such fear, is unwilling to avail himself or herself of the protection of that country, or a stateless person, who, being outside of the country of former habitual residence for the same reasons as mentioned above, is unable or, owing to such fear, unwilling to return to it."

[27] Article 2(c) and Article 15 (c) of the Qualification Directive.

[28] Article 267 TFEU now grants a normal jurisdiction for the Court of Justice to give preliminary rulings. Previously, under the EC Treaty, the right to ask preliminary rulings was limited to the highest national courts, see Article 68 EC Treaty.

[29] *Case C-465/07 Meki Elgafaji, Noor Elgafaji v Staatssecretaris van Justitie [2009] ECR I-00921.* On Elgafaji, see Chap. 7, Raitio, and Chap. 10, Vedsted-Hansen.

viewed. In a more recent case of *B*,[30] the Court answered the question of whether and under what criteria a person can be excluded from protection as a refugee if there is a suspicion that the person has committed a "serious non-political crime" or "acts against purposes of the United Nations."[31] Therefore, through the Court of Justice it is possible to achieve uniformity for the qualification of a refugee or any other concept employed by the asylum Directives.

However, the national authorities may not be prepared to alter their views on how asylum or subsidiary protection obligations are to be viewed. As has been pointed out by Vested-Hansen, the Dutch authorities in *Elgafaji* arguably adopted a stricter interpretation of subsidiary protection than the Court of Justice.[32] It remains for the national authorities to interpret the facts of the case and through this there is a possibility for the authorities to take different views on factual situations and how they fit into the legal provisions. However, if these national interpretations vary too much or the national authorities depart from the line taken by the Court of Justice, it is possible for the Commission to bring enforcement proceedings against a Member State for not complying with the Directives[33] and enforce the EU obligations against the Member State. Here, it is hoped that the Commission will take a pro-active role to guard that the Union criteria will develop objectively, consistently and with respect to the protection of fundamental rights.

Meanwhile, divergences continue to exist and as a result the Dublin system has been fiercely criticised.[34] As an alternative for the Court of Justice proceedings, it is possible for individuals to bring the proceedings to the ECtHR on the application or interpretation of the asylum acquis by the Member State authorities. There are, indeed, currently 960 cases pending in the ECtHR on the application of the Dublin

---

[30] *Joined Cases C-57/09 and C-101/09 Bundesrepublik Deutchland v B*, judgment of 9 November 2010.

[31] See Articles 12(2)(b) and (c) of the Qualification Directive. The Court of Justice answered here that the person is not necessarily excluded from the protection on the basis that the person is or has been a member of an organisation listed on Common Foreign and Security Policy (Common Position 2001/931/CFSP) lists on combating terrorism. There needs to be serious reasons for the person to have committed such acts and individual responsibility must be attributed to the person concerned.

[32] See Chap. 10, Vedsted Hansen.

[33] Under Article 258 TFEU.

[34] See for example, UNCHR Discussion Paper, "The Dublin II Regulation", April 2006, http://www.unhcr.org/refworld/docid/4445fe344.html (accessed 14 August 2011); ECRE, "Report on Application of Dublin II Regulation in Europe", March 2006, available from http://www.ecre.org/topics/areas-of-work/protection-in-europe/135.html (accessed 14 August 2011). From academic writers, see for example Brandl, "Distribution of Asylum Seekers in Europe? Dublin II Regulation Determining the Responsibility for Examining an Asylum Application", in de Sousa and De Bruyncker, The Emergence of European Asylum Policy, (2003) Bruylant, Hurwich, "The 1990 Dublin Convention: A Comprehensive Assessment", (1999) 11 IJRL, pp. 648–677, Marx, "Adjusting Dublin Convention: New Approaches to Member State Responsibility for Asylum Applications", (2001) 3(1) EJML, pp. 7–21, and Noll, "Formalism and Empiricism: Some Reflections on the Dublin Convention on the Occasion of Recent European Law", (2001) 70 Journal of International Law, pp. 161–182.

system.[35] These cases concern the return of the asylum seekers to third countries and whether there have been breaches of principle of non-refoulement, and the access of asylum seekers to asylum procedures as well as generally treatment of asylum seekers. Most cases concern Greece, which has reportedly had problems relating to the treatment of asylum seekers and access of asylum seekers to asylum procedures.[36] Two cases are worth mentioning here. First, the ECtHR has given interim judgments and suspended the application of the Dublin system and halted the return of asylum seekers to Greece, Italy and Malta. One such example concerned a transfer of an Afghan asylum seeker from Hungary to Greece, because it could be proven that Greece would not give proper treatment to him. The young Afghan applicant had requested for asylum in Greece and while the application was pending he was left to live in the streets homeless without any social or legal assistance. In addition, he was arrested and detained in jail and mistreated by the police.[37] Second, in M.S.S. versus Belgium and Greece,[38] the first case to be decided on the point of transfer of asylum seekers to another Member State, the ECtHR decided that transfer of an asylum seeker from Belgium to Greece was not compatible with the ECHR obligations. Both Greece and Belgium were condemned on the basis of Articles 3 and 13 ECHR. Greece was held liable on the basis of the detention conditions that asylum seekers are subjected to, the actual living conditions which the applicants find themselves in and the lack of procedural guarantees. The Court recognised that the living conditions as well as procedural guarantees were provided under both national law as well as EU Directives; however, it noted how in practice the Greek authorities had failed the applicant. Belgium was held responsible for returning the applicant to Greece even though it could be proven that the Belgian authorities had relevant knowledge of the situation in Greece regarding the conditions facing the applicant as well as the possibility that there would be refoulement of the applicant back to Afghanistan. Finally, Belgium was also held in breach for not providing adequate remedy to appeal against the expulsion order.

---

[35] European Court of Human Rights, Fact Sheet, "The Dublin Cases", August 2010, http://www.echr.coe.int/NR/rdonlyres/26C5B519-9186-47C1-AB9B-F16299924AE4/0/FICHES_Dublin_Cases_EN.pdf (accessed 14 August 2011).

[36] See for example ECRE, Letter to Jacques Barrot, Vice-President of the European Commission, "RE: The treatment of asylum seeker in Greece and reform of the Dublin Regulation", 3 April 2008, available from http://www.statewatch.org/news/2008/apr/eu-greece-ecre-dublin-letter.pdf (accessed 14 August 2011), and more recently, ECRE, Letter to the European Council, "Stop sending asylum seekers to Greece", 29 October 2010, press release available from http:irishrefugeecouncil.ie/media/ECRE-Stop-Transfers-Greece-press-release.pdf (accessed 14 August 2011); or UNCHR, "Observations of Greece as a country of asylum", December 2009, http://www.unhcr.org/refworld/docid/4b4b3fc82.html (accessed 14 August 2011).

[37] See for example, ECRE Information Note, ECRE Interim Measures (rule 39) to stop Dublin transfers according to which transfers to Greece, Malta and Italy have been halted by the ECtHR, available from http://cmr.jur.ru.nl/cmr/docs/ecre.rule39.pdf (accessed 14 August 2011).

[38] Case of M.S.S. versus Belgium and Greece, Application No. 30696/09, Judgment of 21 January 2011, see also Press Release issued by the Registrar of the Court, No. 043, 21 January 2011, "Belgian authorities should not have expelled asylum seeker to Greece".

1.3 From Minimum Standards to Uniformity: New TFEU Provisions and European Asylum Support Office

At the Union level the problems on application of the common asylum system and that the Member States do not grant the same level of protection for the asylum seekers have been recognised. The CEAS has entered the second stage and asylum Directives are proposed to be recast, strengthening the protection of asylum seekers and qualification for refugees.[39] The Commission has taken the initiative and the new proposals aim for considerable strengthening of the common asylum system.[40]

These new measures will be adopted under the new TFEU provisions which allow the Union to adopt measures which set out the "uniform standards" in asylum protection.[41] This means that the new measures can also potentially aim for further uniformity than the previous minimum harmonisation provision under the EC Treaty. Furthermore, for the first time qualified majority voting with the full involvement of the European Parliament is applied in adoption of all asylum measures.[42] This could mean that it is possible to raise the protection standards to a higher level because individual Member States do not hold the veto power anymore and the European Parliament might intervene in the negotiation process if the result is not satisfactory. In addition, the binding Charter of Fundamental Rights now obliges the EU legislation in asylum to take into account that there is a right to asylum as well as it contains the principle of non-refoulement, consolidating these principles into the core of Union law.[43]

However, it must also be recognised that by simply creating further obligations under Union law for the Member States cannot solve these problems. The Dublin system of allocating responsibility to a single Member State has created pressures in particular for the Southern Member States. In most cases, Dublin gives the responsibility for the Member State which border a person first crossed when entering into the Union. Most irregular arrivals come from Africa or Middle-East[44] and they cross the Union borders from South: Greece, Malta or

---

[39] Proposed new measures are: COM(2008)820 final on Dublin Regulation, COM (2008) 815final on minimum conditions for reception conditions, COM(2009)554 final on minimum standards on procedures in Member States for granting and withdrawing international protection, COM(2009)551final on minimum standards on qualification and status of third country nationals or stateless persons as beneficiaries of protection and the content of the protection granted.

[40] See Chap. 7, Raitio, for the recast Dublin Regulation, Chap. 10, Vedsted-Hansen, for recast minimum procedures and qualification Directive proposals, and Chap. 9, Vandvik, for reception conditions reform.

[41] Article 78(2) TFEU.

[42] Previously Article 67(4) EC Treaty allowed qualified majority voting with the involvement of the European Parliament on when the Council had previously adopted by unanimity Community legislation defining the common rules and basic principles in asylum.

[43] Articles 18 and 19 of the Charter.

[44] See Chap. 7, Raitio, and Chap. 9, Vandvik.

Italy.[45] As a consequence, the asylum systems in these Member States have become overwhelmed and the Member States cannot deal with the number of arriving migrants, including asylum seekers. This was also noted by the European Parliament when it discussed the ECtHR decision in *M.S.S. versus Belgium and Greece*.[46] Similarly, the ECtHR also noted that the Union legislation and the national legislation that are in place in Greece would comply with the fundamental rights standards for the protection of asylum seekers. However, the Member State practice is not in compliance with the legislative provisions.

Therefore, in addition to the formal unification of the asylum systems, to support the actual realisation of the rights under the Directives, there is a need for practical support for the Member States facing pressures in trying to comply with the legislation. The Member States agreed in 2000 to set up the European Refugee Fund and according to the new Decision[47] on the priorities of the Fund, it is aimed at improving in the Member States "the grant of reception conditions for refugees, displaced persons and beneficiaries of subsidiary protection, to apply fair and effective asylum procedures and promote good practices in the field of asylum so as to protect the rights of persons requiring international protection and enable Member States asylum systems to work efficiently."[48] The majority of the early funds will be distributed for the Member States under the objective criteria relating to the number of asylum seekers.[49] For instance, the UNHCR is working with the funding provided by the European Refugee Fund to assess the implementation of the Asylum Procedures Directive.[50]

---

[45] According to the IND statistics presented at the conference, Italy does not have that many asylum applicants. However, there are according to the statistics many irregular immigrants arriving through Italy. The problem could be that Italy is not allowing these persons the entry to the asylum procedures. Some statistical confirmation for this can be seen for example from UNHCR Report, Asylum Levels and Trends in Industrialised Countries 2009, http://www.unhcr.org/4ba7341a9.html (accessed 14 August 2011), according to which there has been 42% decrease in asylum applications in Italy, p. 5. See further on this Chap. 8, Ascoli.

[46] European Parliament, State of European asylum system, after the recent decision of the European Court of Human Rights, 75518, 15 February 2011, http://www.europarl.europa.eu/en/media-professionals/content/20110215SHL18429/html/State-of-European-asylum-system-after-the-recent-decision-of-the-European-Court-of-Human-Rights-75518 (accessed 14 August 2011).

[47] Decision 573/2007/EC of the European Parliament and of the Council of 23 May 2007 establishing the European Refugee Fund for the period of 2008–2013 as part of the General Programme "Solidarity and Management of Migration Flows" and repealing Council Decision 2004/904/EC, OJ 2007/L144/pp. 1–21.

[48] See European Commission, The European Refugee Fund III, http://ec.europa.eu/home-affairs/funding/refugee/funding_refugee_en.htm (accessed 14 August 2011).

[49] For the period of 2008–2013 the Fund has 628 million Euro and 566 million Euro will be distributed to the Member States. 62 million Euro is reserved for other Union actions, such as supporting practical cooperation between Member States, ibid.

[50] See further Chap. 5, Hövell.

To help the national authorities further in implementation of the CEAS, the Union has established the Common European Asylum Office (EASO)[51] which started its operation in 2010 in Valletta, Malta. The main role of the EASO is to "facilitate, coordinate and strengthen practical cooperation among Member States" on asylum.[52] It also provides the Union with scientific and technical assistance in regard to the policy and legislation. It can, therefore, provide information to the Union about all matters relating to asylum. For this purpose the EASO can provide information about the best practices,[53] or about the countries of origin.[54] Added value to the information provided by the EASO is that it also has direct link with the UNHCR. The EASO is obliged to work in cooperation with the UNHCR,[55] in its work the EASO is to use the UNHCR guidelines,[56] and the UNHCR representative sits on the management board of the EASO.[57]

The EASO has a specific role in helping the Member States, where a Member State is subject to a particular pressure from the Dublin system. It can gather and analyse information about the situation in that Member State.[58] The EASO can, furthermore, provide operational support by, for instance, helping Member States on initial analysis of the asylum applications or making sure that appropriate reception facilities are made available by Member States.[59]

Therefore, the unification of asylum procedures, treatment of asylum seekers and recognition of persons requiring international protection can also be helped by the practical measures that the Union has adopted in this regard. The EASO may prove to be an influential body in raising the common standards on asylum protection by providing help to those Member States where the system is the weakest. The links with the UNHCR are also important in this regard. These may ensure further the Member State compliance with the international protection provisions.

1.4 The External Borders and Return Operations

So far this Chapter has concentrated on the internal functioning of the CEAS. What remains to be analysed separately is the access of the asylum seekers to the Union territory and asylum procedures. The basic premise here is that the

---

51 Regulation (EU) No 439/2010 of the European Parliament and of the Council of 19 May 2010 establishing a European Asylum Support Office, OJ 2010/L132/pp. 11–28.

52 Article 2 of the Regulation.

53 Article 3 of the Regulation.

54 Article 4 of the Regulation.

55 Recital (10) and Article 50 of the Regulation.

56 Article 12(2) of the Regulation.

57 Articles 25(4) and 27 of the Regulation, as a non-voting member. The representative can also sit in the Executive Committee, only without the right to vote, Article 29(2) of the Regulation and sit in the Consultative Forum, Article 51 of the Regulation.

58 Article 9 of the Regulation.

59 Article 10 of the Regulation.

responsibility for controlling the external border is still a matter for the Member States.[60] Although the Union has adopted new measures on external borders, and for example, FRONTEX[61] has been established, the premise is still the same. Under the TFEU the Union competence is limited in this respect. The Union can develop common policies on border control mechanisms or visas, as well as treatment of aliens who have already crossed the borders,[62] but there is no general competence to adopt common policies on controlling who can enter into the Union.

In this regard, the common policies on asylum only start taking effect when a person has been admitted by the Member State authorities to asylum procedure. The Charter of Fundamental Rights only grants right to asylum and does not mention the right to access to asylum procedures.[63] Similarly, Article 78 TFEU does not mention the right to access to asylum procedures as one of the common policies to be developed by the Union.[64] This is mirrored by the asylum instruments to date. Both the Asylum Procedures Directive[65] and the Qualification Directive[66] take effect from the point in time when a person has submitted his or her application. Therefore, under Union law it remains the Member State's competence to organise that the person has access to the asylum process and in this respect to comply with the protection afforded by the 1951 Refugee Convention and ECHR.

Furthermore, the Union is more involved in the development of return policies for irregularly arriving migrants. In 2008, the Return Directive[67] was adopted which sets out common standards and procedures for returning illegally staying

---

[60] See also Inex, Interview with Director of FRONTEX, Mr. Laitinen, 12 May 2010, http://migrantsatsea.files.wordpress.com/2010/11/incx-laitinen-interview-12may20101.pdf (accessed 14 August 2011).

[61] http://www.frontex.europa.eu/ (accessed 14 August 2011) for information on FRONTEX. See further Chap. 6, O'Dowd, on the role of FRONTEX.

[62] Article 77 TFEU.

[63] Article 18 of the Charter: "The right to asylum shall be guaranteed with due respect for the rules of the Geneva Convention…".

[64] In Article 78 TFEU we find provisions for developing uniform status on asylum and subsidiary protection for nationals of third countries, common system of temporary protection for displaced persons in the event of a massive inflow, common procedures for granting or withdrawing of asylum or subsidiary protection status.

[65] See especially Article 3 which states that the "Directive shall apply to all applications made in the territory…".

[66] The only mention of an asylum application is made in Article 1(g) of the Directive which states that "'application for international protection' means a request made by a third country national or a stateless person for protection from a Member State, who can be understood to seek refugee status or subsidiary protection status, and who does not explicitly request another kind of protection, outside the scope of this Directive, that can be applied for separately".

[67] Directive 2008/115/EC of the European Parliament and of the Council of 16 December 2008 on common standards and procedures in Member States for returning illegally staying third-country nationals, OJ 2008/L348/pp. 98–107.

third country nationals.[68] While this Directive does not allow the return of asylum seekers, it still maintains the principle that asylum seekers are only granted protection once they have been able to apply for asylum.[69]

There is a danger here that these type of return policies will mount to the so-called "push back operations". There are precedents where the Member States of the Union have been summarily returning irregularly entering persons to states such as Turkey (from Greece) or Libya (from Italy).[70] The problem here is that in these cases it is not investigated by the authorities whether there are mixed with irregularly entering migrants also persons who have valid claims for asylum, in other words, whether there is a so-called mixed flow. Especially, the "push back operations" by Italy to Libya have been contested by the UNCHR and currently, cases on this policy are also pending in the ECtHR.[71] What has been particularly problematic here is that Libya is not a party to the 1951 Refugee Convention and the 1967 Protocol and therefore, although Italy and Libya would have bilateral agreements on the treatment of persons returned to Libya, Libya is not under the international obligation to grant protection to asylum seekers and to apply non-refoulement. Therefore, in adopting these types of neighbourhood policies the Union must make sure that the principles on access to asylum procedures and non-refoulement are respected also by Member State authorities.

1.5 Conclusions

All in all, as this short introductory presentation and more fully the book itself shows, there is still much to do in the CEAS "to establish a level playing field, a system which guarantees to persons genuinely in need of protection access to a high level of protection under equivalent conditions in all Member States while at the same time dealing fairly and efficiently with those found not to be in need of protection."[72] It is likely that the negotiations for the creation of a single asylum procedure will take years to come. Asylum is a highly political issue. The EU policies are reflecting the current anti-immigration attitudes from the Member States.[73] In the Stockholm Programme asylum policies are afforded only a page

---

68 Article 1 of the Directive.

69 Recital (9) of the Directive: "a third country national who have applied for asylum in a Member State should not be regarded as staying illegally on the territory of that Member State until a negative decision on the application, or a decision ending his or her right of stay as asylum seeker has entered into force".

70 See Chap. 8, Ascoli, and Chap. 3, Bruin.

71 See Submission by the Office of the UNCHR in the Case of Hirsi and Others versus Italy (Application no. 27765/09).

72 Commission Green Paper on the Future of Common European Asylum System, COM(2007)301 final.

73 Discussed also by O'Dowd in Chap. 6.

and a half and it mainly reiterates that asylum policies need to be strengthened in accordance with the 1951 Refugee Convention. Otherwise, the policies in the Stockholm Programme[74] seem to be concentrating on securing external borders, returning illegal migrants and creating a buffer zone with the neighbourhood region where the persons arriving to Europe can be processed. In this regard, the Programme invites the creation of Regional Protection Programmes with third countries.[75]

Yet, the pressure is still mounting. The Commission has taken a very active role in its new proposals to strengthen the CEAS. It is trying to give substance to the obligations that the Member States need to respect in order to get the single asylum procedure system working. However, as discussed here, simply raising the standards of the Union legislation is not enough. The Union has employed softer measures to also take into account the difficulties faced by the Member States that end up receiving most of the asylum seekers and refugees. These may further help in practical application of the fundamental rights protection standards. In addition, the Union must try to make sure that the Member States are complying with the standards, by enforcement through Union law, if necessary.

If the Member States do not hold on to the international human rights standards in the application of the CEAS, the ECtHR has now shown that it will get involved to ensure that the Member States of the Union are not breaching these obligations. The transfers of asylum seekers are within the Union being frozen and the ECtHR is placing an obligation for the Member State authorities to review the situation in the Member State where the asylum seeker is to be transferred. While this could be construed as a condemnation of the CEAS, it should not be read so harshly. The ECtHR is not saying that there is a major problem with the CEAS itself, but rather that the system as it stands, does not comply with the ECHR standards. The immediate remedy would be simple. The Member State that wishes to transfer an asylum seeker needs to review objectively the situation of the Member State where the transfer is to be made. It cannot simply trust that the other EU Member State is respecting the standards of the treatment of asylum seekers or respecting the principle of non-refoulement. The Member State must take into account the evidence if it tells that the situation is not safe for the asylum seeker and not to return the person in that case.

Furthermore, it needs to be realised that the external border policy is still in the hands of the Member States. The Union action is far too limited here for it to be able to intervene and it is difficult for the Union to strengthen the right of asylum seekers to access the asylum procedures in the borders or international sea areas. This is a crucial piece that is still missing from the CEAS and meanwhile as this is the situation, the only ECtHR is able to intervene if there are problems. Perhaps, once more cases reach the Court of Justice, the situation will change. It may start interpreting the right to asylum as including the right to access to asylum procedures. Without it, the right to asylum under Union law is here simply very limited.

---

[74] *Supra* n. 11, Sect. 1.2.

[75] *Supra* n. 11, Sect. 1.2, p. 33.

Chapter 2
Conference on Recent Developments in European and International Asylum Policy and Law

Nebahat Albayrak

Contents

2.1 Introduction 15
2.2 Where are We Now in Europe in 2009? 16
2.3 How to Continue in Europe in 2009? 17
2.4 Regional Protection Programmes 18
2.5 Resettlement in Europe 18
2.6 Root Causes 19
2.7 Global Forum for Migration and Development 19
2.8 Food for Thought and Discussion 19

2.1 Introduction

We recently celebrated the birth of Gerrit Gerritszoon, better known as Desiderius Erasmus, one of the greatest thinkers of his time, and name giver to the Erasmus University, Rotterdam. Erasmus held the view that 'In a free state, the tongues too should be free.' Centuries later, in 1951, the same body of thought was included in the Convention on Refugees. One of the underlying principles in this convention is that asylum must be granted to anyone who is prosecuted in his or her own country on account of his or her political beliefs.

Much has happened between 1951 and 2009. The world has changed; it has become smaller. Nowadays, most refugees are mainly on the run due to war and

Nebahat Albayrak, (former) Minister for Aliens' Affairs, The Netherlands.

N. Albayrak (✉)
e-mail: N.Albayrak@tweedekamer.nl

F. A. N. J. Goudappel and H. S. Raulus (eds.), *The future of asylum in the European Union*, DOI: 10.1007/978-90-6704-802-6_2,

regional conflicts. Some asylum seekers who come knocking on our doors are not refugees in the proper sense of the word, but people who are looking for a better life, one without poverty and crime. They arrive here through smuggling routes which are often operated by ruthless criminals. We often see images of the dramas that take place during trips by boats or in trucks.

In our countries, most of these people end up living on the fringes of society where they are exploited, and worse. All around the world people are on the run from violence and suppression; people who are completely displaced, who have no means at all, and who have nowhere to go. To put it briefly, migrant flows are more and more mixed and present with new challenges again and again. I sincerely believe that we can deal with these challenges together. Netherlands makes a difference for some people. Europe can really make a difference. If we want that, we must act in concert, and that is where our major challenges currently lie.

2.2 Where are We Now in Europe in 2009?

We have, relatively speaking, already achieved much in this young and politically sensitive European policy area; think, for instance, of Tampere and the Hague programmes. However, the asylum systems within the European Union have not yet been sufficiently harmonised; nor are the regulations, the policies or the methods of implementation the same.

As far as the regulations are concerned, there are still different statuses, forms of residence, and different rights and obligations attached to them. The differences in policies can, for instance, be found in the country-specific asylum policies, with the Member States assessing the situations in the countries of origin according to different criteria. It should not be that one Member State recognizes just a few asylum seekers as refugees, whereas another Member State grants this status much more frequently.

The consequence of this is that a Member State with a generous asylum policy pays the price, with a large influx. We might mention in this context, for instance, the large number of Iraqis that went to Sweden in 2008, and the many Somalis that we currently receive in the Netherlands.

Anyway, at the level of implementation, it has become evident that asylum applications are assessed differently in similar situations.

All this undermines the confidence in the asylum system. Member States cannot take it for granted that equal cases produce equal results. The asylum seeker cannot rely on his or her asylum application being similarly successful in all Member States. Finally, among the citizens in our societies, the confidence in the asylum system, and with that the support for the protection of refuges, is being undermined.

2.3 How to Continue in Europe in 2009?

I am convinced that we are on the right track with Tampere, the Hague programmes, and shortly the Stockholm programme. We must energetically continue to harmonise our regulations, policy and methods of implementation. In that respect, I would like to emphasise the following points.

First of all, a continued 'top down' harmonisation, by aligning the different asylum systems further on the basis of [European] legislation. As we all know, 2009 is an important year.

The Commission has prepared various proposals on asylum issues which will be discussed in Brussels, namely proposals for amending the procedure and the qualification directives. In addition, we are on the eve of the third Multi-Year Programme for Justice and Home Affairs 2010–2014: the so-called Stockholm programme. The Dutch Cabinet will have soon informed both the houses which position it has adopted on this programme.

Meanwhile, our objectives in the area of asylum are: at the end of the Stockholm programme in 2014, the third phase of the asylum harmonisation process must have been completed and implemented. In respect of regulations and methods of implementation, the asylum systems of the Member States must, by that time, have been aligned to such an extent that someone in need of protection stands the same chance in all Member States. It may sound futuristic, but I am convinced that it is realistic, all it takes is dedication, vision and strategy.

Talking about strategy, harmonisation through practical cooperation among the Member States is an option. This cooperation could stimulate 'bottom up' harmonisation, for instance, by exchanging knowledge, best practices and skills. A fine example of this—and one which is currently underway—is the 'Coherent Plan for Iraq'. A Dutch initiative, in which the Netherlands is investing much through the Temporary Desk on Iraq, which started in Brussels, in March 2008. In a lightweight organisational structure, it will provide support in the areas of protection, resettlement and returns to the Member States to stakeholders such as the UNHCR, the European commission, and the academic world and to the countries involved such as Syria, Iraq and Jordan. I consider this an example of concrete, practical cooperation in the area of asylum among several Member States.

I am confident that now the European Asylum Agency is on its way to prove to be useful in this area.

But neither this Asylum Agency nor Frontex will be the panacea for the problems currently being encountered; the Member States will remain responsible for ensuring continued cooperation and harmonisation of the overall asylum process.

The third very relevant dimension is that the Court of Justice has played an increasingly important role in the interpretation of the European asylum rules. In doing so, the Court has a harmonising influence. In February of this year, for instance, the Court delivered its first preliminary ruling on the Qualification Directive, which contains the minimum criteria in the area of asylum, in the Dutch

Elgafaji case. The ruling endorses the necessity of harmonising the European asylum policy to prevent differences among the Member States in assessing the situations in the countries of origin.

I have informed the Parliament that in my opinion the judgment of the ECJ will not have significant implications for asylum practices in the Netherlands. However, the ECJ does indicate that in a situation of 'armed conflict', an'exceptional situation' can be said to exist.

In such a situation, the degree of indiscriminate violence reaches such a high level, that a civilian who returns to the relevant country or region solely on account of his presence on the territory of that country or region, faces a real risk. My aim is to achieve a harmonised interpretation and application of the Qualification Directive.

During the Justice and Home Affairs Council of 26 and 27 February 2008, I already requested attention for joint alignment between the Member States in respect of, for example, the terms 'armed conflict' and 'exceptional situation'. The Commission could also play a part in this process.

2.4 Regional Protection Programmes

In addition to all this, the relationship with third countries is crucial to the European asylum policy. Consider, for instance, an improvement in the regional protection programmes. By aiming at improved protection and building-up capacity in the receiving countries, we show solidarity with the countries that take responsibility for much larger number of refugees. In addition, we provide a future to these refugees in areas closer to their homes. Together with my colleague Minister Koenders, the Minister for Development Cooperation, I have written a letter to the Lower House on this subject. We are currently implementing the measures described in this letter in respect of those countries.

2.5 Resettlement in Europe

Meanwhile, we have drawn attention to and taken successful action in the area of resettlement at the European level. In this context, Europe is likely to make a much larger difference than an individual Member State. For this reason, I have involved myself in this issue for some time. This involvement started more than a year ago with a letter to my European colleagues. And I see progress, and that really stimulates me. It encourages me to believe even more in Europe.

We recently completed a resettlement mission, in which I was accompanied by interested colleagues from Belgium and Luxembourg, and Belgium has decided to pursue resettlement. I am looking forward to the resettlement communication from the Commission that we may expect in mid-2009, as a follow-up from the Hague programme.

I am pleased to inform that Europe has decided for a first EU-resettlement project, in which it will resettle 10.000 Iraqi refugees (at the end of 2008). The Netherlands will take its share in the resettlement of Iraqis. Resettlement is one of the three pillars of a European Coherent Plan on Iraq, which I have proposed at a Ministerial Conference in Paris last year.

2.6 Root Causes

The fact that we provide protection to refugees at the European level is a good and important thing to do, but I consider it even more important to ensure that people do not have to leave their home at all. We focus on measures to promote sound administration and security, which—as you know—is the basis of the fragile state policy of this cabinet. This forces us to look further, at policy level as well. In the Netherlands we do this, for instance, in respect of migration and development. We attempt to link good governance in a country of origin, to the economic and development relationships that the Netherlands and Europe have with such a country, but also to sustainable return.

As individual Member States, we can only make small differences in the relationships with the third countries.

Europe must therefore assume its role as a global player. Here too, I am convinced that Europe can make a difference. Together we carry more weight, with more results.

In elaboration to this, with the new administration in the US—why not consider a more strategic approach by Europe together with the US and Canada, for instance in the area of resettlement?

2.7 Global Forum for Migration and Development

I would also like to mention is that I am confident that the Global Forum for Migration and Development can play an important role at the global level. This migration dialogue will meet for the third time, in Athens in the autumn of 2009 at a high official and political level, and is slowly but surely exploring the elements of a global model for migration management.

2.8 Food for Thought and Discussion

Finally, I propose several questions for further consideration during this conference. First of all: What more can we do to harmonise the European asylum policy to become a reality? Which concrete obstacles have to be overcome? How can we realise that we actually protect the people for whom the asylum policy is intended?

Given the large number of well-informed specialists, I would even stimulate you to think about the long term. How should we proceed after the Stockholm programme, after 2014?

In this context, I am thinking, for instance, of the possibility of processing asylum applications outside the European Union. This is not feasible in the short term, but once the requirement of a common asylum system has been met, I consider this very well possible.

I am therefore, looking forward to the study on this subject which the Commission has announced to conduct in 2009 in its Asylum policy plan. Is it conceivable that we switch from a supply driven approach to a demand-driven one? That Europe will assume its responsibility for those really vulnerable people who are currently locked up too often in a dead-end situation in refugee camps? A precondition to this context is that we have a grip on illegal migration to the EU. This will involve all kinds of complex questions, such as: Which system of law will be applicable? How is the EU going to deal with the countries of origin? What would be the pull factor of such a centre outside the EU? What would be the role of UNHCR? Apart from this, I would like to add that I think that our policy should always be incorporated in a comprehensive approach, with all aspects of migration being dealt with, including illegal migration.

In short, enough food for thought and discussion for this conference. I am very curious about the views and solutions. Hopefully, we will be able to put them into practice soon. As Desiderius Erasmus once said: if you keep thinking about what you want to do or what you hope will happen, if you don't do it, it won't happen.

Chapter 3
Border Control: Not a Transparent Reality

René Bruin

Contents

3.1 Introduction 21
3.2 At the European Border 25
3.2.1 International Refugee Law 25
3.2.2 EU Law 25
3.2.3 European Human Rights Law 27
3.3 Border Control Activities Undertaken at Sea 29
3.3.1 International Refugee Law and Human Rights Law 29
3.3.2 Jurisprudence 31
3.3.3 EU Law 33
3.3.4 UNHCR 34
3.3.5 Safe Third Countries 35
3.4 Border Control Outside Europe 36
3.4.1 Activities Undertaken at Airports 36
3.4.2 International Refugee Law 37
3.4.3 Jurisprudence 37
3.4.4 EU Law 38
3.4.5 National Jurisprudence, the House of Lords, UNHCR 38
3.5 To Conclude 40
References 42

3.1 Introduction

States have the right to control the entry, residence and the expulsion of aliens. The legitimate interest of States in controlling their borders must be recognized. A person may be deprived of his liberty to prevent him from affecting an

---

René Bruin, is a lawyer and the National Officer of UNHCR in The Hague. The views expressed in this article do not necessarily coincide with the views of UNHCR.

F. A. N. J. Goudappel and H. S. Raulus (eds.), *The future of asylum in the European Union*, DOI: 10.1007/978-90-6704-802-6_3,

unauthorized entry into the country.[1] According to Article 31 of the 1951 Convention relating to the Status of refugees (hereafter: 51CSR) States shall not impose penalties on refugees on account of their illegal entry or presence when coming directly from a territory where their life or freedom is threatened, provided they present themselves without delay to the authorities and show good cause for their illegal entry or presence. Persons have a right not to be returned to their own country, or to any other country, if this results in being seriously harmed. In other words, persons, including refugees, have a right to be protected from refoulement. The prohibition of refoulement is the cornerstone of international refugee and asylum law and is contained in and developed under various international treaties.[2] In the broadest and general terms it protects people from being removed from a country where they are at risk of being subjected to serious human rights violations. As a result the prohibition of refoulement provides a right for people to obtain protection from serious harm in a country other than their own. To ensure that people seeking protection can have access to a procedure in which their claims can adequately be examined access to the territory of the host State is essential if this is the only way to guarantee a fair procedure.

More and more States try to prevent the prohibition of refoulement from being applicable in the first place. States try to prevent aliens from reaching their territory or even from leaving their country of origin. This is not at all a new phenomenon. Hathaway enumerates a number of decisions States from all over the world have taken over the last 70 years to close their borders for aliens.[3] Where it initially started with strict border controls, in the last 20 years, industrialized nations have adopted measures such as visa requirements followed by the sharing of passenger lists and carrier sanctions.[4] Also, industrialized countries are patrolling the shores and territorial waters of asylum producing countries and posting Immigration Liaison Officers (ILOs)[5] at foreign airports.

At first, States took these measures individually, nowadays however, States work together and have institutionalized their common efforts to impede persons

---

[1] Article 5 par 1 (f) European Convention for the Protection of Human Rights and Fundamental Freedoms.

[2] See, for example, Article 33 of the Convention Relating to the Status of Refugees, Article 3 of the Convention against Torture and Other Cruel, Inhuman or Degrading Treatment or Punishment, Article 7 of the International Covenant on Civil and Political Rights, and Article 3 of the European Convention for the Protection of Human Rights and Fundamental Freedoms.

[3] Hathaway 2005, p. 280. He *inter alia* reminds the readers of his book of the whereabouts of the *St. Louis,* carrying Jewish refugees not being allowed to leave the boat in North and South America ending up in the concentration camps in Germany.

[4] Ibid., pp. 291–292.

[5] One can also mention the Rapid Action Teams as deployed by *inter alia* the Dutch authorities in combating human smuggling and trafficking.

from entering their territories. In this context one can point at the sharing of information gathered by the different ILOs and the activities of FRONTEX.[6]

So far these measures aimed at preventing persons from reaching a State's territory have hardly been challenged in a court of law. In fact, they are difficult if not impossible to challenge by individuals while having a significant impact on the individuals' ability to seek protection elsewhere.[7] Certainly, more legal clarity on the legitimacy of these measures is needed.

Access to procedures is under threat. In January 2007 UNHCR has stipulated that border control must not impede asylum requests.[8] UNHCR has stated that practical protection safeguards are required to ensure that border control measures are not applied in an indiscriminate or disproportionate manner and that they do not lead to refoulement. In May 2009 UNHCR heavily criticized Italy for sending back boats with migrants and possibly refugees to Libya. Italian Interior minister Maroni had said: "We are only sending them back to where they come from." HCR Guterres voiced concern: "I appeal to the Italian and Maltese authorities to continue to ensure that people rescued at sea and in need of international protection receive full access to territory and asylum procedures."[9] UNHCR pointed to the fact that the fundamental right to seek and enjoy asylum from persecution set out in the Universal Declaration of Human Rights is guaranteed in the EU Charter of Fundamental Rights. UNHCR's concerns remain unheard. Neither EU Member States nor the European Commission has expressed concern with regard to the conduct of the Italian authorities. European Commission President Barroso responded by telling an Italian newspaper he will unveil new plans to combat illegal immigration to Europe within weeks: "By June 10, the EC Vice-President Jacques Barrot and myself will present new proposals with three aims: to prevent sea tragedies, protect the principle of free movement and defend people's right to asylum." Barroso said that Europe must "provide a strong answer" to "illegal immigration" and must consider creating an EU asylum bureau to examine individual cases. He also underlined people's universal right to claim asylum.[10]

---

[6] FRONTEX started to be fully operational on 3 October 2005. According to the FRONTEX website FRONTEX staff consists of 164 seconded national experts, temporary, auxiliary and contract staff. FRONTEX strengthens border security by ensuring the coordination of Member States' actions in the implementation of Community and EU measures relating to the management of the external borders, working closely with other EU partners responsible for the security of the external borders, such as Europol, CEPOL and EMSA, see http://www.FRONTEX.europa.eu.

[7] The only cases known to me are the Prague airport case in the UK concerning British ILOs stationed at Prague airport in the Czech Republic, *Regina versus Immigration Officer at Prague Airport and Another, Ex parte European Roma Rights Centre and Others*, [2004] UKHL 55, House of Lords, 9 December 2004, available at www.unhcr.org/refworld/docid/41c17ebf4.html, case also published in International Journal of Refugee Law 2005, pp. 217–270 and the Marine I case dealt with by Committee Against Torture, *J.H.A. v Spain*, 21 November 2008, Communication No. 323/2007.

[8] UN High Commissioner for Refugees 2007a, b.

[9] UN News Centre, May 7 2009.

[10] Corriere della Sera, May 8 2009.

In June 2009, the European Commission (EC) issued the communication 'An area of freedom, security and justice serving the citizen' outlining its vision for the next 5 years in the policy areas of justice and home affairs.[11] The proposal entails a more prominent role for FRONTEX and a call to clarify the rules with regard to rescue at sea. In Sect. 4.2.3.1 the European Commission proposes:

> Operational cooperation between Member States through FRONTEX must be improved. The agency must play a central role in the future integrated mechanism for surveillance of external borders. Its operational capabilities must be strengthened, notably through regional or specialized offices, the priorities being powers of command over joint operations on a voluntary basis, use of its own resources, and ability to mobilize more easily the manpower needed to carry out operations.
>
> The types of checks (security, immigration, and customs) at border crossings must be rationalized, in particular by separating private and commercial traffic. In certain cases, this rationalization will involve improvements to existing infrastructures and increased use of new technologies (biometrics, etc.). Closer cooperation between national authorities will allow procedures to be simplified, thus making borders easier to cross. It will also allow optimal use of resources.
>
> Particular attention must be paid to the situation of vulnerable people and groups. In this regard, priority will be given to the needs of international protection and reception of unaccompanied minors. It will be essential to coordinate the activities of FRONTEX and of the European Asylum Support Office to receive people intercepted while crossing external borders. In this context, the European Union will also have to consider a clarification of the international rules in the light of the imperatives of maritime control and surveillance, while preserving the fundamental obligation of rescue at sea.

The sending back of asylum seekers to Libya was not directly addressed in this communication.

To be noticed is the EC urging clarification of the international rules with regard to the rescue at sea, an issue that will addressed later in this paper.

In dealing with refugees seeking protection in Europe three situations can be distinguished. The first situation concerns a refugee reporting himself at the border and submitting an application for asylum. The second situation sees upon the asylum seeker who tries to reach the territory of European country and is intercepted at sea (in territorial waters, at the high seas or in the territorial waters of the country he left). The third situation deals with an asylum seeker trying to leave his country of origin or a first country of asylum. In this article I will first briefly discuss the refugee who presents himself at the border of a European country. The Procedures Directive and the Dublin Regulation will be addressed. Secondly I will focus on extraterritorial control executed by States (albeit in coordinated actions like the FRONTEX activities), with regard to refugees intercepted at sea. Thirdly I will address border control outside Europe, possibly resulting in refugees being prevented from travelling to Europe.

---

[11] Communication from the Commission to the European Parliament and the Council, 'An area of freedom, security and justice serving the citizen', Brussels, COM (2009) 262/4.

The issue at stake in all three situations is access to an asylum procedure for determining who is in need of asylum protection, or more specifically, who has a right to be protected from refoulement.

3.2 At the European Border

3.2.1 *International Refugee Law*

The legal dispute whether or not asylum seekers at the border can benefit from the prohibition of refoulement has come to an end. It is commonly accepted that Article 33 of the 51CSR and the Articles of other treaties[12] containing a prohibition of refoulement are applicable to anyone seeking protection at the border.[13] Article 33 Para 1 reads: "No Contracting State shall expel or return ("refouler") a refugee in any manner whatsoever to the frontiers of territories where his life or freedom would be threatened on account of his race, religion, nationality, membership of a particular social group or political opinion." The Cambridge Expert Roundtable stated clearly in 2001: The principle of non-refoulement embodied in Article 33 encompasses any measure attributable to the State which could have the effect of returning an asylum seeker or refugee to the frontiers of territories where his or her life or freedom would be threatened or where he or she is at risk of persecution, including interception, rejection at the frontier or indirect refoulement.'[14] The European Court on Human Rights has judged clearly that there is a right not to be refouled if one presents himself at the border.[15]

3.2.2 *EU Law*

European law reflects in this regard international refugee law. Article 3 of the Procedure Directive obliges EU Member States to accept applications for asylum made on the territory, including at the border or in the transit zones of the Member States. Persons looking for protection within the EU are confronted with the Schengen acquis, including the Dublin Regulation.[16] In Article 3 (1) of the Dublin

[12] Article 3 Convention against Torture; Article 7 International Covenant on Civil and Political Rights, Article 3 European Convention on Human Rights.

[13] Wouters 2009, pp. 48–55.

[14] Feller et al. 2001, p.178.

[15] ECtHR Amuur versus France 25 June 1996, Appl. No. 19776/92 and Gebremedhin versus France. 26 April 2007, Appl. No. 25389/05.

[16] Council Regulation (EC) No 343/2003 of 18 February 2003 establishing the criteria and mechanisms for determining the Member State responsible for examining an asylum application lodged in one of the Member States by a third-country national, Official Journal of the European Union 25 February 2003, L50/1.

Regulation Member States have agreed to examine the application of any third-country national who applies for asylum at the border or in their territory.

Two remarks have to be made. First, by applying common criteria for the identification of persons genuinely in need of international protection and by the approximation of rules and procedures, the EU Member States aim at limiting secondary movements. However, examination of the claim does not mean examination of its merits *per se*. Asylum claims can be rejected and declared inadmissible. According to the Procedures Directive a claim can be declared inadmissible based on the fact that another State has already granted refugee status, or because the other State is deemed to be the first country of asylum or is considered a safe third-country.[17] Article 26 (dealing with first country of asylum) and Article 27 (on the safe third-country concept) of the Dublin Regulation contain strict requirements as regards to the safety and access to the country considered to provide protection. Secondly, the application —in principle—be examined by one Member State only.

When having access to a procedure the asylum seeker has a legal right to stay in the country pending the assessment of his application. This includes asylum seekers claiming asylum at the border. Article 35 of the Procedures Directive, dealing with border procedures, contains a reference to Article 7 (1) Procedures Directive, according to which: "Applicants shall be allowed to remain in the Member State, for the sole purpose of the procedure, until the determining authority has made a decision in accordance with the procedures at first instance set out in this chapter. This right to remain shall not constitute an entitlement to a residence permit."

As already mentioned, if a claim is admissible it will be examined by a single Member State. The Dublin Regulation however does not create obstacles for an asylum seeker to apply in another EU State. States can and will in most cases refer the asylum seeker to the country responsible for the examination of the claim, but in accordance with Article 3 (2) of the Dublin Regulation that State may choose to examine the merits of the claim despite not being the primary responsible State.[18]

---

[17] Council Directive 2005/85/EC of 1 December 2005 on minimum standards on procedures in Member States for granting and withdrawing refugee status, see Article 25, 1 (sub a, b, c).

[18] Article 3 Dublin regulation reads: 1. Member States shall examine the application of any third-country national who applies at the border or in their territory to any one of them for asylum. The application shall be examined by a single Member State, which shall be the one which the criteria set out in this chapter indicate is responsible. 2. By way of derogation from Para 1, each Member State may examine an application for asylum lodged with it by a third-country national, even if such examination is not its responsibility under the criteria laid down in this Regulation. In such an event that Member State shall become the Member State responsible within the meaning of this Regulation and shall assume the obligations associated with that responsibility. Where appropriate, it shall inform the Member State previously responsible, the Member State conducting a procedure for determining the Member State responsible or the Member State which has been requested to take charge of or take back the applicant.

3.2.3 European Human Rights Law

In the absence of a complete and substantive harmonization of European asylum law, EU Member States are forced to assess an asylum claim before removing a person. This idea is underlined by the European Court in 2000 and 2008. In 2000 the Court considered in the case of T.I vs. United Kingdom[19]:

> … that the indirect removal in this case to an intermediary country, which is also a Contracting State, does not affect the responsibility of the United Kingdom to ensure that the applicant is not, as a result of its decision to expel, exposed to treatment contrary to Article 3 of the Convention. Nor can the United Kingdom rely automatically in that context on the arrangements made in the Dublin Convention concerning the attribution of responsibility between European countries for deciding asylum claims. Where States establish international organizations, or *mutatis mutandis* international agreements, to pursue cooperation in certain fields of activities, there may be implications for the protection of fundamental rights. It would be incompatible with the purpose and object of the Convention if Contracting States were thereby absolved from their responsibility under the Convention in relation to the field of activity covered by such attribution (see e.g. Waite and Kennedy v. Germany judgment of 18 February 1999, *Reports* 1999, Section 67). The Court notes the comments of the UNHCR that, while the Dublin Convention may pursue laudable objectives, its effectiveness may be undermined in practice by the differing approaches adopted by Contracting States to the scope of protection offered.

In 2008, in K.R.S versus United Kingdom, the Court reaffirms the above considering that this ruling must apply with equal force to the Dublin Regulation, created within the framework of the "third pillar" of the European Union. The European Court however puts emphasis on the possibility of lodging a complaint before the Court while asking for interim measures concluding that the transfer to another EU Member State will not jeopardize the right to not be refouled. The Court considered:

> Quite apart from these considerations, and from the standpoint of the Convention, there is nothing to suggest that those returned to Greece under the Dublin Regulation run the risk of onward removal to a third-country where they will face ill-treatment contrary to Article 3 without being afforded a real opportunity, on the territory of Greece, of applying to the Court for a Rule 39 measure to prevent such. It is true that the Greek authorities, in their letters of 31 October and 4 November 2008, have not specifically addressed this matter, even though they were requested to do so. However, the Court notes in this regard that assurances were obtained by the Agent of the United Kingdom Government from the Greek "Dublin Unit" – in particular in the letter dated 11 July 2008 from the Head of Aliens Division (Asylum Section) of that unit – that asylum applicants in Greece have a right to appeal against any expulsion decision and to seek interim measures from this Court under Rule 39 of the Rules of Court. There is nothing in the materials before the Court which would suggest that returnees to Greece under the Dublin Regulation,

---

[19] ECtHR, March 7 2000, Application no. 43844/98, T.I versus United Kingdom; the ECtHR reiterated this in K.R.S. versus United Kingdom, see ECtHR December 2 2008, Application no. 32733/08, K.R.S. versus United Kingdom,available at: http://www.unhcr.org/refworld/docid/49476fd72.html. The Court finds that this ruling (T.I vs. UK) must apply with equal force to the Dublin Regulation, created within the framework of the "third pillar" of the European Union.

> including those whose asylum applications have been the subject of a final negative decision by the Greek authorities, have been, or might be, prevented from applying for an interim measure on account of the timing of their onward removal or for any other reason.

Access to a procedure in the second country seems to be guaranteed, but a decision on the merits is not guaranteed. In general one can argue that EU States do not examine requests if others States are first responsible.

Asylum seekers who are expelled and who will transit another European country during the deportation, are treated differently. In spite of the jurisprudence of the ECtHR and in contravention with Article 3 (1) of the Procedures Directive stating that this Directive shall apply to all applications for asylum made in the territory, including at the border or *in the transit zones* (emphasis, RB) of the Member States, deportees seem not to benefit from this ruling. In practice they are prevented from applying for asylum in order not to frustrate the deportation.

By way of example the following is a true story. A rejected asylum seeker from Afghanistan was expelled by Sweden. He was in transit at Schiphol airport and therefore in the Netherlands for about two or three hours. The man was a bisexual and according to country of origin information with respect to Afghanistan, this can be an impediment for expulsion. Open homosexual relations are not allowed in Afghanistan given conservative social mores. In addition to gays and lesbians risking violence from family or community members, most interpretations of the applicable criminal law indicate that homosexual acts would lead to severe punishment were they come to the attention of the authorities. The Swedish lawyer asked for an interim measure with the Human Rights Committee but did not receive an answer at the time of expulsion. She then asked Amnesty International and the Dutch Council for Refugees for help. UNHCR also got involved. Dutch Immigration services and the Ministry of Justice were informed the man wanted to apply for asylum. No asylum application, however, was lodged. The Swedish authorities continued the deportation to Afghanistan. Amnesty International and the Dutch Council for Refugees wrote a letter to the State Secretary of Justice asking for clarification.[20] The State Secretary of Justice answered that the man did not apply for asylum.[21] It might well be he was not allowed to do so, although his intention to claim asylum in the Netherlands was clearly communicated beforehand by the two NGOs.

This case is quite similar to a case which Amnesty International dealt with in January 2005. The United States of America used Schiphol Airport during the expulsion of Mr Abd al-Rahman al-Musa, affiliated to the Muslim Brotherhood, to Syria.[22] Amnesty urged the Dutch authorities to give the man the opportunity to apply for asylum. Amnesty's request was denied and not handled with the required attention. The man ended up in a Syrian cell.

---

[20] Letter to the State Secretary of Justice dated 19 December 2008, dir/en/2008/358.

[21] Letter of the State Secretary of Justice dated 11 March 2009, KUBIS/22830.

[22] The man was arrested upon arrival in Syria, see Amnesty International MDE24 005/2005, 26 January 2005.

To conclude, while access to an asylum procedure at a European border is in general guaranteed, access however does not mean the merits of the claim are examined. Certainly a person who is being deported and transiting a European airport does not seem to have access to an asylum procedure.

3.3 Border Control Activities Undertaken at Sea

Activities undertaken at sea can, in principle, be derived from two legal systems, (1) the duty to rescue persons in distress under international maritime law and (2) the control of borders under general international public law. Duties to render assistance to persons in distress at sea are found in the United Nations Convention on the Law of the Sea, the International Convention for the Safety of Life at sea and the International Convention on Maritime Search and Rescue. The right to control the border is stated in Article 2 of the United Nations Convention on the Law of the Sea. Article 33 of that Convention extends the right to control to a zone contiguous to its territorial sea. The coastal State may prevent infringement of its customs, fiscal, immigration or sanitary laws and regulations within its territory or territorial sea. Rescue at sea entails the obligation to treat persons with humanity, subject to the capabilities and limitations of the ship. It may result in delivering the rescued persons to the nearest port of call. Here Maritime law collides with border control. In practice States are not always willing to allow ships to enter their ports and disembark the rescued persons. Den Heijer rightly points at the amendment of the International Maritime Organization Safety Committee to the SOLAS and SAR Conventions adopted in 2004 clarifying disembarkation is to be effected as soon as reasonably practicable,[23] but reality is often different.

3.3.1 International Refugee Law and Human Rights Law

Border control should also be in accordance with international refugee law. The prohibitions of refoulement contained in, *inter alia*, Article 33 51CSR, Article 3 Convention against Torture, Article 7 International Covenant on Civil and Political Rights and Article 3 European Convention on Human Rights, oblige State parties not to return an alien to his country of origin when there is a real risk of serious harm. This implies that after rescuing people at sea, the obligation exists to identify who is in need of and has a right to protection from refoulement. Such an obligation requires a proper (asylum) procedure. It is impossible for a proper asylum procedure to take place on board of a vessel at sea. Furthermore, Article 4 of the ECHR's Fourth Optional Protocol prohibits the collective expulsion of aliens.

[23] Den Heijer 2009, footnote 65.

This Article requires individual examination of each decision on expulsion. The sending back of a person to his country of origin without guaranteeing access to a fair procedure is clearly in violation with international refugee and asylum law.

In 2004 the Human Rights Committee issued General Comment Number 31.[24] In Paragraph 10 of this Comment, the Committee considers:

> States Parties are required by article 2, paragraph 1, to respect and to ensure the Covenant rights to all persons who may be within their territory and to all persons subject to their jurisdiction. This means that a State party must respect and ensure the rights laid down in the Covenant to anyone within the power or effective control of that State Party, even if not situated within the territory of the State Party. As indicated in General Comment 15 adopted at the twenty-seventh session (1986), the enjoyment of Covenant rights is not limited to citizens of States Parties but must also be available to all individuals, regardless of nationality or statelessness, such as asylum seekers, refugees, migrant workers and other persons, who may find themselves in the territory or subject to the jurisdiction of the State Party. This principle also applies to those within the power or effective control of the forces of a State Party acting outside its territory, regardless of the circumstances in which such power or effective control was obtained, such as forces constituting a national contingent of a State Party assigned to an international peace-keeping or peace-enforcement operation.

The Human Rights Committee clearly states the responsibility of a State vis-à-vis anyone under actual control of the State and urges States to abide to their international commitments.[25]

In General Comment Number 2, the Committee Against Torture stipulated the same even more explicitly:

> Article 2, paragraph 1, requires that each State party shall take effective measures to prevent acts of torture not only in its sovereign territory but also "in any territory under its jurisdiction." The Committee has recognized that "any territory" includes all areas where the State party exercises, directly or indirectly, in whole or in part, de jure or de facto effective control, in accordance with international law. The reference to "any territory" in article 2, like that in articles 5, 11, 12, 13 and 16, refers to prohibited acts committed not only on board of a ship or aircraft registered by a State party, but also during military occupation or peacekeeping operations and in such places as embassies, military bases, detention facilities, or other areas over which a State exercises factual or effective control. The Committee notes that this interpretation reinforces article 5, paragraph 1 (b), which requires that a State party must take measures to exercise jurisdiction "when the alleged offender is a national of the State." The Committee considers that the scope of "territory" under article 2 must also include situations where a State party exercises, directly or indirectly, de facto or de jure control over persons in detention.[26]

[24] General Comment 31: "The Nature of the General Legal Obligation Imposed on States Parties to the International Covenant on Civil and Political Rights".

[25] See for a comprehensive analysis of extraterritorial responsibility to ensure the rights contained in the ICCPR, in particular the right to be protected from refoulement, Wouters 2009, pp. 372–376.

[26] See for a comprehensive analysis of extraterritorial responsibility to ensure protection from refoulement under Article 3 CAT, Wouters 2009, pp. 435–437.

Similar views have been expressed by the European Court of Human Rights in its case law.[27]

3.3.2 *Jurisprudence*

The Committee against Torture (CAT) dealt with this situation in the so-called *Marine I* case. This case concerned a search and rescue operation conducted by Spain in January 2007 off the coast of West Africa. According to the facts as established by CAT the Spanish maritime rescue tug *Luz de Mar* sailed from Tenerife in the Canary Islands, Spain, in response to a distress call sent by the cargo vessel *Marine I*, which had capsized in international waters with 369 immigrants from various Asian and African countries on board. On 4 February 2007, the *Luz de Mar* reached the *Marine I* and towed it. At that time, diplomatic negotiations began between Spain, Senegal and Mauritania regarding the fate of *Marine I*, as a result of which the two ships remained anchored off the Mauritanian coast for eight days. On 9 February, a Spanish Civil Guard patrol boat carrying members of the non-governmental organization Médecins du Monde, a representative of the Spanish Ministry of the Interior and Civil Guard personnel, accompanied by a delegation from Guinea, which had come to identify persons of African origin aboard the *Marine I*, tried to reach the place where the ships were anchored. However, the operation was hampered by poor sea conditions. On 11 February, the operation resumed, with the additional presence of Spanish Red Cross personnel and Mauritanian health personnel. After boarding the *Marine I*, members of the operation provided health care to the passengers, who were in a poor state of health. On 12 February, the Spanish and Mauritanian Governments concluded an agreement that allowed the passengers of the *Marine I* to disembark in the port of Nouadhibou, Mauritania, the same day. In the hours that followed, the Spanish national police force proceeded to identify the immigrants who had landed. According to the facts as established by CAT, of these migrants, 35 persons of Asian origin were transferred to the Canary Islands to initiate asylum application procedures on the advice of the Spanish Commission for Refugee Assistance (CEAR). Another 35 persons, of African origin, were transferred to the Canary Islands on 13 February on an aircraft chartered by Spain. In March they ended up in Guinea. On 14 February 2007, the immigrant identification process was completed. According to the complainant, all but 23 of the alleged victims signed voluntary repatriation agreements and were repatriated to India or Pakistan with the assistance of the International Organization for Migration (IOM). During the recognition procedure,[28] the alleged victims declared that the reason for their

---

[27] Ibid., pp. 205–220.

[28] To set up a recognition procedure aimed at identifying and sending persons back is a bit strange.

departure from India was fear of ostensible persecution as a result of the conflict in Kashmir. The 23 alleged victims, who refused to sign voluntary repatriation agreements, remained in detention under Spanish control in Nouadhibou.[29]

Spain rescued the asylum seekers in international waters reacting to a distress call of the *Marine I* and a request for assistance made by the Senegalese authorities. Spain acted according to Article 98 (1) and (2) of the UN Convention on the Law of the Sea (in conjunction with the International Convention on Maritime Search and Rescue, Annex, Chap. 3, Sect.3.1.7). It was up to Spain to *retrieve the persons in distress, provide for their initial medical or other needs, and deliver them to a place of safety*" (SAR Convention, Annex, Chap. 1, Sect. 1.3.2). The place of safety will normally be the nearest by port.[30] Even after their search and rescue operation Spain kept a supervisory role during the entire period of the asylum seekers detention in Nouadhibou. The Committee Against Torture held Spain responsible because Spain "maintained control over the persons on board the *Marine I* from the time the vessel was rescued and throughout the identification and repatriation process that took place at Nouadhibou". Thereby the Committee referred to its General Comment Number 2 as already mentioned above.[31]

The position taken by the Committee Against Torture seems to be the same as the position taken by the European Court of Human Rights in case a state party to the Convention boards a vessel at the high seas.[32] The case concerned drugs smugglers being intercepted at the high seas. The Court considered:

> Having made that clear, the Court notes, on the one hand, that it is not disputed that between 13 June 2002 (the date on which the *Winner* was intercepted) and 26 June 2002 (when it arrived in Brest harbour) the *Winner* and its crew were under the control of French military forces, so that even though they were outside French territory, they were within the jurisdiction of France for the purposes of Article 1 of the Convention.

Previously, the ECtHR dealt with another case relevant while dealing with this subject.

In 2001, the Court dealt with the complaint of a group of Albanians who tried to reach the coast of Italy by sea.[33] They failed to reach the border or even the territorial waters of Italy because their ship was seriously damaged by an Italian war vessel and sank. Fifty-eight passengers drowned. The survivors claimed the Italian war vessel had deliberately damaged their boat, in order to prevent the

---

[29] According to a reconstruction made by UNHCR the 35 African asylum seekers ended up in Guinea. With money of the Spanish authorities they returned home. Not all of the 35 Asian asylum seekers applied for asylum, only 13 of them. On April 23 276 of the 299 persons still in Mauritania returned home with the help of IOM. According to the organization lodging the complaint with CAT, the organization did so also on behalf of these 23 persons.

[30] Wouters 2009, pp. 435–438.

[31] The Committee Against Torture referred to General Comment 2, adopted 24 January 2008, CAT/C/GC/2.

[32] ECtHR 10 July 2008, Application nr. 3394/03, case of Medvedyev and others versus France.

[33] ECtHR, Xhavara and 12 Others versus Italy and Albania, 11 January 2001, Appl. No. 39473/98.

passengers' entry into Italy. The complaint was declared inadmissible because the national legal remedies had not been exhausted. Nevertheless the Court decided that Italy, being a State party to the Convention, had a responsibility in this case, irrespective of where the incident took place, be it inside or outside the territorial waters.

3.3.3 EU Law

In the process of creating an internal market, the European Member States have abolished the internal borders and adopted a Common European Asylum System. As a result stronger external border management was established. The prohibition of refoulement was incorporated in the Schengen Borders Code. It was specified that immigration controls are to be conducted without prejudice to the rights of refugees and persons requesting international protection, in particular as regards nonrefoulement.[34] Article 13 of the Schengen Borders Code guarantees an individual decision on a claim for (asylum) protection is taken. Article 13 reads:

> A third-country national who does not fulfill all the entry conditions laid down in Article 5(1) and does not belong to the categories of persons referred to in Article 5(4) shall be refused entry to the territories of the Member States. This shall be without prejudice to the application of special provisions concerning the right of asylum and to international protection or the issue of long-stay visas. 2. Entry may only be refused by a substantiated decision stating the precise reasons for the refusal. The decision shall be taken by an authority empowered by national law. It shall take effect immediately.

Stronger border management has led to the creation of FRONTEX. The legal basis for FRONTEX was Articles 62 (2) (a) and 66 EC Treaty.[35] According to these Articles: "The Council... shall... adopt... measures on the crossing of the external borders of the Member States which shall establish standards and procedures to be followed by Member States in carrying out checks on persons at such borders" (Article 62 (2) (a) and "...shall take measures to ensure cooperation between the relevant departments of the administrations of the Member States in the areas of visas, asylum, immigration and other policies related to freemovement of persons" (Article 66).

---

[34] Article 3 b of the Regulation (EC) No 562/2006 of the European Parliament and of the Council of 15 March 2006 establishing a Community Code on the rules governing the movement of persons across borders (Schengen Borders Code), 13 April 2006, Official Journal of the European Union L 105/1. See also Recital 20 of its preamble.

[35] Now, after the Treaty of Lisbon, the legal basis used for FRONTEX is Articles 74 and 77(1)(b) and (c) TFEU, see newly proposed Regulation amending the 2007 Regulation establishing FRONTEX, COM (2010)61 final.

FRONTEX activities in the Mediterranean raise the question, whether in the mixed flows of migrants trying to reach the European shores, the alien who is looking for protection will not be the victim of a too strict cordon.[36]

The Borders Code deals with border control activities at the border but also with control at the high seas and even in the territory of a third-country, as Den Heijer noted with a reference to Annex VI 3.1.1 of the Schengen Borders Code. He points to the fact that the Schengen Borders Code seems to be on the one hand restricted to geographical territory but on the other hand to be extended to measures of extra-territorial control leading to anomalies with regard to the definition of the activities of border guards.[37]

Also, in Annex VI Sect. 1.2.2, extra-territorial checks are mentioned. This paragraph reads:

> By way of derogation from point 1.2.1 and in order to facilitate rail traffic flows of high-speed passenger trains, the Member States on the itinerary of these trains from third countries may also decide, by common agreement with third countries concerned, to carry out entry checks on persons in trains from third countries in either one of the following ways: in the stations in a third-country where persons board the train.

3.3.4 UNHCR

UNHCR has closely followed EU discussions with respect to the Schengen Borders Code and on interception and rescue at sea, including in the context of FRONTEX coordinated operations.

UNHCR commented that Article 4 par 3 of the Schengen Borders Code[38] is lacking an explicit reference to Article 31 of the 51 CSR. Further, UNHCR noted that Article 5 Para 4 does not stipulate an obligation for Member States to grant, to all persons seeking protection, access to their territory and asylum procedure.[39]

---

[36] FRONTEX is more and more active in the Mediterranean. The Associated Press reported May 19 2009 the EU agency, known as FRONTEX, has sent 40 officers from 20 countries to work with 165 Greek border guards in the exercise. Border guards from new EU member Bulgaria are also assisting. Athens is seeking greater assistance from the European Union to help stop immigrants illegally crossing over its rugged borders with Turkey or reaching dozens of islands in the Aegean Sea. FRONTEX officers are using heartbeat and carbon dioxide detectors, along with heat cameras and other sensors to scan vehicles, and are watching the border with a surveillance helicopter and aircraft.

[37] Den Heijer 2010.

[38] Without prejudice to the exceptions provided for in Para 2 or to their international protection obligations, Member States shall introduce penalties, in accordance with their national law, for the unauthorized crossing of external borders at places other than border crossing points or at times other than the fixed opening hours. These penalties shall be effective, proportionate and dissuasive.

[39] UNHCR Observations on the access to the territory and the asylum procedure for persons seeking protection in the European Union, June 2006, Page 3, Para 12.

UNHCR is concerned that at present Member States have very divergent approaches to responding in rescue/interception activities. A major challenge is how to identify people seeking protection among those who are travelling toward the EU. In an advisory opinion on the extra-territorial application of non-refoulement obligations under the 51 CSR UNHCR has stressed that Article 31 51 CSR unambiguously contains an obligation not to send back a refugee or an asylum seeker, wherever a State exercises jurisdiction, including at the frontier, on the high seas or on the territory of another State.[40]

UNHCR called on the EU to make an explicit commitment to protection of the sensitive issue of border management and even suggested the adoption of a new EU legal instrument which clearly outlines Member States' protection responsibilities when their vessels intercept or rescue persons at sea.[41] UNHCR emphasizes the right to seek asylum and also points at the EU Charter of Fundamental Rights.[42]

3.3.5 *Safe Third Countries*

The United Nations Convention on the Law of the Sea obliges States to disembark rescued persons at a safe port. One could argue—as UNHCR did[43]—that rescued or intercepted asylum seekers have the right to be disembarked at a safe port, in a country where their asylum claim will be processed adequately and fairly. UNHCR takes as a starting point, (a) that the prohibition of refoulement has extra-territorial scope, and (b) that the North African countries are not—automatically—to be considered safe third countries.

Concerns arise when persons are removed to a third-country which is not safe. Cooperation (agreements with regard to returning persons) with third countries which are not signatories to the 51 CSR and to other human rights treaties and which are without functioning asylum systems does not guarantee a fair and effective asylum procedure. If disembarkation of rescued/intercepted people is foreseen in such countries, it cannot be ensured that refugees will receive protection. The State disembarking the rescued persons has a responsibility in this regard.

---

40 UN High Commissioner for Refugees 2007a, b.

41 UNHCR, 'Response to the European Commission's Green Paper on the Future Common European Asylum System, September 2007, p. 50. A reference is made to Executive Committee Conclusion on Protection Safeguards in Interception Measures, no. 97 (LIV) 2003.

42 Article 19 Paras 1 and 2 of the EU Charter on Fundamental rights read as follows: 1. Collective expulsions are prohibited. 2. No one may be removed, expelled or extradited to a State where there is a serious risk that he or she would be subjected to the death penalty, torture or other inhuman or degrading treatment or punishment.

43 UNHCR Observations on the access to the territory and the asylum procedure for persons seeking protection in the European Union, June 2006, Page 3, Para 12.

The Dublin Convention and the subsequent Regulation guarantee that an application can be lodged in at least one EU Member State. According to Article 3 of the Dublin Regulation it is required for the asylum seeker at least to be at the border or in a transit zone. An asylum claim can be declared inadmissible if the asylum seeker has stayed in a country of first asylum deemed to be safe or in a third safe country. Article 3 of the Procedures Directive obliges a State to examine every asylum claim lodged in the territory of the responsible EU Member State. Persons intercepted in the territorial waters should be treated equally and not sent back to countries not designated as safe third countries.

Article 3 of the Procedures Directive is not applicable if a vessel intercepts a refugee at the high seas or in the territorial waters of another non-EU Member State.[44]

Border control activities based on the Schengen Borders Code are not restricted to EU territory. If conducted outside the EU it seems to be access and individual decision taking must be guaranteed. Border guards have duties vis-à-vis persons seeking refuge also while acting abroad. This seems to me also in line with the obligations derived from CAT and ECHR. CAT General Comment number 2 stipulates the obligations vis-à-vis anyone under a State's jurisdiction. Article 3 CAT and Article 3 ECHR in conjunction with Article 1 ECHR clarify the responsibility of the State intercepting persons at sea. In my view it is therefore prohibited to disembark asylum seekers in a country that cannot be considered safe. If returned to a country not considered to be a safe country (or detained in a country outside Europe)—as a consequence of activities deployed by European States—the person concerned will, in my opinion, has a right to challenge the conduct of the border officials and ultimately lodge a complaint to CAT or the ECtHR.

3.4 Border Control Outside Europe

In the previous paragraph some remarks have been made with regard to border control at the high seas and in territory in third countries outside Europe. This paragraph sees upon activities at airports outside Europe.

3.4.1 Activities Undertaken at Airports

Border activities undertaken at airports find their basis in bilateral agreements between the country deploying civil servants and the country to where they are

[44] Weinzierl 2007.

deployed. Immigration Liaison Officers[45] (ILOs) undertake activities based on an agreement with the State where they are stationed. Immigration Liaison Officers check the identity and travel documents of persons who are seeking to leave a country.[46]

3.4.2 International Refugee Law

The prohibition of refoulement contained in Article 3 Convention against Torture, Article 7 International Covenant on Civil and Political Rights and Article 3 European Convention on Human Rights, oblige State parties not to return a person to his country of origin when there is a real risk of serious harm. This obligation has no territorial limitation. When a person is de facto under the control of a State, this State has the obligation to ensure protection from refoulement, except for the prohibition of refoulement contained in Article 33 of the 51 CSR. This Article is not applicable because Article 1A of the 51 CSR stipulates clearly that one must be outside his own country in order to be a refugee and be eligible for protection under this Convention.

3.4.3 Jurisprudence

There is until now no jurisprudence on this subject of an international supervisory body with regard to the prohibition of refoulement. The Human Rights Committee has addressed the topic of the right to leave one's own country in General Comment 27.[47] In Para 10 the HRC considers:

> The practice of States often shows that legal rules and administrative measures adversely affect the right to leave, in particular, a person's own country. It is therefore of the utmost importance that States parties report on all legal and practical restrictions on the right to leave which they apply both to nationals and to foreigners, in order to enable the Committee to assess the conformity of these rules and practices with article 12, Para 3. States parties should also include information in their reports on measures that impose sanctions on international carriers which bring to their territory persons without required documents, where those measures affect the right to leave another country.

As far as I know States have not complied with this request by HRC.[48]

---

[45] Council Regulation (EC) 377/2004 on the creation of an immigration liaison officers network, 19 February 2004, Official Journal of the European Union 2.3.2004, L64/1.

[46] Besides the network of Liaison Officers the Netherlands has situated a Rapid Action Team in Nigeria to check direct flights to the Netherlands in order to detect victims of trafficking.

[47] General Comment No. 27: Freedom of movement (Article 12): 02/11/99, CCPR/C/21 REV.1/Add.

[48] No reference has been made to the issue in the latest Concluding observations of the Human Rights Committee with regard to France and United Kingdom, see for France CCPR/C/FRA/CO/4, 31 July 2008 and for the United Kingdom CCPR/C/GBR/CO/6 30 July 2008.

3.4.4 EU Law

The activities of ILOs are outlined in the EC Regulation on the creation of an Immigration Liaison Officer's network.[49] Article 2 clarifies Immigration Liaison Officers to be active in the collection and exchange of information to combat illegal immigration. No mention is made of advising of national border officials or carriers being part of their job-description.

3.4.5 National Jurisprudence, the House of Lords, UNHCR

In dealing with the issue of carrier sanctions and the work of ILOs, UNHCR has intervened in the case of *Regina vs. the Immigration Officer at Prague Airport and another* before the British House of Lords.[50] UNHCR urged States to abide to the principle of good faith. UNHCR explained that different aspects to 'good faith' as a *general* principle of international law must be distinguished. These include the obligations of States, (1) to settle disputes in good faith; (2) to negotiate in good faith; (3) having signed a treaty, not to frustrate the achievement of its object and purpose prior to ratification; (4) having ratified a treaty, to apply and perform it in good faith and not to frustrate the achievement of its object and purpose; (5) to interpret treaties in good faith, in accordance with their ordinary meaning considered in context and in the light of their object and purpose (the principle *pacta sunt servanda*); (6) to fulfill in good faith obligations arising from other sources of international law; and (7) to exercise rights in good faith.

In the same intervention, UNHCR underlined the principle of nonrefoulement entailing the right not to be forced to remain in the country where one fears persecution. UNHCR pointed, *inter alia*, to a 1967 resolution adopted by the Committee of Ministers of the Council of Europe acknowledging that member States should "ensure that no one shall be subjected to refusal of admission at the frontier, rejection, expulsion or any other measure which would have the result of compelling him to return to, *or remain in* [emphasis, RB] a territory where he would be in danger of persecution…".[51] The House of Lords argued Article 33 51CSR not to be applicable since a foreign national applying for refugee status must, to qualify as a refugee, be outside his country of nationality.[52] This is, according to the Lords, unambiguously expressed in the Convention definition of a

---

[49] Council Regulation (EC) 377/2004) on the creation of an Immigration liaison officers network 19 February 2004, Journal of the European Union, L 64/1, Article 2.

[50] UN High Commissioner for Refugees 2004.

[51] Res. (67) 14 on Asylum to Persons in Danger of Persecution, adopted 29 June 1967.

[52] *Regina versus Immigration Officer at Prague Airport and Another, Ex parte European Roma Rights Centre and Others*, [2004] UKHL 55, United Kingdom: House of Lords, 9 December 2004, available at http://www.unhcr.org/refworld/docid/41c17ebf4.html.

refugee. Reference was made to Para 88 of the UNHCR *Handbook on Procedures and Criteria for Determining Refugee Status* (1992), according to which:

> It is a general requirement for refugee status that an applicant who has a nationality be outside the country of his nationality. There are no exceptions to this rule. International protection cannot come into play as long as a person is within the territorial jurisdiction of his home country.

This reasoning is followed in the academic literature.[53] The good faith argument is not considered to be convincing and rightly so.

According to ECRE Immigration Liaison Officers and Airline Liaison Officers are deployed by the UK (which has a network responsible for 128 countries), the Netherlands (posted in 13 countries, covering 56 countries) and France. Among new EU Members, Romania has ILOs/ALOs posted in 26 countries, most of which are EU Member States.[54] In some cases, EU Member States have undertaken joint initiatives.[55]

It may be that carriers and ILOs will be confronted with a person not having the right documents but claiming to be in need of international protection. What are they supposed to do? Is there any protection-sensitive activity to be discerned? Do the persons prevented from leaving have any possibilities for legal redress?

Hathaway is looking for a way out by pointing at the right to leave one's own country as contained in Article 12 (2) ICCPR.[56] In that case, the country of origin is the primary duty bearer. This should be further addressed because it might turn out to be difficult for a person to find international protection while being persecuted by his own government. Weinzierl[57] points also at Article 12 (2) ICCPR and refers to General Comment 27 (dated 1999) of the HRC, in which the Committee with respect to Article 12 (2) ICCPR calls on the States to include information in their reports on measures that impose sanctions on international carriers which bring to their territory persons without required documents, where those measures affect the right to leave another country. It is apparent she concludes from this that violations of the ICCPR's right to leave can not only be committed by those States that are to be left, but also by potential countries of destination.

But how to seek redress if stopped at the border while leaving one's own country and trying to enter Europe?

---

53 Hathaway 2005, p. 312.

54 Other non-EU countries have stationed ILOs as well. Canada has so-called Canadian "Migration Integrity Officers" in countries of transit. They have an unknown impact with regard to access to Canadian territory, but this appears to be significant. Canada maintains a large number of officers abroad, whose primary focus is interdiction. It is unclear what instructions Officers are given in cases where they identify individuals with protection concerns.

55 European Council on Refugees and Exiles 2007, available at http://www.unhcr.org/refworld/docid/4766464e2.html.

56 Ibid., pp. 309–312.

57 Weinzierl 2007, p. 48.

HRC's call in 1999 to provide more information with respect to the effects of ILOs is still to be answered. On 29 May 2008, the European Parliament raised the following question to the Commission: "To what extent has the introduction of Directive 2001/51/EC(2) (carrier sanctions) resulted in fewer asylum applications? To what extent has the deployment of ILOs influenced the number of asylum applications in Member States?" Mr Barrot on behalf of the Commission on 18 July 2008 answered it was not possible on the basis of the information submitted by the ILOs to make any assessment of the influence of the ILOs' activities on the number of asylum applications presented in Member States. He also clarified that at present the bi-annual ILO reports are restricted Council documents, and the decision to de-classify them is to be taken by the Council.

In December 2008 a report was issued by the Refugee Council in the United Kingdom: "Remote Controls: how UK border controls are endangering the lives of refugees."[58] In the research report it is stated that out posted UK immigration officials, as well as the government and private sector actors are relied upon by the Government to implement UK immigration controls. They are neither tasked with nor trained in refugee protection. The report states that immigration and airline officials have no knowledge of systematic procedures to follow in order to identify refugees and to ensure that they are protected. The researchers have not found publicly available information, as to who is stopped, whether they are refugees in need of protection, or what happens to them after they are intercepted.

In sum, the activities of the ILOs are not governed by any international treaty. It can be argued that being agents of the State,[59] States can be held responsible for their conduct. Not to permit leaving one's country of origin could constitute an infringement of the right contained in Article 12 (2) ICCPR. If as result of the activities of ILOs the person concerned ends in detention and being tortured or ill-treated it can be conceived as to be an infringement of the right not to be tortured and ill-treated as contained in Article 3 and 16 CAT, Article 3 ECHR and Article 7 ICCPR.

3.5 To Conclude

In principle, international law does safeguard the right to seek asylum, not only on the territory—which includes the territorial sea—of the country of refuge, but also at the border. Even at the high seas and in territorial waters of another country, the prohibition of refoulement applies. International treaties like CAT, ICCPR and

[58] Refugee Council in the United Kingdom 2008.

[59] International Law Commission, Draft Articles on the Responsibility of States for Internationally Wrongful Acts. Article reads: The conduct of any State organ shall be considered an act of that State under international law, whether the organ exercises legislative, executive, judicial or any other functions, whatever position it holds in the organization of the State, and whatever its character as an organ of the central Government or of a territorial unit of the State.

ECHR reflect the idea of States being responsible for extra-territorial conduct if the persons concerned are under the effective control of States. The EU Dublin Regulation and EU Procedures Directive guarantee asylum seekers on the territory and at the border access to the asylum procedure, at least in one EU country. If border control based on the competencies in the Schengen Borders Code has been undertaken at the high seas or even in third countries the obligations of States with respect to the principle of non-refoulement might be extended likewise.

Although legal obligations seem to exist, increasingly access to territory and (asylum) protection procedures is being denied. Persons are prevented from taking a plane to European airports. Persons are returned to countries where they have departed from without being allowed to lodge an asylum application. Only few complaints were lodged with an international supervisory body. Access to a legal remedy is hard to find.

Activities at EU border points are not always transparent. It is unclear what legal basis permits EU States to create obstacles to applying for asylum when persons are deported from one country to the country of origin, transiting an EU airport. In such a situation a State must allow an asylum claim to be lodged. This is certainly true when NGOs or UNHCR indicate the willingness of the deportee to apply for asylum and inform the State of the possible grounds for persecution and provide relevant country of origin information indicating the risk of serious problems upon return.

With regard to activities at sea, be it on the high seas or in the territorial waters of a non-European country, States appear to be reluctant to live up to the standards as entailed in the Schengen Borders Code and in views and judgments of supervisory bodies. It seems to become European policy to just send the potential refugee claimant back to the country from where he was when trying to reach the coast of Europe.

Competencies and responsibilities of States vis-à-vis persons intercepted outside Europe, be it at the high seas, in the territorial waters of a third-country or at the airports of countries outside the EU, are not well defined, even though the Schengen Borders Code in Annex VI does not limit the activities and therefore the responsibilities to the external borders. But practice shows different interpretations exist as to the responsibilities. One cannot deny that UNHCR urging for a specific EU legal document clarifying the responsibilities outside the EU touched upon a critical point. According to the EC Communication of June 2009 the European Union will have to consider a clarification of the international rules in light of the imperatives of maritime control and surveillance, while preserving the fundamental obligation of rescue at sea. It is to be noted that the EC did not mention the rules have to be clarified in the light of the prohibition of refoulement.

Immigration Liaison Officers conduct activities in secret. Certainly they do hinder access to Europe. Although the Human Rights Committee urged States in 1999 to provide information, no information is currently available. The European Council should lift the secrecy of the Council documents. In order to generate transparency and credibility the bi-annual ILO reports are to be de-classified.

Lawyers helping aliens looking for legal remedies might explore the possibilities to lodge a complaint with the Human Rights Committee based on Article 12 (2) ICCPR.

In general one can argue that extra-territorial entry management must be accompanied by corresponding safeguards. FRONTEX for example should not undertake any activity without a European port of embarkation being guaranteed. On board vessels deployed in interception activities independent observers should be present. Sending persons fleeing persecution back to countries outside the EU that have not made commitments to protect refugees is not the solution.

References

Den Heijer M (2009) The fight against illegal migration and death at the border. In: Snyder, Thym (eds) Europe—a Continent of Immigration? Legal challenges in the construction of European migration policy, Bruylant, Brussels (To be published)

Den Heijer M (2010) Europe beyond its borders: refugee and human rights protection in extraterritorial immigration control. In: Ryan B, Mitsilegas V (eds) Extraterritorial immigration control: legal challenges. Brill Academic Publishers, Leyden, Intersentia, Antwerpen (To be published)

European council on refugees and exiles (2007) Defending refugees' access to protection in Europe. http://www.unhcr.org/refworld/docid/4766464e2.html

Feller E, Türk V, Nicholson F (2001) Refugee protection in international law. Cambridge University Press, Cambridge

Hathaway JC (2005) The rights of refugees under international law. Cambridge University Press, Cambridge

Refugee Council in the United Kingdom (2008) Remote controls: how UK border controls are endangering the lives of refugees. http://www.refugeecouncil.org.uk/policy/position/2008/remotecontrols/remote_controls_report.html

UN high commissioner for refugees (2004) European Roma rights centre and others v. Immigration officer at prague airport. http://www.unhcr.org/refworld/docid/41c1aa654.html

UN High Commissioner for Refugees (2007a) Refugee protection and mixed migration: a 10-point plan of action. http://www.unhcr.org/refworld/docid/45b0c09b2.html

UN High Commissioner for Refugees (2007b) Advisory opinion on the extraterritorial application of non-refoulement obligations under the 1951 convention relating to the status of refugees and its 1967 protocol. http://www.unhcr.org/refworld/docid/45f17a1a4.html

Weinzierl R (2007) The demands of human and EU fundamental rights for the protection of the European union's external borders. German Institute for Human Rights, Berlin

Wouters K (2009) International legal standards for the protection from Refoulement. Intersentia, Antwerpen

Chapter 4
The EU Qualification Directive and Refugees *Sur Place*

Sylvie Da Lomba

Contents

4.1 Introduction 43
4.2 The Recognition of International Protection Needs *Sur Place* 45
4.3 Protection Needs Based on Post-Departure Activity 49
4.4 Manufactured Asylum Claims *Sur Place* 53
4.4.1 The Issue of Good Faith 53
4.4.2 The Qualification Directive and Manufactured Asylum Claims 57
4.5 Conclusion 61
References 63

4.1 Introduction

Refugees are commonly understood to have left the country of origin owing to fear of persecution. The need for international protection is therefore assumed to be the cause of their flight. While this account reflects the experience of most refugees, it is accepted that needs for international protection may arise after leaving the country of origin, i.e. *sur place*.[1] Thus, while the profile of refugees *sur place* may be considered atypical, it does not set them apart from other persons in need of

[1] UNHCR 1992, paras 94–96.

S. Da Lomba (✉)
University of Strathclyde, Glasgow, UK
e-mail: sylvie.da-lomba@strath.ac.uk

F. A. N. J. Goudappel and H. S. Raulus (eds.), *The future of asylum in the European Union*, DOI: 10.1007/978-90-6704-802-6_4,

international protection and refugees *sur place* are subject to the same international protection regime.[2] In line with international standards, Council Directive 2004/83/EC on minimum standards for the qualification and status of third country nationals or stateless persons as refugees or as persons who otherwise need international protection and the content of the protection granted (hereafter the Qualification Directive) recognises the existence of international protection needs *sur place*.[3] However, in contrast to the Convention relating to the Status of Refugees (hereafter the 1951 Convention),[4] the Qualification Directive does so expressly. It provides for the introduction of 'common concepts of protection needs arising *sur place*' and states that such needs may result in the recognition of refugee or subsidiary protection status.[5] The author contends that, while the insertion of provisions dealing with refugees *sur place* boded well for the protection of refugees *sur place* within the EU, the Directive's response to international protection needs *sur place* is ambivalent.

The Qualification Directive aims to identify "persons *genuinely* in need of international protection."[6] This aim must be pursued with due regard for the 1951 Convention and other relevant international instruments.[7] The Directive does not and cannot supersede the 1951 Convention and the EU Member States remain

[2] *Infra* Sect. 4.2.

[3] Council Directive 2004/83/EC of 29 April 2004 (OJ L 304/12 of 30 September 2004). The Directive was adopted as part of the five-year programme of EU legislation on asylum agreed by the Tampere Conclusions (European Community Tampere European Council Presidency Conclusions 15 and 16 October 1999, reproduced in (1999) 11(4) International Journal of Refugee Law, p. 738). The Directive was adopted on the basis of Article 63(1)(c) of the Treaty establishing the European Community. For a comprehensive analysis of the Qualification Directive, see Storey 2008 and Lambert 2006.

[4] See Sect. 4.2 *infra*. References to the 1951 Convention are understood to include the 1967 Protocol relating to the Status of Refugees.

[5] Council Directive 2004/83/EC of 29 April 2004 (OJ L 304/12 of 30 September 2004). The concept of 'person eligible for subsidiary protection' is defined in Article 2(e). It covers third country nationals who do not qualify for refugee status but who 'would face a real risk of suffering serious harm as defined in Article 15' if returned to the country of origin (Article 2(e)). On subsidiary protection, see McAdam 2005 and Piotrowicz and Van Eck 2004 (This article provides an analysis of subsidiary protection in the proposals for a Qualification Directive).

[6] Council Directive 2004/83/EC of 29 April 2004 (OJ L 304/12 of 30 September 2004) Rec. 6

[7] These include the European Convention on Human Rights 1950 (ECHR) and the United Nations Convention against Torture and Other Cruel, Inhuman or Degrading Treatment or Punishment 1987 (CAT) Peers and Rogers 2006, p. 333.

bound by their obligations under this instrument.[8] In this respect, the Directive asserts the Convention as "the *cornerstone* of the international legal regime for the protection of refugees"[9] and reiterates that the establishment of a Common European Asylum System (CEAS) is "based on the full and inclusive application of the (1951) Convention,"[10] Consequently the concept of 'genuine European refugee' must be shaped by reference to the EU Member States' international obligations and must cover refugees *sur place*.[11] Yet the Qualification Directive's approach to refugees *sur place* shows difficulty in accepting some of these refugees as 'genuine'. The Directive seems to establish a hierarchy between asylum claims *sur place* based on events that occurred in the country of origin post-departure and claims that rely on actions engaged in since leaving that country. While the former are looked upon favourably, the latter are suspected of being manufactured. Whether this is indeed the case, however, should not be a consideration which decides who is deserving of international protection as this would engage the EU Member States' international obligations. With this in mind, this paper focuses on the Qualification Directive's approach to asylum claims *sur place* based on post-departure activity, with an emphasis on manufactured asylum claims.

4.2 The Recognition of International Protection Needs *Sur Place*

The 1951 Convention does not explicitly envisage the case of refugees *sur place*. However, it does not require fear of persecution to arise before the asylum seeker leaves his or her country of origin. The UNHCR Handbook emphasises that the

---

[8] See Storey, *supra* n. 3, Sect. 4.1, pp. 7–8. The EU Member States remain equally bound by obligations arising from other relevant international instruments. See Peers and Rogers, *supra* n. 7, Sect. 4.1, p. 333.

[9] See *supra* n. 6 at Rec. 3. Emphasis added.

[10] See *supra* n. 6, Rec. 2.

[11] On the concept of 'genuine European refugee', see, for example, El-Enany 2008, p. 313.

alienage requirement contained in the refugee Convention definition[12] "(…) does not mean that [the asylum seeker] must have left it (i.e. the country of origin) on account of well-founded fear"[13] and decision-makers have interpreted the 1951 Convention as encompassing international protection needs *sur place*.[14]

We have noted that, unlike the 1951 Convention, the Qualification Directive makes express reference to international protection needs *sur place*.[15] It specifies that such needs may result in the grant of refugee status or subsidiary protection.[16] In accordance with UNHCR guidelines,[17] the Qualification Directive identifies two types of circumstances that may give rise to international protection needs *sur place*. First, "[a] well-founded fear of being persecuted or a real risk of suffering serious harm may be based on events which have taken place since the applicant left the country of origin."[18] Such events include "(…) a *coup d'état*, change of government, significant change in government policy, outbreak or escalation or armed conflict, or the disclosure of the names of asylum applicants to officials in the country of origin."[19] Secondly, a person may become a refugee *sur place* as a result of actions undertaken since leaving the country of origin.[20] Activity *sur*

---

[12] 1951 Refugee Convention, Article 1(A)(2). '[i]nternational protection cannot come into play as long as a person is within the territorial jurisdiction of his home country' UNHCR 1992, *supra* n. 1, Sect. 4.1, para 88. Goodwin-Gill and McAdam note that '(…) the fact of having fled, of having crossed an international frontier, is an intrinsic part of the quality of refugee, understood in the ordinary sense' Goodwin-Gill and McAdam 2007, p. 63. The alienage requirement, however, has been called into question. According to Hathaway, '[t]here is nothing intuitively obvious about this requirement: many if not most of the persons forced to flee their homes in search of safety remain within the boundaries of their state' see Hathaway 1991, p. 29. See also Shacknove 1985, pp. 274 and 277. In Hathaway's opinion, three factors explain the inclusion of the alienage requirement in the Convention definition, namely limited resources, concern about state participation and respect for state sovereignty. See Hathaway 1991, pp. 29–33.

[13] UNHCR 1992, *supra* n. 1, Sect. 4.1, para 94.

[14] For example, from the time the 1951 Convention entered into force, the French *Commission des Recours des réfugiés* (CRR) found that well-founded fear of being persecuted could arise post-departure (CCR, *Nejad Nehmed*, 662, 4 November 1954, referred to in Tiberghien 1988, p. 389. Refugee status, however, was refused in this case. The CCR took the view that the form of prosecution that the asylum seeker was likely to face upon return to his country of origin owing to political activities carried out in France did not amount to persecution within the meaning of Article 1(A)(2) of the 1951 Convention. See also *Danian v. Secretary of State for the Home Department* [2000] Imm AR 96 (English Court of Appeal).

[15] See *supra* n. 6, Sect. 4.1, Rec. 18 and Article 5.

[16] Ibid., Article 5(1) and (2).

[17] UNHCR 1992, *supra* n. 1, Sect. 4.1, paras 95 and 96.

[18] See *supra* n. 6, Sect. 4.1, Article 5(1). This in line with para 95 of the UNHCR Handbook (*supra* n. 1).

[19] UNHCR 2005, p. 44. UNHCR notes, for instance, that economic migrants may become refugees *sur place* as a result of such events. See UNHCR 2007, para 20.

[20] See *supra* n. 6, Sect. 4.1, Article 5(2). This is consistent with para 96 of UNHCR 1992, *supra* n. 1, Sect. 4.1.

place may also include "(...) associating with refugees already recognized, or expressing his political views in his country of residence (...)."[21] In *Mbanza v. Secretary of State for the Home Department*, the English Court of Appeal held that a person who faced a well-founded fear of persecution as a failed asylum seeker if returned to his or her country of origin should be bestowed refugee status.[22] Further examples include conversion to a religion not tolerated by the authorities of the country of origin or unauthorised stay abroad, where it is punished by severe sanctions.[23]

Asylum claims *sur place* must be assessed on the same basis as other claims for refugee status.[24] However, while this principle is accepted in respect of asylum claims *sur place* based on events that occurred in the country of origin during the

---

[21] Ibid., para 96.

[22] *R. v Secretary of State for the Home Department Ex p. Mbanza* (1996) Imm AR 136. The UK Government adopted a non-returns policy for Zimbabwean nationals in January 2002 (Home Office press notice STAT001/2002, *Home Secretary Suspends Removals to Zimbabwe*, 15 January 2002). The policy ended in November 2004. The UK Government considered that it acted as an incentive to come to the UK for people who were not in need of international protection (HC Deb 16 November 2004 c78-WS). Removals to Zimbabwe resumed immediately but were subsequently suspended until the hearing of a test case (G. Garton Grimwood, *Asylum Seekers from Zimbabwe*, SN/HA/3391, Home Affairs Section, House of Commons Library, 13 March 2009, p. 3-13). The UK Asylum and Immigration held that failed asylum seekers did not as such face a real risk of being subjected to persecution or ill-treatment if returned to Zimbabwe (*HS (returning asylum seekers) Zimbabwe CG* [2007] UKAIT 00094; *AA (Risk for involuntary returnees) Zimbabwe CG* [2006] UKAIT 00061; and *SM and Others (MDC –internal flight—risk categories) Zimbabwe CG* [2005] UKAIT 00100). The Tribunal, however, identified risk categories; these include: persons who are or suspected of being politically active in opposition to the regime in place (*SM and Others (MDC –internal flight—risk categories) Zimbabwe CG* [2005] UKAIT 00100, paras 42–43), including anyone who cannot demonstrate positive support for Zanu-PF or alignment with the regime (*RN (Returnees) Zimbabwe CG* [2008] UKAIT 00083, para 216); 'those whose military history discloses issues that will lead to further investigation by the security services upon return to Harare Airport' (*AA (Risk for involuntary returnees) Zimbabwe CG* [2006] UKAIT 00061, para 72); 'those in respect of whom there are outstanding and unresolved criminal issues' (*AA (Risk for involuntary returnees) Zimbabwe CG* [2006] UKAIT 00061, para 72); and 'those seen to be active in association with human rights or civil society organisations where evidence suggests that the particular organisation has been identified by the authorities as a critic or opponent of the Zimbabwean regime' (*HS (returning asylum seekers) Zimbabwe CG* [2007] UKAIT 00094, para 51). In February 2009, the Parliamentary Under Secretary of State at the Home Office declared that, although returns to Zimbabwe were not currently enforced, failed asylum seekers who were not in need of international protection could expect to be returned (HL Deb 23 February 2009 Col WA7). In respect of failed asylum seekers' removals to the Democratic Republic of Congo, the UK Asylum and Immigration Tribunal found that there was insufficient evidence that they constituted a risk category (*BK(DRC CG)[*2007] UKAIT 00098). On rejected asylum claims and international protection needs *sur place*, see Clayton 2008, pp. 455–456.

[23] See UNHCR 2005, *supra* n. 19, Sect. 4.2, p. 44.

[24] Ibid.

asylum seeker's absence,[25] it is called into question in respect of claims that rely on post-departure activity. "[Decision-makers] are wary that an asylum seeker might engage in activities in a country of potential refuge for the purpose of creating a claim *sur place*."[26] For example, Musalo observes that post-departure religious conversions are often suspected of being manufactured.[27] These claims are therefore met with circumspection and manufactured claims are seen as a form of asylum abuse.[28] In this context, continuity and good faith are seen as indicative of the existence of a need for international protection *sur place* while their absence casts doubt on the 'genuineness' of the claim. Yet Goodwin-Gill and McAdam point out that

> there is no rational basis for distinguishing between an individual whose opinions and activities in the country of refuge represent a continuation of opinions and activities begun in the country of origin, and one whose political engagement only begins when he or she has left their homeland (…) Equally, there is no rational basis for distinguishing (…) between the innocent bystander to whom political opinions are imputed by the persecutor, and the less than innocent bystander whose self-interested actions lead the persecutor also to impute political opinions to the person concerned.[29]

Besides there is no authoritative basis for demanding continuity and good faith. Indeed neither is a condition for refugee status under the 1951 Convention.[30] The UNHCR handbook stipulates that "[w]hether [post-departure] actions are

---

[25] See, for instance, *supra* n. 6, Sect. 4.1, Article 5(1) and Article 8(1) of the Commission's Proposal for a Qualification Directive (Document COM(2001) 510 final of the Commission of the European Communities, Proposal for a Council Directive on minimum standards for the qualification and status of third country nationals and stateless persons as refugees or as persons who otherwise need international protection (hereafter the Commission's Proposal). The drafting of both provisions shows that this type of asylum claim *sur place* is not deemed problematic.

[26] Musalo et al. 2007, p. 200.

[27] Musalo 2002, p. 49.

[28] In *Shirazi v. Secretary of State for the Home Department*, Sedley L.J. said

> I am conscious of the ever-present risk of creating a back to door to asylum by allowing claims to apostasy on the part of nationals of theocratic states to establish without more a well-founded fear of persecution. That, no doubt, makes great caution appropriate in deciding (…) on the question off causation which can arise in the case of refugees sur place' (*Shirazi v. Secretary of State for the Home Department* [2003] EWCA Civ 1562, para 32 (English Court of Appeal).

However, Sedley L.J. had stressed that the status of refugee *sur place* was recognised in international law (see para 19).

[29] Goodwin-Gill and McAdam, *supra* n. 12, Sect. 4.2, p. 89. In *Ward*, the Supreme Court of Canada held that '[t]he political opinion ascribed to the claimant and for which he or she fears persecution need not necessarily conform to the claimant's true beliefs' (*Canada (Attorney General) v. Ward*, [1993] 2 S.C.R. 689).

[30] The issue of continuity is discussed in Sect. 3 and the concept of good faith for the purpose of seeking refugee status is examined in Sect. 4.

sufficient to justify a well-founded fear of persecution must be determined by a careful examination of the circumstances.[31] Decision-makers must examine whether:

> The applicant's convictions and/or conduct have come, or are likely to come, to the attention of the authorities in his or her country of origin[[32]]; and
> Whether there is a reasonable possibility that on return the applicant would experience persecution for a reason related to a 1951 Convention.[33]

It remains the case that asylum claims *sur place* based on post-departure actions arouse suspicion. The author argues that this suspicion pervades the Qualification Directive's approach to these claims. Indeed the Directive places must emphasis on continuity and singles out manufactured asylum claims, thereby raising the issue of good faith.

4.3 Protection Needs Based on Post-Departure Activity

The Qualification Directive readily accepts that international protection needs *sur place* may arise out of events that occurred in the country of origin post-departure. Article 5(1) reads that "[a] well-founded fear of being persecuted or a real risk of suffering serious harm may be based on events which have taken place since the applicant left the country of origin."[34] The Directive's approach to claims that rely on post-departure actions, however, is rather ambivalent.

---

[31] UNHCR 1992, *supra* n. 1, Sect. 4.1, paras 96 and 83.

[32] Ibid, para 96.

[33] UNHCR 2005, *supra* n. 19, Sect. 4.2, p. 44. In Goodwin-Gill and McAdam's opinion, '[i]t might be argued that, in a refugee status case, the "likelihood of persecution" must be established on a balance of probabilities'. See Goodwin-Gill and McAdams, *supra* n. 12, Sect. 4.2, p. 54. This is in line with UNHCR guidelines. According to the latter, '[t]he adjudicator should consider the applicant's fear well-founded if there is a reasonable possibility that the applicant would face some form of harm if returned to the country of origin or habitual residence'. See UNHCR 2005, n. 19, Sect. 4.2, p. 44. See also UNHCR 1992, *supra* n. 1, Sect. 4.1, para 42. The author contends that in certain circumstances it may also be necessary to determine whether post-departure actions may give rise to well-founded fear of persecution at the hands of non-state actors. See, for example, CRR, *M.M*, 27 April 2006, available at http://www.commission-refugies.fr/centre_recherche_18/thematique/motifs_reconnaissance_qualite_refugie_m77/religion_m195/christianisme_m197/?deplier=2073#art2073 (accessed 13 July 2009). The Qualification Directive expressly recognises non-state agents as potential actors of persecution or serious harm (see *supra* n. 6, Sect. 4.1, Article 6(c)).

[34] The UNHCR Annotated Comments on the Qualification Directive did not include remarks on Article 5(1), thereby suggesting that its drafting was deemed satisfactory (UNHCR, UNHCR Annotated Comments on the EC Council Directive 2004/83/EC of 29 April 2004 on Minimum Standards for the Qualification and Status of Third Country Nationals or Stateless Persons as Refugees or as Persons who otherwise need International Protection and the Content of the Protection Granted (OJ L 304/12 of 30 September 2004) (hereafter the UNHCR Annotated Comments).

Article 5(2) of the Qualification Directive reads, *inter alia*, that "[a] well-founded fear of being persecuted or a real risk of suffering serious harm may be based on activities which have been engaged in by the applicant since he left the country of origin (…)" Article 5(2), however, specifies that post-departure activities may give rise to well-founded of persecution or real risk of suffering serious harm '*in particular* where it is established that the activities relied upon constitute *the expression and continuation of convictions or orientations held* in *the country of origin*.'[35] It is argued that the wording of Article 5(2) makes it susceptible of diverging interpretations. This in itself is problematic as it goes against the goal of establishing 'common concepts of protection needs arising *sur place*' and 'common criteria for the identification of persons genuinely in need of international protection' set out in the Qualification Directive.[36] In Teitgen-Colly's opinion, the term 'in particular' makes it clear that a need for international protection *sur place* may arise in the absence of continuity.[37] This reading of Article 5(2) is in line with that advocated by UNHCR. Commenting on Article 5(2), UNHCR stressed that

> Even where it cannot be established that the applicant has already held the convictions or orientations in the country of origin, the asylum-seeker is entitled to the right of freedom of expression, freedom of religion and freedom of association (…) Such freedoms include the right to change one's religion or convictions, which could occur subsequent to departure e.g. due to disaffection with the religion or policies of the country of origin, or greater awareness of the impact of certain policies.[38]

This interpretation of Article 5(2) is also consistent with the approach adopted in a number of European jurisdictions. In the UK, for instance, it is accepted that refugee status may be granted owing to well-founded fear of persecution based on post-departure actions.[39] In France, the CRR has bestowed refugee status on persons who had left their country of origin for reasons of personal convenience and subsequently engaged in political activities in France resulting in their facing a well-founded fear of being persecuted upon return.[40] In contrast to Teitgen-Colly, Battjes contends that "[Article 5(2)] comes close to stating the "continuation of

---

[35] Emphasis added.

[36] See *supra* n. 6, Sect. 4.1, Rec. 18 and 6.

[37] Teitgen-Colly 2006, p. 1522.

[38] See *supra* n. 34, Sect. 4.3, p. 56.

[39] *YB (Eritrea) v Secretary of State for the Home Department* [2008] EWCA Civ 360 and *Shirazi v Secretary of State for the Home Department*. See *supra* n. 28, Sect. 4.2.

[40] CRR, *Jean*, 9.358, 25 April 1978, referred to in Tiberghien, *supra* n. 14, Sect. 4.2, p. 390 and CRR, *Ba*, 10.232, 27 November 1979.

convictions" as a condition for well-founded fear or real harm."[41] It is the author's view that, while both readings of Article 5(2) are plausible, the former should prevail as a restrictive reading of Article 5(2) would amount to introducing a condition which is not present in the Convention refugee definition. Furthermore, it would be at variance with the definition of "person eligible for subsidiary protection."[42]

The author contends that, short of making continuity an eligibility criterion, the emphasis that Article 5(2) places on continuity risks creating a presumption, albeit not absolute, that claims based on activities engaged in since leaving the country of origin lack credibility and are likely to be manufactured. This analysis finds support in the Commission's Proposal for a Qualification Directive[43]; According to Article 8(2) of the Commission's Proposal,

> A well-founded fear of being persecuted or otherwise suffering serious unjustified harm may be based on activities which have been engaged in by the applicant since he left his country of origin, save where it is established that such activities were engaged in for the sole purpose of creating the necessary conditions for making an application for international protection. That is not the case where the activities relied upon constitute the expression and continuation of convictions held in the country of origin, and they are related to the grounds for recognition of the need for international protection.[44]

As in the case of Article 5(2) of the Qualification Directive, Article 8(2) could be read as affirming continuity as a condition for establishing well-founded fear of persecution or real risk of suffering serious harm. At the very least, it risked instating a presumption that a lack of continuity points to a lack of credibility. Yet we have seen that the characterisation of continuity as a condition for refugee status would infringe the 1951 Convention. The Commission explained that "[a] claim shall be most readily established where activities relied upon constitute the expression and continuation previously held in the country of origin (...) Continuity of this kind is not however an absolute requirement but may give an

---

[41] Battjes 2006, p. 261. This restrictive approach is, for instance, adopted in Denmark. Adjudicators there may refuse refugee status '(...) if the activities are not a "natural continuation or prolongation of the activities" carried out in the country of origin (...)' See Musalo et al., *supra* n. 26, Sect. 4.2, p. 200. The Qualification Directive, however, is not binding on Denmark. In accordance with Articles 1 and 2 of the Protocol on the position of Denmark, annexed to the Treaty on European Union and the Treaty establishing the European Community, Denmark did not take part in the Directive (See *supra* n. 6, Rec. 40).

[42] Article 2(e) of the Qualification Directive reads that

> "person eligible for subsidiary protection" means a third country national or a stateless person who does not qualify as a refugee but in respect of whom substantial grounds have been shown for believing that the person concerned, if returned to his or her country of origin, or in the case of a stateless person, to his or her country of former habitual residence, would face a real risk of suffering serious harm as defined in Article 15, and to whom Article 17(1) and (2) do not apply, and is unable, or, owing to such risk, unwilling to avail himself or herself of the protection of that country.

[43] See *Supra* n. 25, Sect. 4.2.

[44] Ibid.

indication as to the credibility of the application."[45] The Commission's explanations, however, were in themselves equivocal. On the one hand, the use of the term 'requirement' suggested that continuity was construed as a requirement for international protection. On the other hand, the last part of the second sentence seemed to indicate that continuity should be addressed as a credibility matter.

Article 8(2) of the Commission's Proposal raised a further issue that of exclusion from international protection status owing to bad faith. It is contended that the phrase 'save where it is established that such activities were engaged in for the sole purpose of creating the necessary conditions for making an application for international protection' could be interpreted as permitting bars to refugee or subsidiary protection status on account of bad faith. Yet the 1951 Convention does not contain a good faith requirement[46] and does not allow bars to refugee status on that basis.[47] The Commission made clear that manufactured claims could result in the grant of international protection status,[48] but specified that "(...) Member States [were] entitled to start that from the premise that [opportunistic] activities [did] not in principle furnish grounds for a grant of [international protection status] and [should] have serious grounds for questioning the credibility of the applicant."[49] It is apparent from the Commission's explanations that Article 8(2) with its emphasis on continuity sought to target manufactured claims with a view to addressing asylum abuse.[50] It is argued that the ambiguous wording of Article 8(2) revealed a reluctance to grant international protection status on the basis of manufactured asylum claims *sur place*. Like Article 8(2), Article 5(2) establishes a strong linkage between continuity and credibility. However, it no longer elicits the question of good faith. In *YB (Eritrea) v. Secretary of State for the Home Department*, for example, Sedley L.J. pointed out that "(...) it [was] evident from the way art 5(2) [was] formulated that activities other than bona fide political protest [could] create refugee status *sur place*."[51] Besides, to conclude otherwise would cause internal consistency. Indeed we will see in the next section that Article 4(3)(d) as well as Article 20(6) and (7) of the Qualification Directive clearly indicate that international protection status may be granted on the basis of manufactured well-founded fear of persecution or real risk of suffering serious

---

45 Ibid.

46 See Goodwin-Gill, *supra* n. 12, Sect. 4.2, p. 89.

47 1951 Convention, Article 1(D), (E) and (F). On the Convention exclusion clauses, see, *supra* n. 1, paras 140–163; UNHCR, *Guidelines on International Protection. Application of the Exclusion Clauses* (Article 1 F of the 1951 Convention)', HCR/GIP/03/05, 4 September 2003; and Gilbert 2003.

48 See *supra* n. 25, Sect. 4.2, pp. 16–17.

49 Ibid., p. 17.

50 Ibid., p. 16 The Commission stressed that Article 8(2) aimed, *inter alia*, to address 'the issue of abuse in *sur place* cases'.

51 *YB (Eritrea) v Secretary of State for the Home Department*, *supra* n. 39, Sect. 4.3, para 15.

harm.[52] The Qualification Directive, however, remains concerned with manufactured asylum claims *sur place*.

4.4 Manufactured Asylum Claims *Sur Place*

The suspicion that surrounds asylum claims *sur place* based on post-departure activity is manifest in the Qualification Directive. The concern is that actions may be undertaken for the sole purpose of creating an international protection need *sur place*. As a result two conflicting considerations shape the Directive's approach to manufactured asylum claims: asylum abuse and compliance with international obligations. There seems to be an underlying belief that asylum seekers who have manufactured their claim have not 'legitimately' sought protection in the EU and are not "genuinely in need of international protection."[53] Yet, observance of the EU Member States' international obligations compelled the Directive to accept that such claims could give rise to international protection needs *sur place*.

4.4.1 The Issue of Good Faith

Manufactured asylum claims beg the question whether asylum seekers must act in good faith. Grahl-Madsen postulates that "[t]he principle of good faith implies that a Contracting State cannot be bound to grant refugee status to a person who is not a *bona fide* refugee."[54] He concedes that well-founded fear of persecution may be founded on imputed political opinion,[55] but operates a distinction "between those who unwittingly or unwillingly have committed a politically pertinent act, and those who have done it for the sole purpose of getting a pretext for claiming refugeehood."[56] Consequently he takes the view that the latter should be excluded from the 1951 Convention on account of bad faith.[57] In *Re HB*, the New Zealand

[52] Ibid., This point was made by Sedley L.J. in respect of Article 4(3)(d) in *YB* (*YB (Eritrea) v Secretary of State for the Home Department*.

[53] The EU seeks to 'progressively [establish] an area of freedom, security and justice open to those who, forced by circumstance, *legitimately seek protection in the Community*'. See *supra* n. 6, Sect. 4.1, Rec. 1 (emphasis added). With this in mind, '[t]he main objective of this Directive is, on the one hand, to ensure that Member States apply common criteria for the identification of persons genuinely in need of international protection, and, on the other hand, to ensure that a minimum level of benefits is available for these persons in all Member States'. See *supra* n. 6, Rec. 6.

[54] Grahl-Madsen 1966, p. 251.

[55] Ibid., Grahl-Madsen; On the concept of imputed political opinion, see, for instance, Goodwin-Gill, *supra* n. 12, Sect. 4.2, pp. 87 and 89.

[56] See *supra* n. 54, Sect. 4.4.1, p. 251.

[57] Ibid.

Refugee Status Appeals Authority (RSAA) endorsed Grahl-Madsen's approach and ruled that bad faith constituted a bar to refugee status. The reasoning of the RSAA, however, is particularly weak.[58] The RSAA explained that "[its] decision to interpret the Refugee Convention as requiring, implicitly, good faith on the part of the asylum seeker turn[ed] on a *value judgment* that the Refugee Convention was intended to protect only those in genuine need of surrogate international protection (...)."[59] It went on to specify that the good faith principle should "be applied with caution"[60] and that an exclusion from refugee status could only take place in "clear cases".[61] The RSAA's analysis of good in faith was not only unconvincing, but it was also redundant as the RSAA had already established that the appellant did not have a well-founded fear of being persecuted for a Convention reason.[62]

Good faith is a fundamental principle of public international law.[63] This principle, however, is concerned with the conduct of parties which have bound themselves by international treaty[64] and does not bind individuals[65] Pursuant to Article 1(A)(2) of the 1951 Convention states party are under the obligation to recognise as refugees persons who have a well-founded fear of persecution for a Convention reason.[66] In *R. Secretary of State ex p Adan*, the English Court of Appeal held that "the Convention's very purpose is plainly to afford international protection to persons falling within objectively defined classes."[67] The Convention does not require people who seek international protection who act in good faith.[68] UNHCR emphasises that "[t]here is no logical or empirical connection between

[58] Goodwin-Gill 2000, p. 665.

[59] 'Refugee Appeal No. 2254/94 Re HB (21 September 1994)' reported as case abstract in 7 *International Journal of Refugee Law* (1995) p. 352 (emphasis added).

[60] Ibid.

[61] Ibid., The RSAA, however, failed to elaborate on these points.

[62] Ibid., para 6(1) p. 353. In this case, an Iranian national had claimed he had a well-founded fear of being persecuted because he had purchased a copy of *The Satanic Verses* by Salman Rushdie in Japan and brought it back to Iran. He later admitted that his asylum claim was based on an untrue statement. He submitted a subsequent application and alleged that the Iranian authorities now knew that he had applied for asylum in New Zealand and that he had claimed falsely to have acquired *The Satanic Verses*. The RSAA found that there '[was] no real chance of the appellant being subjected to persecution for his (false) claim to have been in possession of The Satanic Verses' (ibid., p. 333). See Goodwin-Gill, *supra* n. 58, Sect. 4.4.1, p. 665.

[63] Shaw 2003, pp. 97–98. See also Kolb 2006.

[64] Judgment of Brooke L.J. in *Danian v. The Secretary of State for the Home Department*, see *supra* n. 14.

[65] See also Lambert, *supra* n. 3, p. 172.

[66] Refugee status is declarative not constitutive. See UNHCR 1992, *supra* n. 1, Sect. 4.1, para 28. The Qualification Directive stresses that '[t]he recognition of refugee status is a declaratory act'. See *supra* n. 6, Sect. 4.1, Rec. 14.

[67] *R v. Secretary of State ex p Adan* [1999] INLR 362, p. 383 E–F.

[68] Goodwin-Gill 2007, *supra* n. 12, Sect. 4.2, p. 89. This is confirmed in UNHCR 2005, *supra* n. 19, Sect. 4.2, p. 45.

well-foundedness of the fear of being persecuted or of serious harm, and the fact that the person may have acted in a manner designated to create a refugee claim."[69] In *Danian*, for example, the English Court of Appeal reiterated that recognition of refugee status was not contingent on good faith.[70] L.J. Brooke took the view that UNHCR's guidance stated the law accurately and went on to say that

> I do not accept the Tribunal's [the Immigration Appeal Tribunal] conclusion that a refugee *sur place* who has acted in bad faith falls outwith the Geneva Convention and can be deported to his home country notwithstanding that he has a genuine and well-founded fear of persecution for a Convention reason and there is a real risk that such persecution may take place.[[71]]

In addition to an inclusion clause,[72] the 1951 Convention contains exclusion clauses.[73] Article 1(F) shows that the drafters of the Convention were not averse to the idea that some persons, who otherwise have the characteristics of a refugee, are not worthy of international protection status.[74]

Bad faith, however, is not a cause for exclusion under the Convention. Furthermore, to construe good faith as a condition for international protection could also engender breaches of Article 33.[75] Indeed this provision affords protection against refoulement to all asylum seekers irrespective of whether they have acted in good faith. The introduction of a good faith requirement could also conflict with the EU Member States' obligations under Article 3 of the ECHR that "prohibits in absolute terms torture or inhuman or degrading treatment or

---

69 *Supra* n. 34, Sect. 4.3, p. 17.

70 *Danian v. Secretary of State for the Home Department, supra* n. 14. See also *YB (Eritrea) v Secretary of State for the Home Department, supra* n. 39, Sect. 4.3.

71 See *Danian v. Secretary of State for the Home Department, supra* n. 14, Sect. 4.2. See also the judgment of Buxton L.J. in *Danian v. Secretary of State for the Home Department*, ibid., para 15.

72 1951 Refugee Convention, Article 1(A).

73 See *supra* n. 47, Sect. 4.3.

74 Article 1(F) of the 1951 Convention reads
The provisions of this Convention shall not apply to any person with respect to whom there are serious reasons for considering that.

(a) He has committed a crime against peace, a war crime, or a crime against humanity, as defined in the international instruments drawn up to make provision in respect of such crimes;
(b) He has committed a serious non-political crime outside the country of refuge prior to his admission to that country as a refugee;
(c) He has been guilty of acts contrary to the purposes and principles of the United Nations.

75 The only limitation to the principle of non-refoulement is to be found in Article 33(2) of the 1951 Convention. It reads that '[t]he benefit of the present provision [Article 33(1)] may not, however, be claimed by a refugee whom there are reasonable grounds for regarding as a danger to the security of the country in which he is, or who, having been convicted by a final judgement of a particularly serious crime, constitutes a danger to the community of that country'. For a discussion of the status of the principle of non-refoulement, see Allain 2001, p. 533.

punishment irrespective of the victim's conduct."[76] This prohibition is equally absolute in expulsion cases.[77]

Attempts to characterise good faith as a condition for refugee status seek to prevent asylum abuse.[78] While this is a legitimate goal, it cannot be pursued at the expense of international obligations. In *Mbanza*, Millet L.J. explained that

> The solution (...) does not lie in propounding some broad principle of abuse of the system or attempting to pervert the course of justice in order to justify a breach of the United Kingdom's international obligations, but in bearing in mind the cardinal principle that it is for the applicant to satisfy the Secretary of State that he has a well-founded fear of persecution for a Convention reason.[79]

Both the English Court of Appeal and the New Zealand RSAA expressed concern over abuse.[80] In *Danian*, Brooke L.J. stressed that the court's ruling should not be read as giving a 'green light' to asylum seekers who act in bad faith.[81] However, while the English Court of Appeal addressed bad faith as a credibility issue in line with UNHCR guidelines,[82] the RSAA construed it as bar to refugee status notwithstanding New Zealand's obligations under the 1951 Convention.[83]

The absence of a good faith condition does not mean that bad faith on the part of asylum seekers has no bearing on the determination process. UNHCR acknowledges that manufactured claims may be difficult to assess, but recommends that this issue be dealt with as an evidentiary and credibility matter.[84] In *Danian*, the UNHCR representative expressed the view that "the misuse of asylum system may eventually be detrimental to the interests of *bona fide* asylum-seekers and genuine refugees. For this reason, UNHCR would not object to a more stringent evaluation of the well-foundedness of a person's fear of persecution in cases involving opportunistic claims."[85] The UNHCR representative, however, failed to explain what amounted to "a more stringent evaluation". Brooke L.J.

---

[76] European Court of Human Rights, *Chahal* (1996) 23 EHHR 413, para 79. The absolute nature of this prohibition distinguishes Article 3 of the ECHR from Article 33 of the 1951 Refugee Convention.

[77] European Court of Human Rights, *Chahal* (ibid.). See also *Saadi v. Italy*, Application No. 37201/06, judgment of 28 February 2008, paras 127 and 137–148 available at http://www.unhcr.org/refworld/docid/47c6882e2.html (accessed 13 July 2009).

[78] See Goodwin-Gill 2007, *supra* n. 12, Sect. 4.2, p. 89.

[79] See *R. v Secretary of State for the Home Department Ex p. Mbanza*, *supra* n. 22, Sect. 4.2.

[80] See *Danian v. Secretary of State for the Home Department*, *supra* n. 14, and *Re HB*, *supra* n. 59, Sect. 4.4.1. See also *Shirazi v. Secretary of State for the Home Department*, *supra* n. 28, Sect. 4.2, para 32.

[81] Ibid.

[82] Ibid.

[83] See *supra* n. 59, Sect. 4.4.1.

[84] See *supra* n. 34, Sect. 4.3, p. 17.

[85] See *supra* n. 14, Sect. 4.2.

ruled that whether an asylum seeker can show a well-founded fear of persecution "(...) will largely turn on his credibility, and an applicant who has put forward a fraudulent and baseless claim for asylum is unlikely to have much credibility left."[86] He indicated that the asylum seeker's "credibility was likely to be low",[87] but emphasised that the asylum seeker's application must nonetheless be "*rigorously scrutinised*".[88] In *Secretary of State for the Home Department v Ahmed*, the English Court of Appeal explained that

> (...) in all asylum cases there is ultimately but a single question to be asked: is there a serious risk that on return the applicant would be persecuted for a Convention reason? If there is, then he is entitled to asylum. It matters not whether the risk arises from his own conduct in this country, however unreasonable. It does not even matter whether he has cynically sought to enhance his prospects of asylum by creating the very risk on which he then relies - cases sometimes characterised as involving bad faith. When I say that none of this matters, what I mean is that none of it forfeits the applicant's right to refugee status, provided only and always that he establishes a well-founded fear of persecution abroad. Any such conduct is, of course, highly relevant when it comes to evaluating the claim on its merits, i.e. to determining whether in truth the applicant is at risk of persecution abroad. An applicant who has behaved in this way may not readily be believed as to his future fears.[89]

It remains the case that asylum claims *sur place*, including manufactured claims, must be assessed on the same basis as other asylum claims.[90] "Whether (...) [activity *sur place* is] sufficient to justify a well-founded fear of persecution must be determined by a careful examination of the circumstances."[91] The Qualification Directive, however, seems to struggle with this principle.

4.4.2 The Qualification Directive and Manufactured Asylum Claims

The drafting of the Qualification Directive suggests that manufactured asylum claims are unlike any other claims. On the one hand, Article 5(3) of the

---

[86] See *supra* n. 22, Sect. 4.2.

[87] See *supra* n. 14, Sect. 4.2.

[88] Ibid., Emphasis added. In 2006, UNHCR reported that '[t]he assessment of credibility still pose[d] a particular problem for [UK] Home Office decision makers' (Refugee Council, *Refugee Council response to the Home Office Consultation on the Qualification Directive: Implementation of Council Directive 2004/83/EC of 29 April 2004 on minimum standards for the qualification and status of third country nationals or stateless persons as refugees or as persons who otherwise need international protection and the content of the protection granted*, August 2006 available at http://www.refugeecouncil.org.uk/OneStopCMS/Core/CrawlerResourceServer.aspx?resource=71933100-A700-42ED-80B2-145AF9CFC8EA&mode=link&guid=196dccc9f1214a70bbc08ae48cb2966f (accessed 16 July 2009).

[89] *Secretary of State for the Home Department v Ahmed* [1999] EWCA Civ 3003 (English Court of Appeal).

[90] See *supra* Sect. 4.2.

[91] See UNHCR 1992, *supra* n. 1, Sect. 4.1, para 96.

Qualification Directive singles out manufactured subsequent applications for refugee status and 'toys with' the idea of bad faith as a bar to refugee status. On the other hand, Articles 4(3)(d) as well as Article 20(6) and (7) make clear that international protection status may be granted to persons who have manufactured their need for international protection. Article 20(6) and (7), however, allows punitive reductions of benefits for those who have been granted protection on the basis of manufactured claims.

Article 5(3) of the Qualification Directive reads

> Without prejudice to the Geneva Convention, Member States may determine that an applicant who files a subsequent application shall normally not be granted refugee status, if the risk of persecution is based on circumstances which the applicant has created by his own decision since leaving the country of origin.

Article 5(3) is a problematic yet unnecessary provision. It is concerned with asylum abuse and identifies manufactured subsequent asylum claims as a particularly suspicious category of claim.[92] The wording of Article 5(3) suggests an intention to permit bars to refugee on account of bad faith and the insertion of the caveat "[w]ithout prejudice to the Geneva Convention" "(…) clearly discloses doubt as to correctness of such actions in international law (…)." [93] Article 5(3) is reminiscent of Article 8(2) of the Commission's Proposal in its concern over manufactured asylum claims *sur place*.[94] Both provisions come close to introducing a good faith requirement with a view to addressing asylum abuse. Article 8(2), however, was broader in scope; it applied to all manufactured asylum claims *sur place* and considered access to subsidiary protection as well as refugee status. It remains the case that adherence to international obligations precludes the adding of a good faith requirement, albeit in respect of a narrowly defined category of asylum claims *sur place*. Furthermore, a restrictive reading of Article 5(3) would undermine the internal coherence of the Qualification Directive as Article 4(3)(d) and Article 20(6) confirm that refugee status may be granted on the basis of manufactured claims, irrespective of whether these are subsequent.

We have established that, while good faith cannot be construed as a condition for international protection status, bad faith may be addressed as a credibility and evidentiary matter.[95] This approach not only ensures compliance with the 1951

[92] Subsequent applications are considered in the EU Asylum Procedures Directives (Council Directive 2005/85/EC of 1 December 2005 (OJ L 326/13 of 13.December. 2005). Article 32 requires the EU Member States to have in place specific procedures to deal, *inter alia*, with fresh asylum claims after a first application has been rejected or withdrawn. These procedures derogate from the basic principles and guarantees set out in Chapter II of the Asylum Procedures Directive. Applications based on well-founded fear of persecution as a failed asylum seeker constitute subsequent claims within the meaning of Article 32. See *supra* n. 22, Sect. 4.2.

[93] See Goodwin-Gill 2007, *supra* n. 12, Sect. 4.2, p. 89.

[94] See *supra* n. 25, Sect. 4.2.

[95] See *supra* Sect. 4.1.

Convention, but it is also in line with Article 4(3)(d) of the Qualification Directive.[96] Indeed Article 4(3)(d) reads that

> The assessment of an application for international protection is to be carried out on an individual basis and includes taking into account (...) whether the applicant's activities since leaving the country of origin were engaged in for the sole or main purpose of creating the necessary conditions for applying for international protection, so as to assess whether these activities will expose the applicant to persecution or serious harm if returned to that country.

It is apparent from Article 4(3)(d) that whether opportunistic post-departure activities create a well-founded fear of persecution will depend on "whether the requirements of the refugee definition are in fact fulfilled taking into account all the relevant facts surrounding the claim."[97]

Article 4(3)(d) is not the only provision in the Qualification Directive which indicates that refugee status may be conferred on persons who have manufactured their need for international protection. Indeed Article 20(6) provides that

> Within the limits set out by the Geneva Convention, Member States may reduce the benefits of this Chapter, granted to a refugee whose refugee status has been obtained on the basis of activities engaged in for the sole or main purpose of creating the necessary conditions for being recognised as a refugee.

Thus Article 20(6) makes clear that manufactured claims, including subsequent ones, may result in the recognition of refugee status.[98] Similarly Article 20(7) indicates that subsidiary protection may be granted on the basis of such claims. However, this is done begrudgingly. Indeed both provisions permit punitive reductions of rights. Yet such reductions may engage the EU Member States' obligations under the 1951 Convention and international human rights instruments.[99] Teitgen-Colly takes the view that reduction of benefits can be consistent with the 1951 Convention, but observes that "its evocation confirms the atmosphere of suspicion (...) in connection with asylum applications, while discrediting the assessment of the need for protection."[100] The author agrees with Teitgen-Colly's analysis of the significance of allowing reduction of rights, but takes the view that punitive reductions lack basis in the Convention and international law.[101] Hathaway points out that "[i]t was explicitly decided in drafting Article 2 of the Refugee Convention that there should be no possibility of

---

[96] See *supra* n. 34, Sect. 4.3, p. 17.

[97] Ibid.

[98] *See* Storey, *supra* n. 3, Sect. 4.1, p. 27.

[99] See Battjes, *supra* n. 41, Sect. 4.3, p. 485.

[100] See Teitgen-Colly, *supra* n. 37, Sect. 4.3, p. 1538.

[101] Hathaway 2003, p. 12. Hathaway made this point in relation to Article 16 of the EU Reception Standards Proposal (Document COM(2001) 181 final of 3 April 2001). Article 16 provides for reduction and withdrawal of reception conditions in a number of cases, for example where the asylum seeker has not claimed refugee status 'as soon as reasonable practicable' (Article 16(2)).

withdrawing refugee rights for reasons insufficient to justify either expulsion or the withdrawal of refugee status."[102] Moreover, we have seen that international law does not require individuals who act in good faith.[103] It is contended that the possibility for punitive reductions of rights may be analysed as an attempt to introduce a *quasi*-good faith requirement by the back door. In any case, curtailments of rights cannot fall short of the minimum standards set out in the 1951 Convention,[104] nor can they fall below the EU Member States' international human rights obligations.[105] Significantly another caveat evinces doubt as to the legality of the proposed actions. Indeed Article 20(1) reads that "[t]his chapter [content of international protection] shall be without prejudice to the rights laid down in the Geneva Convention."[106] The Qualification Directive contains more generous provisions,[107] but some of the 1951 Convention obligations are only

---

[102] Ibid., Article 2 of the 1951 Convention reads that '[e]very refugee has duties to the country in which he finds himself, which require in particular that he conform to its laws and regulations as well as to measures taken for the maintenance of public order.'

[103] See Lambert, *supra* n. 3, Sect. 4.1, p. 172.

[104] See, for instance, UNHCR's comments on Article 20(1) of the Qualification Directive. See *supra* n. 34, Sect. 4.3, p. 35.

[105] In *Pretty v. UK*, the European Court of Human Rights provided guidance as to the level of suffering, physical or mental, required to engage Article 3 of the ECHR. The Court held

> As regards the types of 'treatment' which fall within the scope of Article 3 of the Convention, the Court's case law refers to 'ill-treatment' that attains a minimum level of severity and involves actual bodily injury or intense physical or mental suffering. Where treatment humiliates or debases an individual showing lack of respect for, or diminishing, his or her human dignity or arouses feelings of fear, anguish or inferiority capable of breaking an individual's moral and physical resistance, it may be characterised as degrading and also fall within the prohibition of Article 3. The suffering which flows from naturally occurring illness, physical or mental, may be covered by Article 3, where it is, or risks being, exacerbated by treatment, whether flowing from conditions of detention, expulsion or other measures, for which the authorities can be held responsible. (*Pretty v. UK* (2002) 35 EHHR 1, para 52).

This issue also arises in respect of the conditions for the reception of asylum seekers in the EU. See Da Lomba 2009, pp. 332–334.

[106] Commenting on Article 20(1) of the Qualification Directive, UNHCR noted that international and regional human rights treaties that may be more generous than the 1951 Convention may be applicable. See *supra* n. 34, Sect. 4.3, p. 35.

[107] For example, the 1951 Convention provides that refugees shall be granted the most favourable treatment accorded to foreign country nationals as regards the right to engage in wage-earning employment (Article 17(1)). Conversely, the Qualification Directive guarantees access to employment for Convention refugees on *the same basis as nationals* (Article 17(1) and (2)).

partially reflected in the Directive.[108] In any case, only the rights not guaranteed in binding international instruments could potentially be reduced. In this respect, UNHCR points out that, since the 1951 Convention does not provide for punitive sanctions for asylum seekers who engaged in activity *sur place* for the sole purpose of gaining refugee status, Member States' discretion to reduce rights on this ground is limited.[109] UNHCR also stresses that non-discriminatory treatment of all refugees is a basic principle of international refugee law.[110] These limitations equally apply to reduction of rights for persons granted subsidiary protection status.[111]

The Qualification Directive singles out manufactured asylum claims *sur place*. Bars to refugee status on account of bad faith may be ruled out, but the 'genuineness' of manufactured protection needs is certainly called into question.

4.5 Conclusion

One of the aims of the Qualification Directive is to address international protection needs *sur place*. The Directive's approach, however, reveals a tension between the EU Member States' international obligations, and in particular the obligations arising out of the 1951 Convention, and concern over asylum abuse. The ambiguous drafting indicates that the intended restrictiveness of the Directive's response to protection needs *sur place* had to be curbed in light of the EU Member States' international obligations. Significantly all the provisions dealing with manufactured asylum claims come with the caveat that their application is subject to these obligations. While redundant, these caveats reveal doubt as to these

[108] For example, UNHCR observes that Article 21(2) and (3) of the Qualification Directive, 'which in part reflects the exceptions to the *non-refoulement* principle under Article 33(2) of the 1951 Convention, does not comprehensively reflect the Convention obligations applicable in such a case' (UNHCR Annotated Comments, *supra* n. 34, p. 37). The Directive fails to explain why some rights are expressly incorporated and others are not. For instance, the Qualification Directive does not expressly mention freedom to practise religion and freedom as regards the religious education of refugees' children (Article 4 of the 1951 Convention) and the rights attached refugees' juridical status in the host country (Articles 12–16 of the 1951 Convention). On this issue, see Hathaway, *supra* n. 101, Sect. 4.4.2, pp. 17–18. UNHCR recommended that all 1951 Convention rights be included in national implementation legislation '[f]or the sake of completeness and to avoid oversights in practice' (See *supra* n. 34, Sect. 4.3, p. 35). In Hathaway's opinion, the inclusion of an article stating that all 1951 Convention rights were applicable to recognised refugees would have constituted a simpler option (See Hathaway, *supra* n. 101, Sect. 4.4.2, p. 18).

[109] See *supra* n. 34, Sect. 4.3, p. 36.

[110] Ibid., Article 3 of the 1951 Convention reads that [t]he Contracting States shall apply the provisions of this Convention to refugees without discrimination as to race, religion or country of origin.'

[111] See *supra* n. 34, Sect. 4.3, p. 36.

provisions' conformity to the Convention and other international instruments.[112] It is with great reluctance that the Qualification Directive provides for the recognition of international protection status on the basis of manufactured claims *sur place*. Consequently, while the Directive emphatically affirms the Convention as the cornerstone of refugee protection, the Convention obligations come across as constraints.[113] The result is an ambivalent approach to both refugees *sur place* and the 1951 Convention. The author contends that this equivocation must be removed as it risks undermining the Convention's primacy over the Directive,[114] compliance with the Convention and ultimately refugee protection within the EU. Moreover, restrictive interpretations of the Directive may also engage other international obligations.

The idea of the "genuine European refugee" emerged in the context of restrictive asylum policies that identify asylum abuse as a major problem.[115] Yet who is a 'genuine' refugee and what amounts to asylum abuse are questions that must be framed and addressed by reference to the EU Member States' international obligations. Thus the concept of 'genuine European refugee' must necessarily embrace any person who the 1951 Convention recognises as a refugee, including refugees who have manufactured their need for international protection. In the author's opinion, this calls for a mainstreaming of refugees *sur place* in the Qualification Directive. Moreover, it is argued that such an approach would

---

[112] We have seen that the EU Member States remain bound by their international obligations. See *supra* Sect. 4.1.

[113] The Commission recently stated that '[t]he EU ha[d] made great progress towards creating a common European asylum regime wholly in accordance with the Geneva Convention and other applicable international instruments' (Communication from the Commission to the European Parliament and the Council, An Area of Freedom, Security and Justice Serving the Citizen COM(2009) 262/4 (Communication on the Stockholm Programme), Sect. 5.2.1).

[114] Yet the primacy of the 1951 Convention over the Qualification Directive cannot be taken for granted. Much concern has been expressed as regards the personal scope of the refugee definition contained in the Directive. Indeed, the definition is confined to third country nationals and stateless persons which is not consistent with the Convention definition. This limitation is rooted in Article 63(1)(c) of the TEC which provided the legal basis for the adoption of the Directive. On this issue, see Peers, *supra* n. 7, Sect. 4.1, p. 334 and Storey, *supra* n. 3, Sect. 4.1, p. 8. The House of Lords Select Committee on European Union stressed that international law prevented the scope of the Directive from eroding the EU Member States' obligations under the 1951 Convention (House of Lords Select Committee on European Union's Report on 'Defining refugee status and those in need of international protection', Session 2001–2002, 28th Report, HL Paper 156, para 34). This, however, raises the question of the justiciability of this kind of conflict under Title IV of the TEC (Peers, *supra* n. 7, Sect. 4.1, p. 334). Storey takes the view that these may be addressed through Article 68 of the TEC (Storey, *supra* n. 3, Sect. 4.1, p. 28). However, Peers and Rogers question the European Court of Justice's ability 'to accept a reference that relate[s] to the application of the Directive to a national of a Member State under Title IV of the EC Treaty' (Peers, *supra* n. 7, Sect. 4.1, p. 334).

[115] See, for instance, Communication from the Commission to the European Parliament, the Council, the European and Social Committee and the Committee of Regions, Policy Plan on Asylum, An Integrated Approach to Protection across the EU, COM(2008) 360, para 6 and COM (2009) 262/4, see *supra* n. 113, Sect. 4.5, para 5.2.1.

provide a means to address the 'side effects' of the Directive's ambivalent approach to international protection needs *sur place*, i.e., the risks of diverging national interpretations and internal inconsistency. Commenting on the short-comings of the first phase legislative instruments of the CEAS, the Commission reported that "data show that the recognition of protection needs of applicants from the same countries of origin still varies significantly from one Member State to another.

To some extent, this phenomenon is rooted in the wording of certain provisions of the QD."[116] While the Commission does not expressly refer to the provisions on refugees *sur place*, we have seen that the problem extends to them. The proposed approach to international protection needs *sur place* would render Articles 5(3) as well as Article 20(6) and (7) redundant.[117] It would also necessitate a redrafting of Article 5(2) with a view of removing the focus on continuity. It is the author's view that the second phase of the CEAS provides the EU with a timely opportunity to reconsider its response to refugees *sur place*.[118]

References

Allain J (2001) The jus cogens nature of non-refoulement. Int J Refugee L 13(4):533–558

Battjes H (2006) European asylum law and international law. Martinus Nijhoff, Leiden/Boston

Clayton G (2008) Immigration and asylum law. Oxford University Press, Oxford

Da Lomba S (2009) Les conditions d'accueil des demandeurs d'asile dans l'Union Européenne: une atteinte à la dignité humaine? In: Crépeau F (ed) La Complexe Dynamique des Migrations Internationales. Presses de l'Université de Montréal, Montréal, p 332

El-Enany N (2008) Who is the new European refugee? Eur L Rev 33(3):313–335

Gilbert G (2003) Current issues in the application of the exclusion clauses. In: Feller E, Türk V, Nicholson F (eds) Refugee protection in international law: UNHCR's global consultations on international protection. Cambridge University Press, Cambridge, pp 425–478

[116] COM(2008) 360, see *supra* n. 115, Sect. 4.5, para 3.3. The Commission reported that '[d]espite the existence of a common system of asylum, there is a need for greater uniformity in Member States' handling of asylum applications. the rates of acceptance of applications are currently very variable. In 2007, 25% of first decisions granted protection in the form of either refugee status or subsidiary protection. Behind this average figure there are wide variations: some Member States allow protection in only very few cases, while others have a recognition rate close to 50%'. See COM (2009) 262/4, *supra* n. 113, Sect. 4.5, p. 4.

[117] Significantly the UK did not implement Article 5(3) of the Qualification Directive.

[118] The Hague Programme sets out as the aims of the CEAS in its second phase the establishment of a common procedure and uniform status for persons benefiting from asylum or subsidiary protection before the end of 2010 (Communication from the Commission to the Council and the European Parliament, The Hague Programme: Ten priorities for the next 5 years The Partnership for European renewal in the field of Freedom, Security and Justice 1, COM(2005) 184 final, para 2.3). As required by the Hague Programme, the Commission is due to propose amendments to the Qualification Directive in the course of 2009. See COM (2008) 360, *supra* n. 115, Sect. 4.5, para 3.3). See also COM (2009) 262/4, *supra* n. 113, Sect. 4.5, para 5.2.1.

Goodwin-Gill G (2000) Danian v. secretary of state for the home department, comment: refugee status and 'good faith'. Int J Refugee L 12(4):663–671

Goodwin-Gill GS, McAdam J (2007) The Refugee in international law. Oxford University Press, Oxford

Grahl-Madsen A (1966) The status of Refugees in international law. A. W. Sijthoff, Leiden

Hathaway JC (1991) The law of Refugee status. Butterworths, Toronto

Hathaway JC (2003) What's in a label? Eur J Migr L 5(1):1–21

Kolb R (2006) Principles as sources of international law (with special reference to good faith). Neth Int L Rev 53(1):1–36

Lambert H (2006) The EU asylum qualification directive, its impact on the jurisprudence of the United Kingdom and international law. Int Comp L Q 55(1):161–192

McAdam J (2005) The European Union qualification directive: the creation of a subsidiary protection regime. Int J Refugee L 17(3):461–516

Musalo K (2002) Claims for protection based on religion or belief: analysis and proposed conclusions. Legal and protection policy research series. UNHCR, Department of International Protection

Musalo K, Moore J, Boswell RA (2007) Refugee law and policy, a comparative and international approach. Carolina Academic Press, Durham, North Carolina

Peers S, Rogers N (2006) EU immigration and asylum law, text and commentary. Martinus Nijhoff, Leiden/Boston

Piotrowicz R, van Eck C (2004) Subsidiary protection and primary rights. Int Comp L Q 53(1):107–138

Shacknove AE (1985) Who is a refugee? Ethics: Int J Soc Political Leg Philos 95(2):274–282

Shaw M (2003) International law. Cambridge University Press, Cambridge

Storey H (2008) EU Refugee qualification directive: a brave new world? Int J Refugee L 20(1):1–49

Teitgen-Colly C (2006) The European Union and asylum: an illusion of protection. Common Market L Rev 43(6):1503–1566

Tiberghien F (1988) La Protection des Réfugiés en France. Economica/Presses Universitaires d'Aix-Marseille, Paris/Aix-en- Provence

UNHCR (1992) Handbook on procedures and criteria for determining refugee status under the 1951 convention and the 1967 protocol relating to the status of Refugees. http://www.unhcr.org/refworld/docid/3ae6b3314.html. Accessed 25 May 2010

UNHCR (2005) Refugee status determination, identifying who Is a Refugee. http://www.unhcr.org/refworld/pdfid/43141f5d4.pdf. Accessed 18 May 2009

UNHCR (2007) UNHCR, Refugee protection and international migration. http://www.unhcr.org/refworld/pdfid/462f6d982.pdf. Accessed 18 May 2009

Chapter 5
The Goals of the Common European Asylum System

W. van Hövell

Contents

5.1 Introduction 65
5.2 New EU Legislation: the Need for Change 66
5.2.1 Dublin II and Reception 66
5.2.2 Forthcoming Amendments on Procedures and Qualification Directives 67
5.2.3 Role of the European Court of Justice 68
5.3 Practical Cooperation 68
5.3.1 European Asylum Support Office 69
5.4 Responsibility Sharing in the EU 69
5.5 Migration and Asylum in the EU's External Relations 70
5.6 Conclusion 71

5.1 Introduction

It is nearly ten years since the entry of the Amsterdam Treaty into force, which laid the basis for the first Community legislation on asylum, to be 'in accordance with the 1951 Convention and other relevant treaties.' National asylum legislation based on the common EU minimum standards is, or should be, now in full force in 27 Member States. The European Court of Justice has given its first judgments on asylum cases, and the Council and Parliament are now considering amendments to the first-phase legal instruments; the EU and Member States have recently adopted a programme for the next five years in the Justice and Home Affairs area, including asylum.

This calls for reflection on whether the goals of the Common European Asylum System (CEAS) have been achieved through the steps taken to date. What more

Wilbert van Hövell, Regional Representative, UNHCR Brussels.

F. A. N. J. Goudappel and H. S. Raulus (eds.), *The future of asylum in the European Union*, DOI: 10.1007/978-90-6704-802-6_5,

needs to be done, to ensure a common system that is fully in line with the international refugee law and good practice? I would like to set out a few elements to help us consider these questions, with reference to the current legislative and policy discussions as well as some key challenges foreseen for the near future.

5.2 New EU Legislation: the Need for Change

UNHCR has recently reiterated its view that there are some important gaps and weaknesses in the existing EU asylum instruments. On 3 December 2008, the European Commission proposed amendments to three instruments of the EU asylum *acquis*: the Reception Conditions Directive,[1] the Dublin II Regulation[2] and the Eurodac Regulation.[3] UNHCR has broadly welcomed the Commission's proposals, parts of which address UNHCR's concerns as expressed at the time of their adoption, and in the light of subsequent observations in practice.

5.2.1 Dublin II and Reception

In 2006, UNHCR published a research paper on the implementation of the Dublin Regulation, which revealed significantly diverging approaches and gaps in State practice under the Regulation. Among other things, it found that not all Member States were undertaking full and substantive examinations of the asylum claims of persons returned under Dublin. Contrary to the Regulation, it was also noted that the strict application of the Regulation led in some cases to separation of family members, as well as transfers of children in situations where it was not in their best interests. UNHCR has thus welcomed amendment proposals that would, among other things, strengthen protection for minors in the Dublin system and reinforce obligations to respect family unity.

With regard to Reception Conditions, independent research conducted by the Odysseus academic network in 2006–07, to which UNHCR contributed, showed that many problems resulted from non-implementation of existing provisions of the Reception Conditions Directive. However, there were also other areas where the existing provisions were ambiguous, or left such broad scope for discretion that

---

[1] Council Directive 2003/9/EC of 27 January 2003 laying down minimum standards for the reception of asylum seekers, OJ L 31/18.

[2] Council Regulation (EC) No 343/2003 of 18 February 2003 establishing the criteria and mechanisms for determining the Member State responsible for examining an asylum application lodged in one of the Member States by a third country national, OJ L 50/1.

[3] Council Regulation (EC) No 407/2002 of 28 February 2002 laying down certain rules to implement Regulation (EC) No 2725/2000 concerning the establishment of "Eurodac" for the comparison of fingerprints for the effective application of the Dublin Convention, OJ L 62/1.

they arguably did not establish common standards at all. Among these were provisions on detention of asylum seekers, which under the new proposals, would be more closely regulated, including through more extensive judicial review. The expressed aim of the proposed amendments, to "ensure higher standards of treatment for asylum seekers with regard to reception conditions that would guarantee a dignified standard of living, in line with international law", underlines their high level of ambition.

UNHCR is aware that some Member States feel that the new proposals go further than they would like, in setting high standards that could impose increased costs and limit the 'efficiency' of Member States' administrations. It is recognized that challenging economic and political circumstances may sometimes make it difficult to move beyond existing norms. However, we would recall the words of the European Council in 2008 in its 'Pact on Immigration and Asylum', adopted under the French Presidency, which expressed the goal of achieving a 'higher degree of protection' in the evolving CEAS. The answer to immediate political and resource concerns cannot, in UNHCR's view, lie in reducing or limiting safeguards needed to ensure that asylum systems operate fairly and humanely.

5.2.2 Forthcoming Amendments on Procedures and Qualification Directives

In UNHCR's view, the Qualification Directive[4] has not yet achieved its objectives, neither to facilitate greater harmonisation nor ensure protection for all those who need it. This is due largely to the wide differences in its present interpretation and application by Member States. UNHCR's November 2007 Study on the application of key provisions of this Directive by selected Member States demonstrated that the possibility of finding protection varies dramatically from one Member State to another, for similar categories of applicants.

No official evaluation has been undertaken to date of the Asylum Procedures Directive, despite the fact that proposals for amendment are being prepared and will be issued by the EC in June. To help fill this gap, UNHCR is assessing implementation of the Asylum Procedures Directive [with funding from the European Refugee Fund (ERF)] in a project analysing the level of harmonisation in practice that the instrument has achieved, and protection gaps resulting from its application. So far, we have seen considerable divergence in the approaches to the application of the Directive, and in some cases, lack of clarity about its rules. The findings of this project will be issued in November 2009, in time at least to inform discussions in the Council and Parliament about the amendments.

4 Council Directive 2004/83/EC of 29 April 2004 on minimum standards for the qualification and status of third country nationals or stateless persons as refugees or as persons who otherwise need international protection and the content of the protection granted, OJ L 304/12.

UNHCR hopes that amendments to the Qualification Directive could address some key aspects of the grounds for protection, including the internal flight alternative and exclusion clauses, as well as the content of protected status, including bringing the rights of subsidiary protection beneficiaries more closely in line with those of refugees.

Possible changes to the Procedures Directive could focus on strengthening provisions on access to procedures and on effective remedies; reinforcing procedural guarantees at first instance to increase quality of decisions and limit subsequent applications, as well as limiting the list of grounds for using accelerated procedures.

5.2.3 Role of the European Court of Justice

In addition to the formidable legislative agenda, the EU is also seeing the emergence of a further critical source of law on asylum. The European Court of Justice, in its recent Elgafaji judgment,[5] answered a preliminary ruling request from the Dutch Council of State on one of the most complex and disputed provisions of the Qualification Directive. Most observers agree that the Court's pronouncement helped to clarify the interpretation of the requirement for 'individual targeting' of threats in situations of indiscriminate violence, which could entitle an applicant to subsidiary protection. With at least three new references in the pipeline (on cessation; Palestinians/Article 1D; and exclusion), it is clear that the Court will also play a critical role in interpreting the relationship between international refugee protection principles and the EU *acquis* in the future.

5.3 Practical Cooperation

Outside the legislative sphere, Member States are now also giving considerable priority to 'practical cooperation' as a means of bringing about more harmonisation of practice. UNHCR supports the aim of further practical cooperation among the asylum services of Member States, particularly as a means to facilitate the exchange of good practice and to improve quality. However, this area of activity should be seen as supplementing, and not replacing, the need for legislation to set appropriate standards.

The objective of such cooperation—like all other aspects of asylum harmonisation—must be to ensure better asylum decision-making. This is in the interests of both States and applicants. The gathering and compilation of accurate

[5] ECJ, Case C-465/07 *Meki Elgafaji, Noor Elgafaji* v. *Staatssecretaris van Justitie* [2009] *ECR* I-9919.

information about State practice will be needed to highlight problems as well as positive innovations and performance, in order to bolster the legislative development process and take the CEAS forward towards completion.

5.3.1 European Asylum Support Office

The body which is foreseen to facilitate more practical cooperation in the future is the now established European Asylum Support Office (EASO). UNHCR, along with Member States, welcomed the European Commission's proposal for a Regulation establishing an EASO. There is clearly a need and interest in cooperation on training for asylum officials, the use and production of Country of Origin information, coordinating 'asylum support teams' to help States facing particular demands on their systems and other related activities. UNHCR is ready to cooperate with and provide expert advice to the EASO, and believes that its experience and proven expertise in supporting national asylum systems could contribute significantly to the EASO's work.

5.4 Responsibility Sharing in the EU

Beyond these immediate topics, States will be discussing their objectives for the next phase of development of the CEAS.

A number of States have increasingly underlined their view that the CEAS must, in future, incorporate arrangements more concretely to give substance to the commitment—expressed often in principle—to 'solidarity' among Member States on asylum.

Member States along the Union's southern Mediterranean frontiers have drawn attention to significant numbers of people arriving irregularly at their sea borders, in a way that can exceed the capacity of their asylum, reception and integration systems, among other things (referred to in some contexts as situations of 'particular pressure').

This phenomenon is not the same across all the affected countries, and as such, there is no single or straightforward solution. UNHCR considers that more detailed analysis of the particular strains faced by and needs of each State under such 'pressure' is needed. This could allow for the development of specifically-targeted approaches to addressing the problems, which could involve a number of elements.

The idea of relocation within the EU of people recognised as refugees or other forms of international protection within the EU was endorsed in the Pact of October 2008. UNHCR has expressed its support in principle for such an idea, and would be ready to facilitate transfers from Member States whose capacities are exceeded to other Member States, with the consent of the people involved, and based on rational criteria such as family connections. However, UNHCR considers it important that such internal relocation would not undermine Member States' commitments to resettlement of refugees from countries and regions outside the EU.

UNHCR also supports the continued use of EC funding to address particular needs of States facing capacity problems. Such funds have been used in the past to support innovative partnerships involving governments, non-governmental bodies and international organisations, including an ongoing project to ensure appropriate reception arrangements in the Italian island of Lampedusa.

Political will is, of course, a critical and essential element to ensure that such arrangements can work effectively in practice. The best asylum system is only effective if applicants can gain access to it in practice. In an environment in which controlling irregular migration remains a high priority for all Member States, UNHCR will be encouraging EU institutions, Member States and other stakeholders, to ensure that the next JHA agenda ensures that safeguards are in included in border and migration management systems to ensure that asylum seekers can gain access to territory and procedures in which protection needs can be identified and fulfilled.

5.5 Migration and Asylum in the EU's External Relations

In regard to the 'external dimension' of the EU's asylum and migration policy, Member States have repeatedly affirmed their political commitment to develop international protection standards and capacities outside the Union and to engage in refugee resettlement.

UNHCR has consistently highlighted its support for engagement and cooperation on the part of the EU with third countries, to strengthen their ability to provide international protection. UNHCR has welcomed EU activities directed at building the capacity of third countries to provide asylum, including through the development of legislation, institutions and processes for refugee protection. However, UNHCR has consistently highlighted that the EU's engagement with third countries must be a complementary to, and not a substitute for, the effective provision of protection in the EU for those in need of it. This means that people requesting asylum in the EU or at its borders must be permitted to submit a claim, and to have it determined in a fair procedure in the EU. UNHCR has also encouraged EU States and institutions to ensure that efforts on protection in regions beyond the Union are undertaken in full partnership with the concerned countries, to ensure that they address the real needs and thereby ensure a sense of 'ownership' by those States, which can help ensure sustainability.

UNHCR has supported the concept of 'Regional Protection Programmes', developed by the EC and implemented through UNHCR pilot projects in Belarus and Tanzania, among others. Evaluation of the pilot Regional Protection Programmes is now underway, to consider whether and how to continue to develop the concept in future. In considering how to increase their effectiveness and added value in addressing refugee situations in regions of origin and transit, UNHCR would encourage the devotion of more resources to such programmes in future. There is also a need for greater flexibility in the provision of such support to regions identified as 'RPP' priorities, in order to achieve results where they are needed most.

In mid-2009, the EU is to issue its proposal for an EU resettlement scheme. UNHCR strongly supports efforts to create more resettlement places in the EU, and hopes that a common EU scheme can lend momentum to that endeavour. Consideration should be given to establishing realistic yet ambitious numerical targets for the Union as a whole. The participation of EU countries in global resettlement efforts remains modest, and a significant EU target would help to encourage more participation. Substantial financial support should also continue to be available through the EU to facilitate Member States' resettlement efforts.

A specific arrangement could be established for ensuring that EU Member States actively participate in resettlement of refugees evacuated by UNHCR to the Evacuation Transit Facility (ETF) in Timisoara (Romania). This facility, designed to receive refugees in urgent need of resettlement, could become the hallmark of a strengthened EU commitment to resettlement. EU financial support for the operation of that facility would also be important.

5.6 Conclusion

It is clear that the CEAS has progressed far since the EU decided to move towards a common approach, with extensive legislation now in place, implementation underway, jurisprudence emerging, and practical cooperation advancing. But in terms of its substantive achievements, there is still much work to do. There is a need to remain focused on raising standards in key areas where the current norms do not ensure fair outcomes or humane treatment of asylum seekers. Practical cooperation should be encouraged as a means to reduce persisting divergences between Member States—but this should be in addition to, and not in place of, necessary legislative acts.

UNHCR looks forward to continuing to work with Member States, EU institutions, NGOs, universities and other stakeholders to promote discussion on the way forward. Informed debate, of the kind that forums such as this can facilitate, is an important contribution towards achieving the 'higher standards of protection' to which the European Council (in the Pact of October 2008) has aspired.

Chapter 6
Mutual Recognition in European Immigration Policy: Harmonised Protection or Co-ordinated Exclusion?

John O'Dowd

Contents

6.1 Introduction 73
6.2 Developments 1999–2009 74
6.3 The European Pact on Immigration and Asylum 77
6.4 European Commission's Communication of 10 June 2009 79
6.5 The Stockholm Programme 80
6.6 2008: A Turning Point for EU Immigration Policy? 83
6.7 Extra-territorial Activities and the Rule of Law 98
6.8 Public Opinion and European Migration Controls 103
6.9 Conclusion 106
References 109

6.1 Introduction

The European Union's migration policy and the nature of the instruments adopted under it are likely to have an increasing impact on national migration controls, over the course of the recently adopted Stockholm Programme and beyond. Two recent examples have been the establishment of minimum procedural standards and the increasing application of the mutual recognition principle in relation to decisions on expulsion and refusal of entry to third country nationals. This chapter will examine the influences upon and the impact of Community measures in these two fields—in particular the Return Directive—and seek to assess what each tells us about the political dynamics behind the development of EU policies and actions in these areas, particularly in the context of the Union's search for

J. O'Dowd (✉)
UCD Law School, University College Dublin, Dublin, Ireland
e-mail: john.odowd@ucd.ie

F. A. N. J. Goudappel and H. S. Raulus (eds.), *The future of asylum in the European Union*, DOI: 10.1007/978-90-6704-802-6_6,

legitimacy through public perception of its effectiveness in assisting in the achievement of key policy goals, even if the content of these remains determined largely by national politics and national policy. This assessment may, in turn, give us some idea of the future direction of the Union's policy in the field of immigration and asylum as a whole.

6.2 Developments 1999–2009

Between 1999 and 2008, there was limited progress towards the comprehensive Community law framework for "more efficient management of migration flows at all their stages" envisaged by the Tampere European Council over a decade ago.[1] However, against this general background of limited convergence, Hansen points out that "it is impossible to overstate the importance that the Commission has come to confer upon the issues of repatriation, expulsion, return, and readmission."[2] Two of the specific areas in which there was most progress in the decade following Tampere were the harmonisation of minimum procedural protections and the extension of the principle of mutual recognition of immigration decisions.

Since Tampere, European Community law has increasingly given procedural protection to third-country nationals in national immigration processes, through measures such as the asylum procedures Directive,[3] the family reunification Directive[4] and the long-term residents Directive.[5] These procedural safeguards and remedies have mostly been vaguely defined (for example "the right to mount a legal challenge"),[6] apart from the most recent Directive which makes the nature of

---

[1] Presidency Conclusions Tampere European Council 15–16 October 1999 paras 22–27 http://www.consilium.europa.eu/ueDocs/cms_Data/docs/pressData/en/ec/00200-r1.en9.htm (Last accessed 10 September 2008.) On the lack of progress towards such a framework, see Communication from the Commission on Policy priorities in the fight against illegal immigration of third-country nationals COM (06) 442 final, 19 July 2006.

[2] Hansen and Linköping University and The National Institute for Working Life 2005.

[3] Council Directive 2005/85/EC of 1 December 2005 on minimum standards on procedures in Member States for granting and withdrawing refugee status [2005] OJ L326/13. Ireland and the United Kingdom opted to participate in the adoption and application of this Directive.

[4] Council Directive 2003/86/EC of 22 September 2003 on the right to family reunification [2003] OJ 251/12. Ireland and the United Kingdom did not participate in the adoption or application of this Directive.

[5] Council Directive 2003/109/EC of 25 November 2003 concerning the status of third-country nationals who are long-term residents [2004] OJ L16/44. Ireland and the United Kingdom did not participate in the adoption or application of this Directive.

[6] Council Directive 2003/86/EC Article 18; Council Directive 2003/109/EC Articles 10(2), 20(2).

the guarantees somewhat more explicit.[7] As Cholewinski observed in 2005: "migration instruments adopted under the developing EU migration law hardly distinguish themselves in the degree of legal protection they provide to third country nationals"[8] and "EU measures for irregular migration contain few safeguards for the migrants concerned."[9] The adoption of the Return Directive was an opportunity to redress this deficit; however, as Baldaccini points out in her assessment, it can fairly be regarded as "a codification at EU level of an expulsion regime that is lacking from a perspective of the rights of the individual."[10]

Within the European Union the principle of mutual recognition in the field of migration law and practice is probably most firmly established through the Dublin Convention[11] and the subsequent Regulation.[12] This "clear and workable mechanism for determining responsibility for asylum applications" is sufficiently well known as not to require detailed examination.[13] Although some harmonisation of procedural requirements for the processing of claims for asylum was obviously desirable as a result of the manner in which the Dublin system assigns responsibility for considering applications, it took several years to draft and adopt a directive on minimum procedural requirements.[14] As Ezra points out

> [A] harmonized asylum law did not emerge [from the Dublin Convention]. Rather, the convention simply authorized Member States to examine applications on behalf of all other Member States in accordance with their national law. What has finally emerged is a mutual recognition that the right of asylum seekers to look for shelter elsewhere in the EU should be withheld once the application was rejected by a Member State, this even in the absence of a common asylum policy. ... a more honest approach would have been to first decide on a timetable for achieving a harmonized asylum policy and only then to adopt the above-mentioned measures. The Member States, however, were not ready to follow this reasoning. Instead they favored a coordination of their policies, striving to protect their national interests by limiting the entrance of potential asylum seekers into EU territory and encouraging the notion of unfounded claims for asylum.[15]

---

[7] For example, Council Directive 2005/85/EC Article 39(1) "Member States shall ensure that applicants for asylum have the right to an effective remedy before a court or tribunal, against ..." a series of negative decisions in the asylum process. In general that Directive, as is its main object, sets out a specific procedure which must be followed in dealing with applications for asylum.

[8] Cholewinsky 2005, pp. 237–240.

[9] ibid., p. 241.

[10] Baldaccini 2009, p. 2.

[11] Convention determining the State responsible for examining applications for asylum lodged in one of the Member States of the European Communities-Dublin Convention (1990) [1997] OJ C254/1.

[12] Council Regulation (EC) No 343/2003 of 18 February 2003 establishing the criteria and mechanisms for determining the Member State responsible for examining an asylum application lodged in one of the Member States by a third-country national [2003] OJ L 50/1.

[13] See Report from the Commission to the European Parliament and the Council on the evaluation of the Dublin system SEC (07) 742 COM (07) 299 final.

[14] Lavenex and Wagner 2007.

[15] Ezra and Ludwig-Maximilians-Universität München 2004, p. 98.

This bias towards using mutual recognition to confirm the effect of exclusion from protection under Union law has been reaffirmed in the most recent secondary legislation in the field. In commenting on the proposal for the Return Directive (see below), the UNHCR noted that it requires merely "the mutual recognition of negative asylum decisions:"

> … the proposed Directive would effectively require all Member States to recognize and act on removal decisions issued by others. By implication, it thus requires mutual recognition of negative asylum decisions, whereas the asylum instruments adopted to date do not include any obligation to recognize positive decisions of other Member States. This imbalance—to the detriment of people with recognized protection needs—is reinforced by the current compromise proposal. There are no EU initiatives presently in train to work towards mutual recognition of positive decisions on international protection needs. In UNHCR's view, this remains as an important gap in the asylum acquis.[16]

In regard to the penultimate point made by the UNHCR, one should note that the Commission's Communication of 10 June 2009 did set the end of 2014 as a deadline by which "the EU should formally enshrine the principle of mutual recognition of all individual decisions *granting* protection status taken by authorities ruling on asylum applications"[17] and that the Stockholm Programme, although it is less definite on this issue, points towards a similar conclusion,[18] which is of course presupposed in general terms by the objectives of Article 78 TFEU.[19]

As Cholewinski points out, in relation to the Schengen Implementing Agreement, the adoption of the principle of mutual recognition of decisions made by national immigration administrations creates the risk of unequal treatment of persons in like situations, unless mutual recognition is accompanied by a significant degree of harmonisation in the definition and application in practice of concepts such as threats to public health public policy, public security or to national security.[20]

---

[16] UNHCR, Position on the Proposal for a Directive on Common Standards and Procedures in Member States for Returning Illegally Staying Third-Country Nationals (16 June 2008).

[17] Communication from the Commission to the European Parliament and the Council—An area of freedom, security and justice serving the citizen COM (2009) 262 final, 10 June 2009 Sect. 5.2.1.

[18] The Stockholm Programme—An open and secure Europe serving and protecting the citizens 17024/09 CO EUR-PREP 3 JAI 896 POLGEN 229 (2 December 2009) Sect. 6.2.1 ("The European Council … invites …. the Commission to consider, once the second phase of the CEAS has been fully implemented and on the basis of an evaluation of the effect of that legislation and of the EASO, the possibilities for creating a framework for the transfer of protection of beneficiaries of international protection when exercising their acquired residence rights under EU law …").

[19] Treaty on the Functioning of the European Union Article 78(2)(a)–(b).

[20] Cholewinski, *supra* n. 8, Sect. 6.2, p. 249.

6.3 The European Pact on Immigration and Asylum

The adoption of the Return Directive[21] was the first major result of a new political impetus in 2008 towards further coordination of immigration policy and controls at the European Union level. In the latter half of the year, the most prominent political initiative in this area was the European Pact on Immigration and Asylum,[22] strongly promoted by the French EU Presidency before and during the October 2008 European Council.[23] Whilst the key agreement between the Parliament and Council which paved the way for adoption of the Return Directive was reached in the final weeks of the Slovenian Presidency, it has been persuasively argued that the Parliament felt it opportune to settle this matter before the French Presidency had an opportunity to re-open it in a manner that would widen the gap between the positions taken by the institutions.[24] In assessing recent political developments such as the Pact, it is useful to consider Schain's persuasive analysis of the structural bias in the European Union system as regards the development of policy in this area as well as the political pressures from (and on) national governments to preserve their capacity to give effect to nationally determined immigration policies

> the division of the Council of Ministers into functionally-specific councils militates against tension (or conflict) between pressures for immigration harmonization and expansion, on the one hand, and pressures for harmonization of restriction, on the other. Indeed, with advocacy for restriction concentrated in the Council and advocacy for expansion in the Commission, the 'European level' is structurally biased towards restrictive policies linked to security considerations in the absence of executive leadership. The approach of the European Union to the harmonization of immigration policy has focused on the efforts to enforce exclusion first initiated at the Member State level.[25]

Indeed, Guiraudon pointed out more than a decade ago that the Europeanisation of immigration and asylum policy gave national governments, and specifically those parts of them, such as interior ministries, the opportunity to engage in 'vertical forum shopping' so as to avoid national legal and human rights guarantees for migrants.[26] As she pointed out one of the specific motivations of national political and administrative actors in resorting to European protection was

[21] Directive 2008/115/EC of the European Parliament and of the Council of 16 December 2008 on common standards and procedures in Member States for returning illegally staying third-country nationals [2008] OJ L 348/98. For a detailed analysis, see Carrera et al. 2009, pp. 21–24.

[22] European Pact on Immigration and Asylum Council Document 13440/08 (Brussels, 24 September 2008).

[23] Presidency Conclusions: Brussels European Council-15 and 16 October 2008 Council Document 14368/08 (16 October 2008) p. 8. For the general background see Traynor, Ian "France unveils pact on EU-wide immigration" The Guardian 8 July 2008 p. 16.

[24] Acosta 2009, pp. 37–38.

[25] Schain 2009, p. 104. For other procedural constraints, related to the way the co-decision process operates, see Acosta, *ibid.*, n. 24, pp. 24–25, 38.

[26] Guirodon 2000, p. 251.

to especially weaken and circumvent national judicial protection of migrants.[27] The assessments of the situation by both Guiraudon and Schain seem to be borne out by the background to the adoption of the Return Directive (see below) of which the Pact was an important part.

In the present context, the following are the most relevant aspects of the Pact. "Illegal immigrants" on Member States' territory must leave that territory, each State undertaking to apply this principle effectively, with due regard for the law and for the dignity of the persons involved and preferring voluntary return. "States shall accordingly recognise return decisions taken by another Member State."[28] It was specifically agreed "to put into full effect the Community provisions pursuant to which an expulsion decision taken by one Member State is applicable throughout the European Union, and, within that framework, an alert for such a decision entered in the Schengen Information System (SIS) obliges other Member States to prevent the person concerned from entering or residing within their territory."[29] A range of actions was also proposed to "[m]ake border controls more effective."[30] In these respects, the Pact reflects the areas of immigration policy which the Council has emphasised in recent years, an emphasis that had already shaped the evolution of the Return Directive as it went through the legislative process.[31] The Stockholm Programme confirms the importance of the Pact, both generally, by characterising the Pact as "clear basis for further development" in the field and, specifically, by requiring that measures taken to make the principle of mutual recognition of return decisions should ensure "consistency with the principles of the Pact on Asylum and Migration."[32]

More generally, some authors have seen the Pact as "guided by the principles of nationalism and intergovernmentalism" and as legitimising "certain policy responses and national practices of particular member states at the EU level, and aim[ed] at universalising them in an enlarged Europe."[33] In contrast, other commentators have seen the Pact as something of a missed opportunity, in that immigration and asylum policy are areas where, in their analysis, the European Council can make a constructive political contribution to the development of common policies, which is beyond the capacity of the Union's other institutions.[34] It is thus, they claim "a challenge to a key assumption underpinning European

---

[27] Ibid., pp. 258–259. As she points out "decisions taken at international level have … diminished the role of national courts at the policy implementation level" (ibid., pp. 262).

[28] *Supra* n. 22, Sect. 6.3, p. 7.

[29] Ibid., p. 8.

[30] Ibid., p. 9.

[31] See Acosta, *supra* n. 24, Sect. 6.3, p. 25–36.

[32] The Stockholm Programme—An open and secure Europe serving and protecting the citizens 17024/09 CO EUR-PREP 3 JAI 896 POLGEN 229 (2 December 2009) 5, 67.

[33] Carrera et al. 2008, p. 9.

[34] Angenendt and Parkes 2009, p. 77.

integration, namely that communitarised policymaking procedures are the best means of achieving truly common European migration policies."[35]

Whether, as some fear, the long-term effect of the Pact will be to undermine the Commission's right of initiative and to reverse or impede the communitarisation of immigration and asylum policy, in substance if not in form, or whether it reveals a new way of forging a genuinely common policy will no doubt be played in the implementation of the Stockholm Programme.

6.4 European Commission's Communication of 10 June 2009

As of March 2010, we were still awaiting the Commission's proposals for an action plan to implement the Stockholm Programme (see below).[36] However, the general orientation given by the Tampere European Council a decade ago in relation to policy on return and readmission was reaffirmed by the Commission's Communication of 10 June 2009 (foreshadowing the broad outline of an action plan to be presented under the Stockholm Programme), under which the Union and Member States should

> - envisage the conclusion of new agreements covering the three dimensions of the comprehensive approach: controlling illegal migration (including readmission and support for voluntary return and reintegration), promotion of mobility and legal immigration, and support for development on the lines of the partnerships for mobility;
>
> …
>
> - control illegal immigration and trafficking in human beings more effectively by developing information about migration routes, promoting cooperation on surveillance and border controls, and facilitating readmission by promoting support measures for return.[37]

The Commission developed the notion of "better controls on illegal immigration" as follows

> An effective policy on removal and return in accordance with the law and with human dignity has to be formulated. The rules on return provided for in the Directive will come into force in December 2010. Its implementation will be monitored closely, especially as regards the effective enforcement of expulsion measures, detention, appeal procedures and

[35] Ibid., p. 78.

[36] The European Council of 10/11 December 2009 invited the Commission to present its action plan by June 2010 at the latest: Conclusions of the European Council 10/11 December 2009 DOC/09/6 para 33 available at: http://europa.eu/rapid/pressReleasesAction.do?reference=DOC/09/6&format=HTML&aged=0&language=EN&guiLanguage=en (accessed 4 March 2010).

[37] Communication from the Commission to the European Parliament and the Council—An area of freedom, security and justice serving the citizen COM (2009) 262 final, 10 June 2009 Sect. 5.1.1.

> treatment of vulnerable people. This should go hand in hand with increased operational cooperation between the Member States. In the longer term, and after evaluation of this legislation, the principle of mutual recognition of removal decisions should be implemented. The obligatory recording of entry bans in the SIS will give full effect to this principle.
>
> Giving priority to voluntary return must be promoted and actively encouraged, particularly under the existing financial instruments. Nevertheless, all too often repatriation measures cannot be carried out on account of legal or practical obstacles. In the absence of clear rules, we should study the national needs and practices and consider the possibility of establishing common standards for taking charge of illegal immigrants who cannot be deported. The exchange of information between Member States concerning regularisations should be improved. Guidelines for their implementation could be formulated.[38]

In keeping with the generally bivalent nature of EU policy in the field, the Communication also envisaged the further development of the common asylum regime, involving application of the principle of mutual recognition

> The EU has made great progress towards creating a common European asylum regime wholly in accordance with the Geneva Convention and other applicable international instruments. A common set of standards has been established over the past ten years. The legislative proposals of the second phase of harmonisation need to be adopted quickly with the aim of establishing a single asylum procedure and a uniform international protection status no later than 2012.
>
> ...
>
> ... [B]y the end of 2014 the EU should formally enshrine the principle of mutual recognition of all individual decisions granting protection status taken by authorities ruling on asylum applications, which will mean that protection can be transferred without the adoption of specific mechanisms at European level.[39]

6.5 The Stockholm Programme

The Stockholm Programme, as adopted by the European Council of 2 December 2009 confirms the broad orientations given by the Pact, which it treats as a "clear basis for further development in this field."[40] It is thus not surprising that the terms and concepts employed in the Stockholm Programme contain clear echoes of the Pact and the Commission's subsequent Communication on the subject.

> An effective and sustainable return policy is an essential element of a well-managed migration system within the Union. The European Union and the Member States should

[38] Ibid Sect. 5.14. Compare this with Presidency Conclusions Tampere European Council 15–16 October 1999 paras 22–27, available at: http://www.consilium.europa.eu/ueDocs/cms_Data/docs/pressData/en/ec/00200-r1.en9.htm (accessed 10 September 2008).

[39] COM (2009) 262 final, Sect. 5.2.1.

[40] The Stockholm Programme—An open and secure Europe serving and protecting the citizens 17024/09 CO EUR-PREP 3 JAI 896 POLGEN 229 (2 December 2009) 5. For a general analysis of the Stockholm Programme and its implications for immigration policy, see Collett and European policy centre 2009.

> intensify the efforts to return illegally residing third country nationals. Necessary financial means should be allocated for this purpose. Such a policy must be implemented with full respect for the principle of "nonrefoulement" and for the fundamental rights and dignity of the individual returnees. Voluntary return should be preferred, while acknowledging the inevitable need for efficient means to enforce returns where necessary.[41]

The Stockholm Programme also reiterates the importance of the principle of mutual recognition of return decisions; measures should be taken to improve the implementation of that principle "with a view to ensuring consistency with the principles of the Pact on Asylum and Migration"[42] a formulation which highlights the importance of the Pact in this area of EU policy and action. The Programme also sets out the same general orientations as to relations with third countries (especially as regards the effectiveness of readmission agreements) and the role of FRONTEX in coordinating return operations that were set by the Pact and taken up by the Commission in its approach to the area.[43]

The Programme also repeats the "key objective" of "a common area of protection and solidarity based on a common asylum procedure and a uniform status for those granted international protection" based on "a full and inclusive application of the Geneva Convention on the status of refugees and other relevant international treaties"—all this to be achieved by 2012.[44] Although the need for "due regard … to fair and effective procedures capable of preventing abuse" is acknowledged, the basic principle adopted by the European Council is that "individuals, regardless of the Member State in which their application for asylum is lodged, are offered an equivalent level of treatment as regards reception conditions, and the same level as regards procedural arrangements and status determination … similar cases should be treated alike and result in the same outcome."[45]

Given the awareness of the very significant variations that still exist in the international protection offered by different Member States, the Programme sets ambitious goals, when judged by the degree of progress thus made towards a genuine Common European Asylum System. These include possible accession by the European Union to the Geneva Convention and its 1967 Protocol, greater practical cooperation between the Member States with the assistance of the European Asylum Support Office and intensified efforts to establish, by 2012, a common asylum procedure and a uniform status for those who are granted asylum or subsidiary protection.[46] Longer term measures, whose desirability and feasibility are to be investigated once the Common European Asylum System has been given more substance, include "a framework for the transfer of protection of

---

41 Ibid., p. 66.

42 Ibid., p. 67.

43 Ibid., pp. 67–68.

44 Ibid., p. 69.

45 Ibid.

46 Ibid., pp. 69–70.

beneficiaries of international protection when exercising their acquired residence rights under EU law" and possible joint processing of asylum applications.[47]

The Stockholm Programme thus reflects the well-established formal symmetry in the European Union's approach to asylum and immigration—on the one hand, intensified co-operation to ensure the effectiveness of national decisions to exclude migrants and, on the other, a harmonisation of the standards which those national authorities apply in making decisions on asylum and other forms of international protection. In recent years, the Union has been able much more easily to agree upon and effectively implement measures of the first kind. As a result, those who have long observed the development of European Union policy in the field of migration and its practical impacts may well be sceptical about whether such advances in harmonisation of international protection will really be made over the course of the Stockholm Programme.[48] Such scepticism also seems well-founded on the basis of the nature of the popular legitimacy which the European Union has in many Member States when it intervenes in the field of migration—whereby, it is at least plausible to surmise, the public opinion concerns that strongly prioritise effective migration control over "a full and inclusive application of the Geneva Convention."[49] Angenendt and Parkes highlight another controversial line argument which posits another possible impediment to realising the European Council's objectives on the timescale set out.

> By empowering the Parliament, Commission and Court, institutions viewed by many at member state level as ideological and out of step with the realities of migration regulation, the Lisbon Treaty will make policymaking more complicated. The Treaty will simply sharpen disagreements between the Council of the European Union and the Parliament/Commission, leading to legislative deadlock. Should agreement on EU policies nevertheless be achieved, communitarisation will increase the likelihood that member state governments will resort to the non-implementation of policy in order to express dissatisfaction at the greater influence of the Commission and Parliament on decision-taking.[50]

They also add the national and European Union courts to the list of ideological actors newly empowered, according to this point of view, to disrupt the achievement of a genuinely common policy.

All around, it seems likely that it will be concerns about burden sharing and the distorting effects on free movement of persons within the Union of such a high level diversity of national approaches to international protection will finally produce some more substantial progress towards the Stockholm Programme's aspirations.

---

[47] Ibid., p. 70.

[48] See, for example, the analysis and criticisms of this imbalance in the EU's approach to the control of migration by Hansen, *supra* n. 2, Sect. 6.2; Cholewinski, *supra* n. 8, Sect. 6.2; Lavenex, *supra* n. 14, Sect. 6.2; Ezra, *supra* n. 15, Sect. 6.2; the UNHCR *supra* n. 16, Sect. 6.2; Schain *supra* n. 25, Sect. 6.3 and—in relation to the logic of the Pact—Carrera and Guild, *supra* n. 33. See also the results of the research carried out by the Commission itself, *infra* n. 55, Sect. 6.6 and by the Hungarian Helsinki Committee, *infra* n. 78, Sect. 6.6.

[49] See the text, *infra*, accompanying n. 156 to n. 161, Sect. 6.7.

[50] Angenendt, *supra* n. 32, Sect. 6.3, pp. 80–81.

6.6 2008: A Turning Point for EU Immigration Policy?

In June 2009, the Commission had been able to anticipate with some confidence a greater degree of progress under the Stockholm Programme than was achieved under the Hague Programme largely as a result of a re-orientation of attitudes amongst national governments during 2008–2009. The first major fruit of this re-orientation of the positions adopted by the Member States was a breakthrough on the Return Directive, but which also, later that year, found a broader expression in the Pact.

The text of the Directive agreed in mid-June 2008 by the Council and the Parliament[51] was adopted on 16 December 2008.[52] The Directive's general goal reflects the decision of the Brussels European Council of 4 and 5 November 2004 and is to create "an effective removal and repatriation policy, based on common standards, for persons to be returned in a humane manner and with full respect for their fundamental rights and dignity."[53] The core of this policy's "effectiveness" is the obligation on each Member State to issue a return decision to any third country national staying illegally on its territory, subject to the specific exceptions set out in the Directive.[54] Thus, those holding a valid residence permit or other authorisation giving a right to stay in another Member State shall be required to go to that other Member State's territory and become subject to a return decision only if they fail to comply with this requirement, or where their immediate departure is required for reasons of public policy or national security.[55] Similarly, where another Member State takes back a third country national under bilateral agreements or arrangements existing on the date of entry into force of the Directive, it becomes that Member State's duty to issue and execute a return order.[56]

In addition, the obligation to issue a return decision does not remove a Member State's authority to grant "an autonomous residence permit or other authorisation offering a right to stay for compassionate, humanitarian or other reasons to a third

[51] European Parliament legislative resolution of 18 June 2008 on the proposal for a directive of the European Parliament and of the Council on common standards and procedures in Member States for returning illegally staying third-country nationals (COM(2005)0391—C6-0266/2005—2005/0167(COD)) 20 September 2007. For a review of the draft Directive in the form it was initially proposed see Cassarino and European University Institute 2006.

[52] Directive 2008/115/EC of the European Parliament and of the Council of 16 December 2008 on common standards and procedures in Member States for returning illegally staying third-country nationals [2008] OJ L 348.

[53] Ibid., Recital (2). For a general review of the Directive, see Baldaccini, *supra* n. 10, Sect. 6.2. As she points out (*supra* n. 7, Sect. 6.2) the general reference to fundamental rights obligations in relation to return decisions was, in the course of the legislative process, removed from the main text and confined to the recitals.

[54] Directive 2008/115/EC Article 6(1).

[55] Ibid., Article 6(2).

[56] Ibid., Article 6(3).

country national staying illegally" on its territory.[57] In the same way, a pending procedure for renewing a residence permit or other authorisation offering a right to stay requires the Member State concerned to consider refraining from issuing a return decision, until that procedure is completed.[58]

Despite these exceptions to the obligation to issue a return decision, Baldaccini is right to note the regrettable absence of any explicit reference in this provision to the Member State's obligations under the Community acquis on asylum and immigration or its obligations in respect of the fundamental rights of the third country national.[59]

The Directive envisages that "fair and efficient asylum systems... which fully respect the principle of non-refoulement" are a necessary condition for the legitimacy of the return of illegally staying third country nationals.[60] The Commission's own Policy Plan on Asylum[61] acknowledges considerable evidence which suggests that fair and effective guarantees of asylum are not in place in all Member States: "... data show that the recognition of protection needs of applicants from the same countries of origin still varies significantly from one Member State to another. To some extent, this phenomenon is rooted in the wording of certain provisions of the" Qualification Directive.[62] The Commission has proposed a series of actions to address this problem and to institute "a truly common interpretative approach."[63]

On this score, the UNHCR, in commenting on the proposal for the present Directive reiterated a view it had previously expressed that

> Given the widely acknowledged divergences and concerns around quality in asylum decision-making across the EU, UNHCR considers that this condition [the need for fair and efficient asylum systems in the EU as an essential prerequisite for the EU's return policy] is not met.[64]

As regards the Return Directive itself, the Parliament's rapporteur commented that—

> It is not the task of this directive to establish illegality but merely to ensure a transparent return procedure. On the other hand, the return procedure is linked for the first time to

---

57 Ibid., Article 6(4).

58 Ibid., Article 6(5).

59 Baldaccini, *supra* n. 10, Sect. 6.2, p. 6–7.

60 *supra* n. 54, Sect. 6.6, Recital (8).

61 Communication from the Commission to the European Parliament, the Council, the European Economic and Social Committee and the Committee of Regions—Policy plan on asylum—An integrated approach to protection across the EU COM (2008) 360 final, 17 June 2008.

62 ibid., Sect. 3.3.

63 ibid.

64 UNHCR, Position on the Proposal for a Directive on Common Standards and Procedures in Member States for Returning Illegally Staying Third-Country Nationals (16 June 2008) p. 3. The UNHCR based this assessment on its November 2007 Study on the Implementation of the Qualification Directive: http://www.unhcr.org/cgi-bin/texis/vtx/refworld/rwmain?docid=473050632.

> minimum standards in order to ensure humane treatment. Cooperation at all levels of the return procedure between the national authorities and between Member States is improved. Among other things, a European added value is created. The proposal introduces a ban on re-entry which is valid throughout Europe. This adds value to a strong Europe acting with one voice. However, the key focus is on voluntary return.[65]

In the specific context of procedural guarantees and application the principle of mutual recognition, the most relevant elements of the Return Directive are

- fair and transparent procedures in relation to return decisions
- common minimum legal standards
- requirements of proportionality and effectiveness in relation to the use of coercive measures
- the introduction of an EU-wide ban on entry for those returned to a third-country
- some limitations on the use of detention as a means of giving effect to return decisions
- enhanced administrative cooperation in matters affecting return and re-entry of third country nationals

Although they are largely beyond the scope of the issues treated in this chapter, the provisions of the Directive favouring voluntary departure over mandatory or forced return should be noted.[66] There are, of course, grounds for doubting how effective the preference for voluntary departure will be, particularly in light of the fact that the obligation to set down in the return decision an appropriate period of between seven and thirty days for voluntary departure may be avoided (or a period shorter than seven days fixed) in cases where "there is a risk of absconding, or if an application for a legal stay has been dismissed as manifestly unfounded or fraudulent, or if the person concerned poses a risk to public policy, public security or national security."[67]

> Member States should ensure that the ending of illegal stay of third country nationals is carried out through a fair and transparent procedure.[68]

Specific procedural safeguards are required in relation to return decisions, entry ban decisions and removal decisions and—where applicable—the decision to impose an entry ban. Such decisions must be "issued in writing and give reasons in fact and in law as well as information about available legal remedies."[69]

---

[65] European Parliament Report on the proposal for a directive of the European Parliament and of the Council on common standards and procedures in Member States for returning illegally staying third-country nationals (COM(2005)0391—C6-0266/2005—2005/0167(COD)).

[66] See Baldaccini, *supra* n. 10, Sect. 6.2, p. 7–8.

[67] Ibid., p. 8.

[68] Directive 2008/115/EC Recital (6).

[69] Ibid., Article 12(1). This is accompanied by the qualification that "information on reasons in fact may be limited where national law allows for the right of information to be restricted, in particular in order to safeguard national security, defence, public security and the prevention, investigation, detection and prosecution of criminal offences."

Addressees are entitled to "a written or oral translation of the main elements of decisions related to return ... including information on the available legal remedies in a language the third country national understands or may reasonably be supposed to understand."[70] Nevertheless, Member States may substitute for that a standard form set out in national legislation in respect to "persons who have illegally entered the territory of a Member State and who have not subsequently obtained an authorisation or a right to stay in that Member State."[71]

The European Council on Refugees and Exiles (ECRE) has pointed out that there are several potential shortcomings in these procedural safeguards. For one thing, they fail to guarantee that information will be provided to the third country national in a language which he or she does in fact understand.[72] More fundamentally, ECRE asserts that the exclusion from the full right to translation and information of persons who have illegally entered and not subsequently obtained authorisation or a right to stay constitutes a discriminatory and unjustified limitation of the scope of the procedural guarantees.[73] Broadly, the same type of restriction ("lawfully resident") is contained in Article 1 of the Seventh Protocol to the European Convention on Human Rights (ECHR)[74] (which, in any event,

---

[70] Ibid., Article 12(2).

[71] Ibid., Article 12(3). For purposes of comparison, see Regulation (EC) No 562/2006 of the European Parliament and of the Council of 15 March 2006 establishing a Community Code on the rules governing the movement of persons across borders (Schengen Borders Code) [2006] OJ L 105/1 Article 13(2), Annex V. In addition, "Member States shall make available generalised information sheets explaining the main elements of the standard form in at least five of those languages which are most frequently used or understood by illegal migrants entering the Member State concerned." *supra,* n. 68, Sect. 6.6.

[72] ECRE, *Information Note on Directive 2008/115/EC of the European Parliament and of the Council of 16 December 2008 on common standards and procedures in Member States for returning illegally staying third-country nationals* CO7/1/2009/Ext/MDM (January 2009) p. 17. http://www.ecre.org/files/ECRE_Information_Note_Returns_Directive_January_2009.pdf (Last accessed 11 August 2009).

[73] Ibid.

[74] *Procedural safeguards relating to expulsion of aliens–*

1. An alien lawfully resident in the territory of a State shall not be expelled therefrom except in pursuance of a decision reached in accordance with law and shall be allowed:
   1. to submit reasons against his expulsion,
   2. to have his case reviewed, and
   3. to be represented for these purposes before the competent authority or a person or persons designated by that authority.
2. An alien may be expelled before the exercise of his rights under para 1. a, b and c of this Article, when such expulsion is necessary in the interests of public order or is grounded on reasons of national security.
   Protocol No. 7 to the Convention for the Protection of Human Rights and Fundamental Freedoms
   CETS No.: 117 (Strasbourg, 22 November 1984; entered into force, 1 November 1988.) Article 1.

only twenty-three EU Member States have ratified)[75] and which—unlike Article 4 of the Fourth Protocol to the European Convention—is not directly paralleled in any of the provisions of the Charter of Fundamental Rights of the European Union. However, one difference is that ECRE's complaint concerning unjustified discrimination in favour of the visa overstayer (to use ECRE's example) does not apply there, as the Explanatory Report on the Seventh Protocol makes clear 'an alien whose admission and stay were subject to certain conditions, for example a fixed period, and who no longer complies with these conditions cannot be regarded as being still "lawfully" present.'[76]

Even where the Protocol is not in force or not applicable there may, depending on the right affected, be a violation of the ECHR as a result of a failure to accord adequate procedural protection to a third country national who has been the subject of a return decision or some equivalent measure. The nature of the decision issued and the procedure leading up to it may well be a factor when assessing whether or not a collective expulsion of aliens has taken place. Such a collective expulsion violates Article 4 of the Fourth Protocol to the ECHR, which has been ratified by all EU Member States, apart from Greece and the United Kingdom.)[77] In addition, of course, a collective expulsion now also violates Article 19(1) of the Charter of Fundamental Rights of the European Union.[78] As ECRE has pointed out,[79] referring to the decision in *Čonka v Belgium*, this may be one reason why the practice of issuing standard form to those in receipt of a return decision may lead to a violation of its international human rights obligations by the state concerned. Such a violation occurs if the practice results in the absence of "sufficient guarantees demonstrating that the personal circumstances of each of those concerned had been genuinely and individually taken into account."[80]

ECRE goes somewhat further by stating that "[b]y definition standard forms do not allow any elaboration of the personal circumstances of the individual" and

[75] As of 4 March 2010, Belgium, Germany, The Netherlands, and the United Kingdom had all signed, but not ratified, the Protocol.

[76] *Explanatory Report to Protocol No. 7 to the Convention for the Protection of Human Rights and Fundamental Freedoms (ETS no. 117)* (1984) para 9.

[77] *Prohibition of collective expulsion of aliens*—Collective expulsion of aliens is prohibited. Protocol No. 4 to the Convention for the Protection of Human Rights and Fundamental Freedoms, securing certain rights and freedoms other than those already included in the Convention and in the first Protocol thereto CETS No.: 46 (Strasbourg, 16 September 1963; entered into force, 2 May 1968) Article 4. The opportunity to set out guarantees (whether substantive or procedural) in relation to individual expulsion of aliens was deliberately neglected in the drafting of the Fourth Protocol: *Explanatory Report to Protocol No. 4 to the Convention for the Protection of Human Rights and Fundamental Freedoms, securing certain rights and freedoms other than those already included in the Convention and in the first Protocol thereto* (1963) para 34.

[78] Charter of Fundamental Rights of the European Union (2007/C 303/01) Article 19(1).

[79] ECRE, *Information Note on Directive 2008/115/EC*. See *supra*, n. 72, Sect. 6.6, p. 17.

[80] *Čonka v Belgium* judgment of 5 February 2002, App. No. 51564/99 para 63.

"[c]onsequently, their generalised use would be below the standards laid down in international human rights law and incompatible with ECtHR case-law."[81] This may be an oversimplification; up to the decision in *Čonka*, there was a clear line of decisions holding that it is not the form of the decision issued which is decisive in the such cases, but the extent to which there was in substance a genuine opportunity for the personal circumstances of the individual to be considered in the making of the decision to expel. As the admissibility decision in *Andric v Sweden* put it:

> ... collective expulsion is to be understood as any measure compelling aliens, as a group, to leave a country, except where such a measure is taken on the basis of a reasonable and objective examination of the particular case of each individual alien of the group. Moreover, the fact that a number of aliens receive similar decisions does not lead to the conclusion that there is a collective expulsion when each person concerned has been given the opportunity to put arguments against his expulsion to the competent authorities on an individual basis (see application no. 14209/88, decision of 16 December 1988, DR 59, p. 274)[82]

The partly dissenting opinion of Judge Velaers in *Čonka* points to the potential significance of the majority's reliance on the form of the final decision and in particular the omission of express reference to consideration of the personal circumstances of the applicant, which he considered as introducing 'a purely formal element into the definition of the concept of "collective expulsion"' in a manner inconsistent with *Andric* and other previous cases.[83] In the *Čonka* case, moreover, the majority's doubt as to whether the expulsion might have been collective arose not only from the form of the decision, but from other factors such as prior announcements of and instructions to undertake collective repatriations, the requirement for a large group of individuals to report to the police simultaneously, the difficulty which the persons expelled had in contacting a lawyer and the fact that the asylum process has not been completed in their cases. That the orders directed to them were couched in identical terms was only one such factor. At the same time, in other recent cases, the failure of an order of this general kind (such as one authorising the detention of an immigrant) to refer expressly to the grounds relied upon

---

[81] ECRE, *Information Note on Directive 2008/115/EC*. See *supra*, n. 72, Sect. 6.6, p. 17.

[82] *Andric v Sweden*, admissibility decision of 23 February 1999, App. No. 45917/99 p. 4, citing *A. & Ors v. The Netherlands (Alibaks)*, App. No. 14209/88, Commission decision of 16 December 1988, Decisions and Reports 59, p. 274. To like effect as *Andric*, see *Majic v Sweden*, admissibility decision of 23 February 1999, App. No. 45918/99, five other judgments given on the same day in relation to the same State Party (*Pavlovic*, App. No. 45918/99; *Pranjko*, App. No. 45925/99; *Juric*, App. No. 45924/99; *Andrijic*, App. No. 45923/99; *Maric*, App. No. 45922/99) and *Tahiri v Sweden*, admissibility decision of App. No. 25129/94. See also *Sulejmanovic & autres c Italie* and *Sejdovic et Sulejmanovic c Italie*, l'arrêt du 8 novembre 2002 (règlement amiable) Requêtes nos 57574/00 et 57575/00.

[83] *Čonka, supra*, n. 80, Sect. 6.6. Partly Concurring and Partly Dissenting Opinion of Judge Velaers, para 7. Two other members of the court dissented from the opinion that there had been a violation of Article 4 and for broadly the same reasons: Partly Dissenting Opinion of Judge Jungwiert Joined by Judge Kūris.

by the state concerned has been a significant factor leading to the finding of a violation of Convention rights (under Article 5, in cases involving detention.)[84]

How weighty a factor the form of the order will be in assessing whether a collective expulsion has occurred depends on the surrounding circumstances, as shown by the decision on the point in *Berisha and Haljiti v "the former Yugoslav Republic of Macedonia."*[85] In that case (where two identical decisions issued to spouses who had made a joint application for asylum, based on the same facts) the formula used in *Andric* is invoked, without any reference being made to *Čonka*. The whole procedural history and context of a case has, therefore, to be considered, before concluding that it has been shown that an applicant was a victim of a collective expulsion.

The more substantial issue raised by ECRE is that the use of standard forms in immigration decision-making may be a symptom of, or even a contributory factor to, arbitrary and ad hoc interpretation and application of immigration law, which certainly could be evidence that the personal circumstances of each of those concerned had not been genuinely and individually taken into account.[86]

> A common minimum set of legal safeguards on decisions related to return should be established to guarantee effective protection of the interests of the individuals concerned. Necessary legal aid should be made available to those who lack sufficient resources. Member States should lay down in their national legislation in which cases legal aid is to be considered necessary.[87]

The third-country national will be entitled to "an effective remedy to appeal against or seek review of decisions related to return … before a competent judicial or administrative authority or a competent body composed of members who are impartial and who enjoy safeguards of independence."[88] The authority or body in question shall have the power to review decisions related to return including, if it is not already provided for under national legislation, the possibility of temporarily suspending enforcement.[89] The issue of whether appealing or seeking review should have an automatic suspensive effect (either *ipso facto* or upon the irregular migrant's request) was one of the most controversial points during the legislative process. Although the most extreme position defended by the Council Presidency

---

[84] *Galliani v Romania*, judgment of 10 June 2008, App. No. 69273/01 para 46; *Estrikh v Latvia*, judgment of 18 January 2007, App. No. 73819/01 para 122.

[85] *Berisha and Haljiti v Macedonia*, admissibility decision of 16 June 2005, App. No. 18670/03.

[86] See the study cited by ECRE in this respect: Hungarian Helsinki Committee 2008, *Access to Protection at Airports in Europe: Report on the monitoring experience at airports in Amsterdam, Budapest, Madrid, Prague, Vienna and Warsaw* (2008). http://helsinki.webdialog.hu/dokumentum/Access_at_Airports_Report.pdf (accessed 11 August 2009).

[87] Directive 2008/115/EC Recital (11).

[88] Ibid., Article 13(1). In ECRE's view "the ambiguity of this formulation risks allowing Member States to accommodate practices which may run counter to the objective of granting third country nationals a genuinely effective remedy." ECRE, *Information Note on Directive 2008/115/EC*, *supra*, n. 72, Sect. 6.6, p. 18.

[89] Ibid., Article 13(2).

(that the issue should be left to be governed by national law) was not adopted, the final text is closer to the Council's position during the process than to that of the Commission or the Parliament.[90]

Čonka is relevant in this respect also. There, the Strasbourg Court held that where a Convention provision (such as Article 3 or, in *Čonka* itself, Article 4 of the Fourth Protocol) is applicable to an expulsion decision, the fact that an appeal against or application for review of the decision does not have automatic suspensive effect may be an important factor in holding that the applicant has been denied an effective remedy before a national authority.

> … the notion of an effective remedy under Article 13 requires that the remedy may prevent the execution of measures that are contrary to the Convention and whose effects are potentially irreversible … Consequently, it is inconsistent with Article 13 for such measures to be executed before the national authorities have examined whether they are compatible with the Convention, although Contracting States are afforded some discretion as to the manner in which they conform to their obligations under this provision …[91]

In the specific case, the Court found that the possibility of applying to a national court for a stay on the implementation of the expulsion decision pending a review of its legality did not provide an effective remedy for the applicant (who had been given a period of five days to leave Belgian territory).

> 82. Firstly, it is not possible to exclude the risk that in a system where stays of execution must be applied for and are discretionary they may be refused wrongly, in particular if it was subsequently to transpire that the court ruling on the merits has nonetheless to quash a deportation order for failure to comply with the Convention, for instance, if the applicant would be subjected to ill-treatment in the country of destination or be part of a collective expulsion. In such cases, the remedy exercised by the applicant would not be sufficiently effective for the purposes of Article 13.
>
> 83. Secondly, even if the risk of error is in practice negligible—a point which the Court is unable to verify, in the absence of any reliable evidence—it should be noted that the requirements of Article 13, and of the other provisions of the Convention, take the form of a guarantee and not of a mere statement of intent or a practical arrangement. That is one of the consequences of the rule of law, one of the fundamental principles of a democratic society, which is inherent in all the Articles of the Convention (see, mutatis mutandis, *Iatridis v. Greece* [GC], no. 31107/96, § 58, ECHR 1999-II).[92]

The Court has indicated, however, that the short period (five days) given for departure in *Čonka* was a significant element in the finding that Belgian law did not provide an effective remedy in that case.[93] In addition, provided that the request for protective measures has been examined by the competent national authority, the fact that it was rejected does not necessarily mean that there has been

---

[90] Acosta, *supra* n. 24, Sect. 6.3; Baldaccini, *supra* n. 10, Sect. 6.2, p. 12.

[91] *Čonka, supra,* n. 80, Sect. 6.6, para 79. Citations (to *Jabari v Turkey*, judgment of 11 July 2000 (App. No. 40035/98) para 50 and *Chahal v UK*, judgment of 15 November 1996 (App. No. 22414/93) para 145) omitted.

[92] Ibid., *Čonka,* paras 81–82.

[93] *Sardinas Albo v Italy*, admissibility decision of 8 January 2004, App. No. 56271/00.

a breach of Article 13, since the right to an effective remedy does not mean a remedy that is bound to succeed.[94] Nevertheless, the basic principle laid down in *Čonka* has been reiterated in several subsequent cases.[95] Where the effects of an expulsion are potentially irreversible, and the person to be expelled can make an arguable case that the expulsion will violate one of his or her ECHR rights, Article 13 thus seems to require that there be a framework in national law which, taken as a whole, clearly obliges the authorities to defer the expulsion while an application to review the decision is pending, at the very least for a minimum reasonable period to enable the competent authority to decide the application.[96] Furthermore, there must be legal guarantee that authority will issue protective measures giving the person facing expulsion a sufficient certainty of an effective suspensive remedy.[97] Of course, the two conditions stated at the outset of the paragraph (potentially irreversible effect of the expulsion and the implication of an ECHR right) define only one subset of the cases which fall under the Return Directive.

The third country national will be entitled to obtain legal advice, representation and, where necessary, linguistic assistance; the necessary legal assistance or representation is to be granted on request free of charge in accordance with relevant national legislation or rules regarding legal aid.[98] As Acosta and Baldaccini point out in their commentaries, the scope of the Member States' obligation to provide free legal aid to third country nationals was one of the most difficult political issues to resolve in discussions between the Council and the Parliament and was resolved, not merely by the adoption of the formula now to be found in Article 13, but also on the basis of the Commission's statement emphasizing the possibility of drawing upon the Community Return Fund, for co-financing of the national implementation of this aspect of the Directive.[99] In ECRE's view the discretion given in this regard "severely circumscribes the ability of asylum claimants to access free legal assistance by allowing Member States to introduce a series of

---

[94] *Salah Sheekh v The Netherlands*, judgment of 11 January 2007, App. No. 1948/04 para 154.

[95] *Gebremedhin [Gaberamadhien] v France*, judgment of 26 April 2007, App. No. 25389/05 para 66; *Garabayev v Russia*, judgment of 7 June 2007, App. No. 38411/02 paras 103–107; *Muminov v Russia,* 11 December 2008, App. No. 42502/06 para 102. See also *Mamatkulov and Askarov v Turkey*, judgment of 4 February 2005, App. Nos. 46827/99 and 46951/99 paras 124–128.

[96] See also *Ad hoc Committee of Experts on the Legal Aspects of Territorial Asylum, Refugees and Stateless Persons (CAHAR)—Twenty guidelines on forced return* CM(2005)40finalE adopted by the Committee of Ministers of the Council of Europe 4 May 2005, Guideline 5.3. See the comment on this guideline in *Ad hoc Committee of Experts on the Legal Aspects of Territorial Asylum, Refugees and Stateless Persons (CAHAR)—Comments on the Twenty guidelines on forced return* CM(2005)40 Addendum final 20 May 2005.

[97] *Čonka, supra*, n. 80, Sect. 6.6, para 82.

[98] Ibid., Article 13(3)–(4). Member States may provide that free legal assistance and/or representation is subject to conditions as set out in Article 15(3)–(6) of Council Directive 2005/85/EC on minimum standards on procedures in Member States for granting and withdrawing refugee status.

[99] Acosta, *supra* n. 24, Sect. 6.3, pp. 35–36; Baldaccini, *supra* n. 10, Sect. 6.2, pp. 12–13.

limitations, such as excluding legal aid for judicial review of administrative decisions, limiting the granting of assistance to where appeal or review is likely to succeed, and introducing monetary and temporal restrictions to the provision of legal aid."[100]

The comments of the Ad hoc Committee of Experts on the Legal Aspects of Territorial Asylum, Refugees and Stateless Persons (CAHAR) on Twenty Guidelines on Forced Return adopted by the Committee of Ministers of the Council of Europe specifically address the nature of the legal assistance which should be provided in these cases:

> – the remedy shall be accessible, which implies in particular that, where the subject of the removal order does not have sufficient means to pay for necessary legal assistance, he/she should be given it free of charge, in accordance with the relevant national rules regarding legal aid …
>
> …
>
> Th[is] reference … to the relevant national rules regarding legal aid seeks to preserve the possibility, for the Member States who so choose, to grant legal aid subject to conditions they see fit, provided these are not discriminatory and remain in compliance with their international obligations. It is to be noted, for instance, that some States limit the scope of free legal aid to persons who have an arguable claim that he or she would be subjected to treatment contrary to his or her human rights as set out in Guideline 2.1.[101]

As CAHAR's comments illustrate, there is potential for grounding third country nationals' claim to effective legal assistance in dealing with the immigration process, but only to the extent that an arguable claim can be advanced that their internationally protected human rights stand to be affected by expulsion or similar measures.

> "The use of coercive measures should be expressly subject to the principles of proportionality and effectiveness with regard to means taken and objectives pursued. Minimum safeguards for the conduct of forced return should be established."[102]

Member States will be obliged to take all necessary measures to enforce return decisions if a period for voluntary departure has not been granted or the obligation to return has not been complied with within that period.[103] They may adopt a separate administrative or judicial decision or act ordering the removal[104] and where—as a last resort—they use coercive measures to carry out the removal, such measures shall be proportional and shall not exceed reasonable force and shall be implemented as provided for in national legislation in accordance with

[100] ECRE, *Information Note on Directive 2008/115/EC, supra,* n. 72, Sect. 6.6, p. 18.

[101] *Ad hoc Committee of Experts on the Legal Aspects of Territorial Asylum, Refugees and Stateless Persons (CAHAR)—Comments on the Twenty guidelines on forced return* CM(2005)40 Addendum final 20 May 2005 Commentary on Guideline 5.2.

[102] Ibid., Recital (13).

[103] Ibid., Article 8(1).

[104] Ibid., Article 8(3).

fundamental rights and with due respect for the dignity and physical integrity of the third-country national concerned.[105]

> The effects of national return measures should be given a European dimension by establishing an entry ban prohibiting entry into and stay in the territory of all the Member States. The length of the entry ban should be determined with due regard to all relevant circumstances of an individual case and should not normally exceed five years.[106]

An entry ban is to be the mandatory accompaniment of a return decision where no period for voluntary departure has been granted, or if the obligation to return has not been complied with.[107] In other cases an entry ban is optional.[108] Member States may refrain from issuing, withdraw or suspend an entry ban in individual cases for humanitarian reasons and may withdraw or suspend an entry ban in individual cases or certain categories of cases for other reasons.[109] The entry ban may exceed five years only if the third country national poses a serious threat to public policy, public security or to national security.[110]

For present purposes, the most significant provision is Article 11(4)

> Where a Member State considers issuing a residence permit or another authorisation offering a right to stay to a third-country national who is subject of an entry ban issued by another Member State, it shall first consult the Member State having issued the entry ban and shall take account of its interests in accordance with the provisions of Article 25 of the Convention Implementing the Schengen Agreement.

---

[105] Ibid., Article 8(4). In carrying out removals by air, Member States are to take into account the Common Guidelines on security provisions for joint removal by air, attached to Decision 2004/573/EC: ibid., Article 8(5).

[106] Ibid., Recital (14). The Recital continues: "In this context, particular account should be taken of the fact that the third-country national concerned has already been the subject of more than one return decision or removal order or has entered the territory of a Member State during an entry ban."

[107] Ibid., Article 11(1). Member States may refrain from granting a period for voluntary departure, or grant a period shorter than seven days where there is a risk of absconding, or if an application for a legal stay has been dismissed as manifestly unfounded or fraudulent or if the person concerned poses a risk to public security, public order or national security: ibid Article 7(4). Otherwise a period for voluntary departure of between seven and thirty days is to be given (Article 7(1)) except a longer period is necessary, necessary, taking into account the specific circumstances of the individual case, such as the length of stay, the existence of children attending school and the existence of other family and social links (Article 7(2)).

[108] Victims of trafficking in human beings granted a residence permit pursuant to Council Directive 2004/81/EC of 29 April 2004 on the residence permit issued to third-country nationals who are victims of trafficking in human beings or who have been the subject of an action to facilitate illegal immigration, who cooperate with the competent authorities are not to be subject of an entry ban, provided that the third-country national concerned does not represent a threat to public policy, public security or national security: ibid., Article 11(3).

[109] Ibid.

[110] Ibid., Article 11(2). Member States shall consider withdrawing or suspending an entry ban where a third-country national who is the subject of an entry ban issued on the ground that the obligation to return has not been complied with can demonstrate that he or she has left the territory of a Member State in full compliance with a return decision: Article 11(3).

Article 25 of the 1990 Schengen Convention provides that a residence permit shall be issued for substantive reasons only, notably on humanitarian grounds or by reason of international commitments.[111]

As the Council Proposal for a Return Action Programme (November 2002) put it

> Within an area of freedom, security and justice where inner border control does not exist, the efficient return of illegal residents who have absconded after receiving an expulsion decision issued by one Member State and who have been apprehended in another Member State, is of major importance. In this regard an expulsion decision issued by one Member State should as far as possible and in accordance with national legislation be enforced in another Member State without the latter having to issue a new expulsion decision.[112]

The Return Directive does not repeal the more limited existing Directive on the mutual recognition of decisions on the expulsion of third country nationals.[113]

> The use of detention for the purpose of removal should be limited and subject to the principle of proportionality with regard to means taken and objectives pursued. Detention is justified only to prepare return or carry out the removal process and if the application of less coercive measures would not be sufficient.[114]

Detention of third country nationals is only authorised where other sufficient but less coercive measures cannot be applied effectively in the concrete case and where the detention is in order to prepare return or to carry out the removal process, particularly in the case of a risk of absconding or where the third country national avoids or hampers the preparation of return or the removal process.[115] Any detention shall be for as short a period as possible and only maintained as long as removal arrangements are in progress and executed with due diligence and it remains necessary to ensure successful removal.[116] If it appears that a reasonable prospect of removal no longer exists for legal or other considerations or the other necessary conditions no longer exist, the detention will cease to be justified and the person concerned shall be released immediately.[117]

---

[111] Convention implementing the Schengen Agreement of 14 June 1985 between the Governments of the States of the Benelux Economic Union, the Federal Republic of Germany and the French Republic on the gradual abolition of checks at their common borders [2000] OJ L239/19 Article 25(1).

[112] 14673/02 (MIGR 125 FRONT 135 VISA 172) of 25 November 2002.

[113] Council Directive 2001/40/EC of 28 May 2001 on the mutual recognition of decisions on the expulsion of third country nationals [2001] OJ L149/34. The United Kingdom opted to take part in the adoption and application of this Directive; Ireland did not: ibid Recital (6.) For a review of the national transposition of this Directive, see Carlier and Bruycker 2005, Philippe (eds) *Immigration and asylum law in the EU: current debates = Actualité du droit européen de l'immigration et de l'asile* (Brussels, 2005).

[114] Directive 2008/115/EC Recital 16.

[115] Ibid., Article 15(1).

[116] Ibid., Article 15(1), 15(5).

[117] *supra* n. 114, Sect. 6.6, Article 15(4).

Each Member State shall set a limited period of detention, which may not exceed six months.[118] However, Member States may extend that period, but for a limited period not exceeding a further 12 months in cases where, regardless of all reasonable efforts, the removal operation is likely to last longer

- due to a lack of co-operation by the third country national concerned, or
- due to delays in obtaining necessary documentation from third countries.[119]

Detention shall be ordered, in writing with reasons in fact and in law, by administrative or judicial authorities.[120] When ordered by administrative authorities, the detention shall either be subject to "a speedy judicial review" of its lawfulness[121] or to the right of the person being removed to take proceedings by which the lawfulness of detention shall be subject to a speedy judicial review. The third country national concerned shall be released immediately if the detention is not lawful.[122]

In every case, detention shall be reviewed at reasonable intervals of time either on application by the third country national concerned or *ex officio*. In the case of prolonged detention periods, reviews shall be subject to the supervision of a judicial authority.[123]

As a rule, detention shall take place in specialised detention facilities. If the Member State cannot provide accommodation in a specialised detention facility and must therefore resort to prison accommodation, the detainees are to be kept separated from ordinary prisoners.[124]

Although the Directive envisages that "[c]ooperation between the institutions involved at all levels in the return process and the exchange and promotion of best practices should accompany" its implementation and "provide European added value"[125] it makes no specific provisions for this purpose.

However, the Commission statement accompanying the adoption of the Directive by the Council does envisage a number of actions at the European level to enhance the effectiveness of national migration controls

> the review of the SIS II (under the review clause of Article 24(5) of Regulation (EC) No 1987/2006) could result in an obligation to register in the SIS entry bans issued under the Return Directive.

[118] Ibid., Article 15(5).

[119] Ibid., Article 15(6).

[120] Ibid., Article 15(2).

[121] "to be decided on as speedily as possible from the beginning of detention" ibid.

[122] Ibid. If it is left to the third country national's initiative to begin judicial review proceedings, he or she must be "immediately" informed about the possibility of submitting such an application. Detainees are to be systematically provided with information which explains the rules applied in the detention facility and sets out their rights and obligations: Article 16(5).

[123] Ibid., Article 15(3).

[124] Ibid., Article 16(1).

[125] *Supra* n. 114, Sect. 6.6, Recital (19).

> "in a spirit of solidarity" the Commission is committed to assist Member States in mitigating the financial burden resulting from the provision of free legal aid under Article 13(4) and draws attention to the possibility of using the European Return Fund (Decision No 575/2007/EC) to co-finance national action promoting the application of that provision, as a form of "enhancement of the capacity of competent authorities to take high quality return decisions" (Article 4(3)(a)) to which appropriate legal safeguards, including equality of arms may contribute.[126]

The Commission's assessment under Article 19(2) of "the additional financial and administrative impact in Member States" will consider the additional impact on the administration of justice in the Member States.[127]

At present, there appear to be no plans to offer the same type of support for the implementation of the acquis in relation to expulsion and return as is envisaged in relation to the acquis relating to the Common European Asylum System in the proposal for the establishment of a European Asylum Support Office.[128] At the moment we have, in the field of expulsions and returns merely the possibility of support funding for national (or certain European) actions through the European Return Fund[129] and—without much legislative clarity as to the scope and modes of action—through the assistance which FRONTEX may give to organizing joint return operations by the Member States.[130] Given that the Return Directive in several

[126] Statements on the Proposal for a Directive of the European Parliament and of the Council on common standards and procedures in Member States for returning illegally staying third-country nationals [first reading] 16166/08, Brussels, 2 December 2008 p. 2. The Commission points out that, given priority 4 of the strategic guidelines for the Return Fund (Decision 2007/837/EC), the Community contribution may be up to 75% for actions ensuring a "fair and effective implementation of common standards" on return in Member States, which could include the provision of free legal aid under Article 13(4) and encourages the Member States to take this into account. ibid., p. 3.

[127] Ibid.

[128] Proposal for a Regulation of the European Parliament and of the Council establishing a European Asylum Support Office COM(2009) 66 final, Brussels 18 February 2009 Articles 10, 11.

[129] Decision No 575/2007/EC of the European Parliament and of the Council of 23 May 2007 establishing the European Return Fund for the period 2008–2013 as part of the General Programme Solidarity and Management of Migration Flows [2007] OJ L144.

[130] Council Regulation (EC) No 2007/2004 of 26 October 2004 establishing a European Agency for the Management of Operational Cooperation at the External Borders of the Member States of the European Union [2004] OJ L 349/1 Article 9(1). The Commission now proposes that the legal basis for such financial assistance be clarified—see Proposal for a Regulation of the European Parliament and the Council amending Council Regulation (EC) No 2007/2004 establishing a European Agency for the Management of Operational Cooperation at the External Borders of the Member States of the European Union (FRONTEX) COM(2010) 61 final, 24 February 2010 Article 1(12).

different places refers to the need to respect the principle of non-refoulement in the manner in which it is implemented, it might be appropriate to treat it as, for the purposes of the support role of the European Asylum Support Office, part of the Common European Asylum System acquis.[131] One particular gap identified by the European Council on Refugees and Exiles points out in its Information Note concerning the Directive is that "the Directive lacks any provisions guaranteeing that returns will be properly overseen in order to evaluate whether they are safe, dignified and sustainable... [an] absence of systematic monitoring mechanisms examining the outcome of return policies."[132] All that the Directive provides on this score is as follows:

> Member States shall provide for an effective forced-return monitoring system.[133]

This would seem to be an area where an EU agency such the European Asylum Support Office or FRONTEX could play a useful role and, at least in relation to role which FRONTEX plays in the process, the Commission's proposal of 24 February 2010 appears to attempt to address this lack of effective forced-return monitoring.[134]

The United Kingdom and Ireland did not take part in the adoption of the Directive and are not bound by it in its entirety or subject to its application; Denmark will have six months from the adoption of this Directive to decide whether it will implement it in its national law.[135] The Directive is a development of the Schengen acquis to which Iceland, Norway, Switzerland and Liechtenstein are bound to give effect.[136]

The territory of several Member States forms part of the external frontier of the EU and problems of burden sharing may arise as a result of their location on the routes of major migration flows. In this respect, it is interesting to note the statement which Malta had recorded in the Council minutes, in connection with the adoption of the Directive:

---

[131] Directive 2008/115/EC Recital (8), Article 4(4)(b), Article 5, Article 9(1)(a).

[132] ECRE, *Information Note on Directive 2008/115/EC*, *supra* n. 72, Sect. 6.6, p. 7.

[133] Directive 2008/115/EC Article 8(6).

[134] Proposal for a Regulation of the European Parliament and the Council amending Council Regulation (EC) No 2007/2004 establishing a European Agency for the Management of Operational Cooperation at the External Borders of the Member States of the European Union (FRONTEX) COM(2010) 61 final, 24 February 2010 Article 1(12) (substituting Council Regulation (EC) No 2007/2004 Article 9(3)). See *infra* n. 159, Sect. 6.7 and the accompanying text.

[135] Directive 2008/115/EC Recitals (25)–(27).

[136] Ibid., Recitals (28)–(30).

> Malta declares that it continues to maintain that in view of circumstances prevailing at EU external borders as regards illegal immigration, the subject of detention should remain in the hands of the individual Member States to determine.
>
> In a spirit of compromise, Malta, however, can agree to this proposal, since it leaves the decision to Member States as to whether or not to apply this Directive to the categories of third country nationals listed in Article 2(2)(a) and (b) of the Directive.[137]

The renvoi to national decision, to which Malta refers, is as follows:

> 2. Member States may decide not to apply this Directive to third-country nationals who:
>
> (a) are subject to a refusal of entry in accordance with Article 13 of the Schengen Borders Code, or who are apprehended or intercepted by the competent authorities in connection with the irregular crossing by land, sea or air of the external border of a Member State and who have not subsequently obtained an authorisation or a right to stay in that Member State;
> (b) are subject to return as a criminal law sanction or as a consequence of a criminal law sanction, according to national law, or who are the subject of extradition procedures.

As the European Council on Refugees and Exiles points out in its Information Note, this leaves such persons without any guarantee to an effective remedy under this measure.[138] At the same time, some of the guarantees afforded by the Directive do extend to third-country nationals who fall within Article 2(2)(a):

> … Member States shall:
>
> (a) ensure that their treatment and level of protection are no less favourable than as set out in Article 8(4) and (5) (limitations on use of coercive measures), Article 9(2)(a) (postponement of removal), Article 14(1)(b) and (d) (emergency health care and taking into account needs of vulnerable persons), and Articles 16 and 17 (detention conditions) and
> (b) respect the principle of non-refoulement.

6.7 Extra-territorial Activities and the Rule of Law

In recent years, the European Union and the Member States have increased their efforts to project their control over migration flows outside the territory of the Member States themselves, through co-ordinating their own operations beyond EU territory and through the development of co-operation in this field with third

[137] Statements on the Proposal for a Directive of the European Parliament and of the Council on common standards and procedures in Member States for returning illegally staying third-country nationals [first reading] 16166/08, Brussels, 2 December 2008 p. 1. On Article 2, see Baldaccini, *supra* n. 10, Sect. 6.2, pp. 3–4.

[138] ECRE, Information Note on Directive 2008/115/EC of the European Parliament and of the Council of 16 December 2008 on common standards and procedures in Member States for returning illegally staying third-country nationals CO7/1/2009/Ext/MDM (January 2009) p. 5.

countries. It is in this context that the prospect referred to in the title to this piece ("a Berlin Wall on water") has been evoked.[139] Significant criticisms have been levelled on human rights grounds against some of the practices involved, for example in relation to EU-Libya relations.[140] The Stockholm Programme—in dealing with "the external dimension of asylum"—notes that

> In its dealings with third countries, the EU has the responsibility to actively convey the importance of acceding to, and implementing of, the 1951 Geneva Convention on Refugees and its Protocol.[141]

However, there is a dearth of concrete actions suggested or even contemplated in the Stockholm Programme by which the European Union could contribute in this way to the improvement of standards of international protection in third countries.

More generally, concern has been expressed about the increasing tendency towards the "extra-territorialisation" of European Union migration policy, without an accompanying extra-territorial transfer of the rule of law.[142] Guiraudon pointed out over a decade ago that various forms of 'remote control'—sifting and sorting prospective migrants before they arrive (or are deemed to have arrived) on the national territory—have been a key element in the transformation of immigration policy of the Member States generally and that it is motivated, in part, by the desire to circumvent the judicial protection which migrants may enjoy after having been formally admitted.[143] The specific phenomenon under consideration here involves all forms of collaboration in or implication in the effects of European Union policy in the field of migration by the authorities in third countries.[144] Examples include the immigration liaison officers' network[145] or those joint operations coordinated by the European Borders Agency (FRONTEX) which take place in the territorial waters of a third country.[146] Even where the Union is not

[139] Sassen 2006. For a general account of these developments, see Debenedetti 2006. See also Nsoh 2008.

[140] Hamood 2008.

[141] The Stockholm Programme—An open and secure Europe serving and protecting the citizens 17024/09 CO EUR-PREP 3 JAI 896 POLGEN 229 (2 December 2009) p. 72.

[142] Rijpma et al. 2007.

[143] Guiraudon, *supra* n. 26, Sect. 6.3, p. 259.

[144] Ibid., 13–15.

[145] Established by Regulation (EC) No 377/2004 on the creation of an immigration liaison officers network, [2004] OJ L64/1.

[146] As provided for by Council Regulation (EC) No 2007/2004 of 26 October 2004 establishing a European Agency for the Management of Operational Cooperation at the External Borders of the Member States of the European Union [2004] OJ L 349/1 Article 2(1)(a). See also Regulation (EC) No 863/2007 of the European Parliament and of the Council of 11 July 2007 establishing a mechanism for the creation of Rapid Border Intervention Teams and amending Council Regulation (EC) No 2007/2004 as regards that mechanism and regulating the tasks and powers of guest officers [2007] OJ L199/30.

directly involved it offers encouragement to the Member States to formalise and extend their arrangements for administrative cooperation with third countries—for example, through its support for the conclusion of readmission agreements.[147] As Rijpma and Cremona point out, therefore

> … EU migration policy is a complex network of actions by the EU institutions and the Member States and increasingly depends on the active cooperation of third countries. Fundamental elements of the rule of law where State (or Community) action affects individuals, including protection of human rights and the right to an effective remedy, are put into question where EU policy is carried out within a third country—in particular where there are no common procedural standards or guarantees agreed at Community level. In the case of visas, for example, the refusal of a visa is a matter for national authorities and procedural guarantees are therefore subject to national law.[148]

As the same authors point out, it is particularly important that the "'intermediate' dimension of the rule of law that lies between respect for the fundamental value internally and the promotion of it externally" should be taken into account, particularly when the Member States or agencies of the Union take actions in the territory of a third country which affect the right of admission to the territory of the Member States.[149] This problem of the rule of law potentially being left at home by Member States when they undertake the processing of migrants on the territory of another, non-EU, state will only be accentuated if some of the developments envisaged in the Stockholm Programme come to pass such as "new approaches concerning access to asylum procedures targeting main transit countries, such as protection programmes for particular groups or certain procedures for examination of applications for asylum, in which Member States could participate on a voluntary basis."[150]

Concerns such as those expressed by Rijpma and Cremona have particular relevance to FRONTEX. As another commentator has pointed out

> [W]hen looking at the actual tasks currently undertaken by [FRONTEX], they do not seem to be clearly defined from a legal point of view.
>
> An example which substantiates this lack of legal certainty in some of FRONTEX capacities is its involvement in the Community return policy. Art. 9.1. of the Council Regulation 2007/2004 states that "the Agency shall provide the necessary assistance for organising joint return operations of Member States". However, even though the Agency has already contributed to some return operations carried out by the Member States, until now the precise tasks that FRONTEX is supposed to be carrying out are not specified anywhere and a precise list has not been yet agreed by the Council. This leads to a high degree of juridical uncertainty regarding its activities in a field as sensitive as the return of irregular immigrants where the protection of the individual and the rule of law are so critical.[151]

---

[147] Rijpma and Cremona, *supra* n. 49, Sect. 6.5, p. 15.

[148] Ibid., p. 23.

[149] Ibid., p. 16.

[150] The Stockholm Programme—An open and secure Europe serving and protecting the citizens 17024/09 CO EUR-PREP 3 JAI 896 POLGEN 229 (2 December 2009) p. 73.

[151] Carrera and Centre for European Policy Studies 2007.

The Commission's proposal of 24 February 2010 for a Regulation modifying Council Regulation (EC) No 2007/2004 does seek to do something to address several of these concerns about the effectiveness of legal guarantees in relation to the activities of FRONTEX, particularly in relation to respect for human rights.[152] Thus, the Commission proposes that all border guards and other personnel of the Member States, as well as FRONTEX staff "shall, prior to their participation in operational activities organised by [FRONTEX], have received training in relevant EU and international law, including fundamental rights and access to international protection."[153] A similar requirement would be imposed in relation to the development of a common core curriculum for the training of national border guards, which is to include fundamental rights and access to international protection.[154] The implications of operations in which FRONTEX Joint Support Teams participate are also addressed in the proposed amendments to the Regulation:

> Members of the Frontex Joint Support Teams shall, in the performance of their tasks and in the exercise of their powers, fully respect fundamental rights and human dignity. Any measures taken in the performance of their tasks and in the exercise of their powers shall be proportionate to the objectives pursued by such measures. While performing their tasks and exercising their powers, members of the teams shall not discriminate against persons on grounds of sex, racial or ethnic origin, religion or belief, disability, age or sexual orientation.[155]

Guest officers will also be required, according to the proposal, to comply with Union law "in accordance with fundamental rights" (a new reference) as well as the law of the host Member State.[156]

It is also proposed that FRONTEX ensure that "in its grant agreements with Member States any financial support" for the organising of joint return operations of Member States "is conditional upon the full respect of the Charter of Fundamental Rights."[157] This is certainly a modest improvement on the laconic reference to the use of Union financial means in the original provision though it can hardly in itself change the nature of the obligations placed on FRONTEX or any other institution or body established under the Treaties.

---

[152] Proposal for a Regulation of the European Parliament and the Council amending Council Regulation (EC) No 2007/2004 establishing a European Agency for the Management of Operational Cooperation at the External Borders of the Member States of the European Union (FRONTEX) COM(2010) 61 final, 24 February 2010. The United Kingdom, Ireland and Denmark are not participating in the adoption of this proposal.

[153] Ibid., Article 1(3)(b) (inserting Council Regulation (EC) No 2007/2004 new Article 2(1a)).

[154] Ibid., Article 1(7) (amending Council Regulation (EC) No 2007/2004 new Article 5).

[155] *supra* n. 152, at Article 1(5) (inserting Council Regulation (EC) No 2007/2004 new Article 3b(4)).

[156] Ibid Article 1(13) (substituting Council Regulation (EC) No 2007/2004 Article 10(2) as inserted by Regulation (EC) No 863/2007 of the European Parliament and of the Council of 11 July 2007 Article 6).

[157] Ibid Article 1(12) (substituting Council Regulation (EC) No 2007/2004 Article 9(1)).

The proposal also envisages some strengthening of fundamental rights protection in relation to the return of illegally present third country nationals by air, at least at the levels of standards and monitoring. FRONTEX is to develop a Code of Conduct for the returns by air, to apply during all joint return operations coordinated by the Agency. This Code should describe "common standardized procedures which should simplify the organisation of joint return flights and assure return in a humane manner and in full respect for fundamental rights, in particular the principles of human dignity, prohibition of torture and of inhuman or degrading treatment or punishment, right to liberty and security, the rights to the protection of personal data and non discrimination."[158] In this respect, the proposal seeks to build on the existing forced return monitoring system envisaged—though not more than merely sketched in—by the Return Directive itself.[159]

> The monitoring of joint return operations should be carried out independently and should cover the whole joint return operation from the predeparture phase until the hand-over of the returnees in the country of return. Furthermore, observations of the monitor, which shall cover the compliance with the Code of Conduct and in particular fundamental rights, shall be made available to the Commission and form part of the internal Final Return Operation Report. In order to ensure transparency and a coherent evaluation of the forced-return operations, reports of the monitor shall be included in an annual reporting mechanism.[160]

This monitoring of the compliance of joint return operations with fundamental rights norms will be paralleled, it is proposed, by the inclusion of "a specific analysis on the way the Charter of Fundamental Rights was respected" in the implementation of the FRONTEX Regulation, as part of the independent external evaluation which FRONTEX itself must undergo every five years.[161]

These proposals from the Commission go some way towards addressing concerns that the joint actions of Member States which FRONTEX exists to support and co-ordinate create a gap in the fundamental rights protections which those seeking entry to the EU area of justice, freedom and security should enjoy. However, they do not by any means address the central points made by critics, such as Rijpma and Cremona or Carrera. No further action at European Union level is proposed—at this juncture—to address the variation in the levels of protection given by Member States, even in relation to procedural safeguards for migrants.

The proposal also attempts to ensure greater respect of fundamental rights in the context of arrangements made with third countries. The Commission proposes in that regard that FRONTEX "shall facilitate the operational cooperation between Member States and third countries, in the framework of the European Union

---

[158] Ibid. (substituting Council Regulation (EC) No 2007/2004 Article 9(2)).

[159] Directive 2008/115/EC Article 8(6).

[160] Proposal for a Regulation of the European Parliament and the Council amending Council Regulation (EC) No 2007/2004 Article 1(12) (substituting Council Regulation (EC) No 2007/2004 Article 9(3)).

[161] Ibid., Article 1(23) (inserting Council Regulation (EC) No 2007/2004 new Article 33(2b)).

external relations policy, including with regard to human rights."[162] However, there are proposals for more specific guarantees that this. "Liaison officers shall only be deployed to third countries in which border management practices respect minimum human rights standards"[163] and their contacts with the competent authorities of the third country are to be established and maintained "in compliance with European Union law and in accordance with fundamental rights."[164] The distinction here between "fundamental rights" (as affects the actions of the liaison officers themselves) and "(minimum) human rights" is understandable, given the limited territorial scope of fundamental rights under European Union law. However, given the seriousness of the problems encountered in assuring the compliance of third country authorities with basic human rights standards, as highlighted by authors such as Hamood and Rijpma and Cremona, it is doubtful whether the measures outlined in the Commission's proposal of 24 February 2010 go far enough.[165]

Only a few months before the adoption of the Return Directive, the Court of Justice had strikingly reaffirmed that "the Community is based on the rule of law, inasmuch as neither its Member States nor its institutions can avoid review of the conformity of their acts with the basic constitutional charter, the EC Treaty" and that "the principle of effective judicial protection is a general principle of Community law stemming from the constitutional traditions common to the Member States."[166] In that light, it would seem more necessary than ever to assess the gaps in judicial protection for those denied entry to the territory of the Member States in relation to the substantial contributions which the Member States and Union agencies make to decisions taken in the territory of third countries.

6.8 Public Opinion and European Migration Controls

As has already been pointed out, the application of a form of mutual recognition principle in relation to determination of asylum claims has not resulted in a harmonisation of the substantive criteria adopted in dealing with them.[167] In the same way, the negotiations over the European Immigration Pact, while they have made considerable progress in relation to measures for the control of illegal

---

[162] Ibid., Article 1(16) (substituting Council Regulation (EC) No 2007/2004 Article 14(1)). Author's emphasis.

[163] Ibid., Article 1(16) (inserting Council Regulation (EC) No 2007/2004 new Article 14(2)).

[164] *supra* n. 160, Sect. 6.7, Article 1(16) (inserting Council Regulation (EC) No 2007/2004 new Article 14(3)).

[165] See Rijpma and Cremona, *supra* n. 49, Sect. 6.5 and Hamood, *supra* n. 134, Sect. 6.6.

[166] ECJ, Joined Cases C-402/05 P and C-415/05 P *Kadi* v. *Council* [2008] *ECR* I-06351 paras 281, 335.

[167] See *supra*, Sect. 6.2, p. 4.

immigration—particularly surrounding the issue of removals—have not resulted in the same degree of consensus among the Member States in relation to issues such as collective regularisation ("amnesty") or integration policies towards third country nationals[168]

If a consensus sufficient to sustain a substantive common immigration policy were truly in the process of being created, one would expect to find some of the clearest indications amongst the Members of the European Parliament, who sit at the intersection between the Commission's long-term, strategic policy initiatives and the views of their constituents on this most highly contentious and widely discussed issues. In addition, the Return Directive is the first major measure relating to immigration to be adopted under the co-decision procedure, under which, in form at least, the Parliament and the Council stand on an equal footing.

Research on the attitudes of MEPs has shown that, in the period 1992–2004, the increased salience of migration as an issue at EU level has been accompanied by, if anything, stronger support amongst MEPs for policy in this area to be set at national level, a trend that is particularly pronounced amongst MEPs from those countries which are traditionally the major recipients of immigration.[169] On the other hand, Eurobarometer shows a high level of public support across the European Union for some form of common immigration policy at European Union level, as high as 63% in the most recent survey.[170] The levels of support for decisions in the field of immigration being taken jointly by national governments and the Union varies from a high of 87% in Malta to a low of 32% in Finland (levels of support in other Member States ranging between 40% and 76%.)[171] When asked more specifically in the previous Eurobarometer survey whether they favoured "a common immigration policy towards people from outside the EU" 74% percent of respondents agreed.[172] Of course, the wide variation in

---

[168] See Traynor, *supra* n. 5, Sect. 6.2.

[169] Gallya and Messina 2005. It is interesting also to note that, in the case of a new recipient of migrants such as Ireland, the percentage of MEPs who reported that immigration was "not important" as an issue went from 83% in 1993 to 0% in 2004.

[170] Table of Results—Standard Eurobarometer 72 Annex Vol. 1 (Fieldwork: October–November 2009 Publication: December 2009) http://ec.europa.eu/public_opinion/archives/eb/eb72/eb72_anx_vol1.pdf (Last accessed 5 March 2010). Response to QF3.6. ("... do you think that decisions [in the area of immigration] should be made by the (NATIONALITY) Government, or made jointly within the European Union?") These figures show little significant change as compared with Eurobarometer 69—Public Opinion in the European Union (First Results/Fieldwork: March–May 2008 Publication: June 2008) http://ec.europa.eu/public_opinion/archives/eb/eb69/eb_69_first_en.pdf (Accessed 8 September 2008) Response to QA35a.6 ("... do you think that decisions [in the area of immigration] should be made by the (NATIONALITY) Government, or made jointly within the European Union?").

[171] Ibid. The corresponding figures for the six most populous Member States are: Germany (67%), France (69%), the UK (40%), Italy (72%) and Spain (69%).

[172] Eurobarometer 68—Public Opinion in the European Union (Final Report/Fieldwork: September–November 2007 Publication: May 2008) 131. http://ec.europa.eu/public_opinion/archives/eb/eb68/eb_68_en.pdf (Accessed 8 September 2008) A majority in all Member States agreed with the proposition, ranging from 83% in Greece to 62% in Romania.

responses to these two questions (should immigration policy be made jointly by national governments and the Union and should there be a common immigration policy) suggests that positive sentiments on the latter score do not necessarily translate into support for further communitarianisation of this area of policy.[173]

On the other hand, the public perception of the seriousness of immigration as a problem has declined in recent Eurobarmoter polls, so that across the EU as a whole only 9% of respondents rated it as one of the two main problems facing their country.[174] In only two Member States—the United Kingdom (29%) and Malta (34%) was that figure above 20%.[175] In parallel, the emphasis which respondents say that the European Union institutions should give to immigration has declined in the last two years recent surveys, from 32% of respondents naming it amongst the top three to name priorities for the EU in Spring 2008, to 24% doing so in the most recent survey.[176] In terms of the stress which public opinion places on the added value of European Union action in the field of migration, it is also interesting to note that the three countries in which public opinion accords this greatest priority are three island states, each with strong public and political preoccupations with the effectiveness of controls on migration—Malta, the United Kingdom and Cyprus.

One analysis of public opinion on this question has suggested that

---

173 See also Givens and Luedtke 2003.

174 Eurobarometer 72—Public Opinion in the European Union (First Results/Fieldwork: October–November 2009 Publication: December 2009) http://ec.europa.eu/public_opinion/archives/eb/eb72/eb72_first_en.pdf (Accessed 5 March 2010) Response to QA5 ("What do you think are the two most important issues facing (OUR COUNTRY) at the moment?").

175 Ibid.

176 Standard Eurobarometer 69—Public Opinion in the European Union—Annexes (Fieldwork: March–April 2008 Publication: December 2008) http://ec.europa.eu/public_opinion/archives/eb/eb69/eb69_annexes.pdf (Last accessed 5 March 2010) Response to QA39; Table of Results—Standard Eurobarometer 72 Annex Vol. 1 (Fieldwork: October–November 2009 Publication: December 2009) http://ec.europa.eu/public_opinion/archives/eb/eb72/eb72_anx_vol1.pdf (Last accessed 5 March 2010). Response to QA16 ("European integration has been focusing on various issues in the last years. In your opinion, which aspects should be emphasized by the European institutions in the coming years, to strengthen the European Union in the future?" (maximum 3 answers; 7 prompts).).

> It is certain, or at least very probable, that if the European Union can convince Europeans of its role and utility on policies to regulate immigration, it would benefit substantially at least in terms of opinion. It stands to benefit from a general level of approval, explicitly formulated to a greater or lesser extent, but always present.[177]

It remains to be seen, however, whether the general demand for effective co-ordinated action in the field of migration control necessarily implies widespread public support for the specific institutional role which the Union may come play in this area. It also seems plausible to understand much of the public support for more effective European Union action in the field of immigration as being concerned with the effectiveness of controls on migration, rather than the "full and inclusive application of the Geneva Convention on the status of refugees and other relevant international treaties" which the Stockholm Programme sets as a short-term goal. It also remains unclear how far the Pact represents a new stage in legitimising European Union action in the area of immigration and asylum policy in the eyes of citizens. As Angenendt and Parkes comment, the world situation overtook what the European Council was seeking to achieve in that respect

> Had it not been overshadowed [by the global financial crisis], the Pact would likely have alleviated the public pressure for ad hoc legislative activity and facilitated measured steps towards a common policy. In sensitive policy areas such as this, deliberation may be mistaken for inactivity by European citizens. By dramatising this process of deliberation and highlighting the existing actions of the Community institutions, political tools like the Pact can make a tangible contribution to policymaking.[178]

6.9 Conclusion

Undoubtedly, the entry into force of the Treaty of Lisbon has provided a clearer and more comprehensive scope for European Union action in the field of immigration and asylum. The Charter of Fundamental Rights now sets out, as a matter of Union law, the fundamental right to asylum, which shall be guaranteed with due respect for the Geneva Convention and in accordance with the Treaty on European Union and the Treaty on the Functioning of the European Union.[179] Article 78 of the Treaty on the Functioning of the European Union requires the development of

[177] Public Opinion in the European Union—Standard Eurobarometer 68 Analytical Report (TNS Opinion, 2008) 34. However, criticisms have been expressed concerning the methodological deficiencies of the Eurobarometer surveys as a means of accurately gauging public opinion on these matters: see Lahav 2004 p. 233.

[178] Angenendt and Parkes, *supra* n. 32, Sect. 6.3, p. 95.

[179] Charter of Fundamental Rights of the European Union (2007/C 303/01) Article 18.

"a common policy on asylum, subsidiary protection and temporary protection with a view to offering appropriate status to any third country national requiring international protection and ensuring compliance with the principle of non-refoulement" and sets out the main required elements for the creation of such a common European asylum system, including "partnership and cooperation with third countries for the purpose of managing inflows of people applying for asylum or subsidiary or temporary protection."[180] This seems like a promising basis for realising the goal (repeated in the Stockholm Programme) of "full and inclusive application of the Geneva Convention on the status of refugees and other relevant international treaties" through concrete measures at European Union and national level. However, it is important to note, even at the level of the Treaties, what is missing. Even the minimal procedural guarantees contained in Protocol No. 7 to the European Convention on Human Rights in relation to the expulsion of aliens (which have been accepted by all but four of the Member States)[181] are not explicitly repeated in the Charter, so that the third country national must fall back on the Strasbourg Court's case law in relation to the degree to which an alien can rely on a putative violation of substantive rights under the Convention (as paralleled in the Charter) to claim a violation of the right to an effective remedy for such a right, as a substitute for a right to a fair hearing as such,[182] either under the Convention or the Charter, subject to judicial clarification of the effect of Article 52(3) of the latter.[183]

Whatever the correct interpretation of the Charter provisions, however, the main task facing the Union is to create a code of Union law which provides an effective legal basis for uniform international protection throughout the Member States, delivered primarily by the administrative authorities of the Member States themselves. This is a classic example of the peculiar nature of the Union's executive order. Curtin and Egeberg offer a persuasive analysis of the changing nature of that executive order.[184] Many of the features they identify (such as the "agencification"[185] of border control or the phenomenon of "double hattedness"—whereby "parts of national administrations … becom[e] parts of a multi-level Union administration in which the Commission in particular forms the new executive centre"[186]) can be seen in the review undertaken here of the

[180] Treaty on the Functioning of the European Union Article 78.

[181] See the text accompanying *supra,* n. 74 to n. 76, Sect. 6.6.

[182] *Maaouia v France* judgment of 5 October 2000 App. No. 39652/98. See Spijkerboer 2009.

[183] Ibid., Article 52(3). See the text accompanying *supra* n 91 to n 97, Sect. 6.6 and Lock 2009.

[184] Curtin and Egeberg 2008.

[185] Ibid., p. 640.

[186] Ibid., p. 650.

development of the Union's role in migration control. Certainly, there general conclusion would seem to apply

> [Executive] orders are co-existing in Europe ... The accumulated executive order consists of qualitatively new elements that transcend the inherited intergovernmental order. The persistence of diplomacy and [international governmental organisations] represents recognition and reproduction of a system of states ... Due to its complexity such an order may be rather robust and sustainable ... However, it raises sensitive questions about which actors should be held to account, at what level of order and to whom.[187]

At the very least, effective judicial protection for the individual third-country national ought to form part of such a system of accountability. The way in which the Union's involvement has developed in this area suggests that a greater clarity concerning the competences of Union agencies and the minimum procedural standards which Member States are required to observe is a necessary precondition for this. The Commission's proposal of 24 February 2010 for amendments to the FRONTEX Regulation would, if adopted, go some way towards improving transparency and accountability in relation to the removal of third country nationals from EU territory and in respect of the liaison of FRONTEX officials with third countries. However, these changes, while welcome in themselves, could not been seen as a substitute for a uniform system of clear and effective judicial guarantees for third country nationals, particularly when one considers that an important element in motivating the Member States (or some of them at least) in advancing as far as they have towards common actions and policy in this field appears to have been a desire to weaken and circumvent national judicial protections for migrants.[188]

We have also seen that it has thus far been very much easier to arrive at a consensus on co-ordination of control mechanisms—particularly in the context of illegal immigration—than it is to arrive at an agreement on substantive immigration policy. The application of the Dublin Convention and the subsequent Regulation bear that out and it seems to have been confirmed by the nature of the political compromise arrived at in Cannes in the summer of 2008.[189] This seems to bear out Schain's plausible assessments of the dynamics of the international policy-making process in this area

> ... [T]he most effective actions on immigration taken at the EU level have been strongly oriented towards intergovernmental co-operation for immigration control (visa, asylum, and border control), and exclusion. ...
>
> ...
>
> ... [T]he European context, rather than constraining states in Europe, has enhanced their abilities both to control immigrant entry and to develop more forceful policies on integration, essentially defined at Member State level.
>
> ...

187 ibid., p. 656. References omitted.

188 Guiraudon, *supra* n. 26, Sect. 6.3, p. 259.

189 See Traynor, *supra* n. 5, Sect. 6.2.

> … European institutions and processes have been effective means for Member States to develop more restrictive policies, and avoid the pressures of NGOs and other domestic political forces. They have done this through intergovernmental co-operation, for the most part, and have effectively used European Union institutions to their advantage.[190]

While there may be a prospect that a greater degree of harmonisation will be achieved in relation to the procedural aspects of migration control—leaving the United Kingdom, Ireland and Denmark largely to one side in this regard—it remains much less clear that this convergence will be soon paralleled by a coherent policy towards migration as an economic and social phenomenon and the realisation of the ambitious goals set for a common immigration and asylum system under the new Treaty provisions.

References

Acosta D (2009) The good, the bad and the ugly in EU migration law: is the European parliament becoming bad and ugly? (The adoption of directive 2008/15: the returns directive). Eur J Migr Law 11(1):19–39

Angenendt S, Parkes R (2009) Can further nationalisation facilitate a common EU approach to migration? Int Spectator 44(3):77–96

Baldaccini A (2009) The return and removal of irregular migrants under EU law: an analysis of the return directive. Eur J Migr Law 11(1):1–17

Carlier J, Bruycker P (2005) Immigration and asylum law in the EU: current debates = Actualité du droit européen de l'immigration et de l'asile. Bruylant, Brussels

Carrera S, Centre for European Policy Studies (2007) The EU border management strategy: FRONTEX and the challenges of irregular immigration in the canary islands. http://shop.ceps.eu/downfree.php?item_id=1482 Accessed 10 September 2008

Carrera S, Guild E, Centre for European Policy Studies (2008) Archive of European Integration, The French Presidency' s European Pact on Immigration and Asylum: Intergovernmentalism vs. Europeanisation? http://aei.pitt.edu/9381/ Accessed 5 March 2010

Carrera S, Merlino MS, Centre for European Policy Studies (2009) Liberty and security in Europe,'undocumented immigrants and rights in the EU: addressing the gap between social science reasearch and policy-making'. www.ceps.eu/book/undocumented-immigrants-and-rights-eu-addressing-gap-between-social-sciences-research-and-policy. Accessed 5 March 2010

Cassarino J, European University Institute (2006) The Return Policy: Premises and Implications. http://cadmus.iue.it/dspace/bitstream/1814/6442/1/MIREM RSCAS_RR_2006.pdf Accessed 10 September 2008. Accessed 10 September 2008

Cholewinsky R (2005) The need for effective individual legal protection in immigration matters. Eur J Migr Law 7:237–262

Collett E, European policy centre (2009) Beyond stockholm: overcoming the inconsistencies of immigration policy. www.koningboudewijnstichting.be/uploadedFiles/KBS-FRB/Files/Verslag/EPC%20Working%20Paper.pdf. Accessed 5 March 2010

Curtin D, Egeberg M (2008) Tradition and innovation: Europe's accumulated executive order. West Eur Politi 31(4):639–661

[190] Schain, *supra* n. 25, Sect. 6.3, pp. 106, 109. See also the analysis of Guiraudon, *supra* n. 26, Sect. 6.3, pp. 267–268; a decade earlier, but to the same general effect.

Debenedetti S (2006) Externalization of European asylum and migration policies. http://www.iue.it/RSCAS/research/SchoolOnEuro-MedMigration/2006pdfs/Paper%20Debenedetti%20 2006%20FINAL.pdf Accessed 10 September 2006

Ezra E, Ludwig-Maximilians-Universität München (2004) European integration and refugee protection: the development of asylum policy in the European union. http://edoc.ub.uni-muenchen.de/2680/1/Ezra_Esther.pdf. Accessed 10 September 2008

Gallya L, Messina AM (2005) The limits of a European immigration policy: elite opinion and agendas within the European parliament. J Common Mark Stud 43(4):851–875

Givens T, Luedtke A (2003) Public opinion, issue salience and immigration policy in Europe. Paper presented at the annual meeting of the American political science association, Philadelphia Marriott Hotel, Philadelphia, PA, http://www.allacademic.com/meta/p64286_index.html Accessed 7 August 2009

Guirodon V (2000) European integration and migration policy: vertical policy making as venue shopping. J Common Mark Stud 38(2):251–271

Hamood S (2008) EU-Libya cooperation on migrtaion: a raw deal for refugees and migrants? J Refug Stud 21(1):19–42

Hansen P, Linköping University and The National Institute for Working Life (2005) A superabundance of contradictions: The European Union's Post-Amsterdam Policies on Migrant 'Integration', Labour Integration, Asylum and Illegal Immigration. www.temaasyl.se/Documents/Forskning/Peo%20Hansen%20A%20Superabundance%20of%20Contradictions.pdf. Accessed 10 September 2008

Hungarian Helsinki Committee (2008) Access to Protection at Airports in Europe: Report on the monitoring experience at airports in Amsterdam, Budapest, Madrid, Prague, Vienna and Warsaw. http://helsinki.webdialog.hu/dokumentum/Access_at_Airports_Report.pdf. Accessed 11 August 2009

Lahav G (2004) Immigration and politics in the new Europe: reinventing borders. Cambridge University Press, Cambridge

Lavenex S, Wagner W (2007) Which European public order? sources of imbalance in the European area of freedom, security and justice. Eur Secur 16(3&4):225–243

Lock T (2009) The ECJ and the ECtHR: the future relationship between the two European courts. Law Pract Int Court Tribu 8(3):375–398

Nsoh N (2008) The European union internal exclusion and extra-territorialisation of asylum seekers and migrants into camps: case studies. Ukraine, Libia and Germany. Freie Universität Berlin, Berlin

Rijpma JJ, Cremona M, European University Institute (2007) The extra-territorialisation of EU migration policies and the rule of law. http://ssrn.com/abstract=964190 Accessed 9 September 2009

Sassen S (2006) Migration policy: from control to governance. http://www.opendemocracy.net/people-migrationeurope/militarising_borders_3735.jsp Accessed 10 September 2006

Schain M (2009) The state strikes back: immigration policy in the European union. Eur J Int Law 20(1):93–109

Spijkerboer T (2009) Subsidiarity and 'arguability': the European court of human rights' case law on judicial review in asylum cases. Int J Refug Law 21(1):48–74

Chapter 7
A Few Remarks to Evaluate the Dublin System and the Asylum Acquis

Juha Raitio

Contents

7.1 Introduction 111
7.2 Background 113
7.3 The Problems of the Dublin II Regulation 115
7.4 The Proposals–Dublin III Regulation and Other Current Developments 116
7.5 The Interpretation of the Qualification Directive 2004/83/EC and the Dublin System 120
7.6 Concluding Remarks 122
References 123

7.1 Introduction

The "Dublin system" aims to determine which Member State is responsible for examining an asylum application lodged by a third country national on the territory of one of the Member States of the European Union,[1] Norway and Iceland. Currently, the Dublin system comprises Council Regulation (EC) No 343/2003[2]

[1] Denmark did not originally take part in the adoption of the Dublin II Regulation, but it became applicable to Denmark on 1 April 2006 after the entry into force of an Agreement with the European Community, OJ L 66, 8.3.2006, p. 38. See more thoroughly on this Fabrice 2009, pp. 152–153.

[2] Council Regulation (EC) No 343/2003 of 18 February 2003 establishing the criteria and mechanisms for determining the Member State responsible for examining an asylum application lodged in one of the Member States by a third country national, OJ, L 50, 25.2.2003, p. 1.

J. Raitio (✉)
University of Helsinki, Helsinki, Finland
e-mail: juha.raitio@helsinki.fi

F. A. N. J. Goudappel and H. S. Raulus (eds.), *The future of asylum in the European Union*, DOI: 10.1007/978-90-6704-802-6_7,

(Dublin II Regulation), its Implementing Regulation No 1560/2003[3] and the so-called Eurodac Regulation (EC) No 2725/2000[4] as well as its Implementing Regulation (EC) No 407/2002.[5] The Eurodac Regulation requires fingerprints of all asylum seekers of 14 years old to be taken and transmitted to a Central Unit which compares them with other fingerprints previously transmitted. Similarly, Member States must take the fingerprints of all third country nationals who cross a border irregularly and transmit them to the Central Unit. This helps to establish whether the asylum seeker has made multiple applications in the EU. The EU Asylum policy was based on Article 63(1–2) EC (Article 78 TFEU), which in turn built on Article 61(b) EC.

In this brief article, my aim is to introduce the Dublin system and some features of the Asylum acquis in general as well as to refer to the European Commission Proposal to recast the Dublin Regulation.[6] It aims to ensure a higher degree of harmonisation and better standards of protection for the Common European Asylum System (CEAS). It is adopted at the same time as the recast of the Eurodac Regulation[7] and the recast of Reception Conditions Directive.[8] The recast undergoes considerable scrutiny during the co-decision procedure and certain amendments have already been proposed by the Parliament. The recast has already been commented upon by the European Council on Refugees and Exiles (ECRE) as well as by the United Nations Refugee Agency (UNHCR). The critical comments relate to the question of the Dublin system's impact on the legal rights and the personal welfare of asylum seekers as well as on the uneven distribution of asylum claims among the Member States. Thus, at least for some critical commentators, the Dublin system seems to be unfair both to asylum seekers and to

[3] Commission Regulation (EC) No 1560/2003 of 2 September 2003 laying down detailed rules for the application of Council Regulation (EC) No 343/2003 establishing the criteria and mechanisms for determining the Member State responsible for examining an asylum application lodged in one of the Member States by a third country national, OJ, L 222, 5.9.2003, p. 3.

[4] Council Regulation (EC) No 2725/2000 of 11 December 2000 concerning the establishment of 'Eurodac' for the comparison of fingerprints for the effective application of the Dublin Convention, OJ, L 316, 15.12.2000, p. 1.

[5] Council Regulation (EC) No 407/2002 of 28 February 2002 laying down certain rules to implement Regulation (EC) No 2725/2000 concerning the establishment of 'Eurodac' for the comparison of fingerprints for the effective application of the Dublin Convention, OJ, L 62, 5.3.2002, p. 1.

[6] Proposal for a Regulation of the European Parliament and of the Council establishing the criteria and mechanisms for determining the Member State responsible for examining an application for international protection lodged in one of the Member States by a third country national or a stateless person, COM (2008) 820 final, 3 December 2008, (Dublin III Regulation).

[7] Proposal for a recast of the Regulation of the European Parliament and of the Council concerning the establishment of "Eurodac" for the comparison of fingerprints for the effective application of the Dublin II Regulation, COM (2008) 825 final, 3 December 2008.

[8] Proposal for a Directive of the European Parliament and of the Council laying down minimum standards for the reception of asylum seekers, COM (2008) 815 final, 3 December 2008.

certain Member States.[9] Especially, the Member States from the Mediterranean area have been under pressure as regards the increasing amount of refugees and asylum seekers. On the other hand, a harmonised and humane CEAS seems to be a relative difficult political goal to achieve.

7.2 Background

Steve Peers' description of the background of the Dublin system provides the main source for this cursory presentation.[10] First, Articles 28–38 of the Schengen Convention set out the rules on the responsibility for asylum applications among the Schengen States, with effect from March 1995. These rules were replaced by the essentially identical rules applicable to all Member States set out in the Dublin Convention, in force from September 1997. According to Peers, it was obvious that the Member States adopted the Dublin Convention, because they feared that loosening or abolishing the internal border checks would lead to an increase in multiple asylum applications, which in turn would cause delays and administrative burden to the Member States. Member States needed common rules on how to determine which Member State was responsible for an asylum seeker's application. Otherwise, Member States would take different approaches to determining which other Member State was responsible.[11] As an outcome of this discussion, the Convention drew up a complicated list of conflict rules for determining which Member State had jurisdiction over an application. In this list, for example, aspects concerning family reunion as well as issued residence permits or visas were taken into consideration. However, the Member State in which the application was made was a default.

Peers points out that the Convention was criticized for forcing apart family members, for ignoring the differences in national interpretation of the Geneva Refugee Convention,[12] and for inducing asylum seekers to destroy travel documents and thus avoid the adoption of the conflict rules. The Convention seems to have been disappointing from the very beginning. The huge majority of asylum applications were not identified as subject to it. In the years 1998–1999 only 1.7% of all asylum applications made in the EU actually resulted in the transfer of an asylum seeker pursuant to the rules of the Convention. In 2001, only 4.2% of asylum applications were subject to requests to take responsibility according to the

[9] Parliament (EC), Evaluation of the Dublin system (Own Initiative Report), INI (2008) 2262, 2 July 2008, para 2.

[10] Peers 2006, pp. 318–324 and Peers 2011, pp. 357–368.

[11] See also Craig and de Burca 2008, pp. 257–259. Craig and de Burca have referred to Peers' presentation on this as well.

[12] Convention Relating to the Status of Refugees of 28 July 1951 as amended by the Protocol Relating to the Status of Refugees of 31 January 1967 (Geneva Refugee Convention).

Convention, and 71.4% of these requests were accepted, i.e. only 3% of the total sum of asylum applications.

In this situation the Member States adopted the Dublin II Regulation No 343/2003, which replaced the Dublin Convention from 1 September 2003 onwards. Its main objectives are the following:

- To ensure that the asylum seekers have effective access to procedures for determining refugee status.
- To prevent abuse of asylum procedures in the form of multiple applications for asylum submitted simultaneously or successively by the same person in several Member States.
- To determine as quickly as possible the Member State responsible for the examination of an asylum claim.

The Dublin II Regulation altered the criteria from the original Dublin Convention. The hierarchy of the criteria can be found in Articles 5–14. The hierarchical responsibility criteria are based on the general principle underpinning the Dublin system, namely that the responsibility for examining an asylum application lies with the Member State which played the greatest part in the applicant's entry into or residence in the territories of the Member States, subject to exceptions designed to protect family unity.[13] However, the Dublin II Regulation also contains two important discretionary provisions, namely the sovereignty clause and the humanitarian clause. According to sovereignty clause in Article 3(2), a Member State has always the possibility to decide to examine an asylum application, even it is not responsible according to the criteria of the regulation. Additionally, in Article 15, there is a humanitarian clause according to which regardless of the criteria set out in Articles 5–14, any Member State may bring together family members under certain circumstances based on family or cultural considerations. Any Member State shall retain the right, pursuant to its national laws, to send an asylum seeker to a third country, in compliance with the provisions of the Geneva Refugee Convention. In Articles 16–23, the procedural rules and provisions on administrative cooperation were amended, in particular to accelerate the transfer of asylum seekers and to include some of the details of the previous implementing measures. The Dublin II Regulation establishes mechanisms for requesting another Member State to take back or take charge of an asylum seeker and includes deadlines to be respected by both the requesting and requested Member States.

One could confirm the point put forward in the legal literature that the Dublin II Regulation was not able to address the argument concerning the inefficiency of the Dublin system.[14] Inefficiency refers to the fact that even the Dublin II Regulation

---

[13] Commission staff working document accompanying document to the Report from the Commission to the European Parliament and the Council on the evaluation of Dublin system—Annex to the communication on the evaluation of the Dublin system, SEC(2007) 742 final, p. 6.

[14] Peers 2006, *supra* n. 10, Sect. 7.2, p. 321; Craig and De Burca, *supra* n. 11, Sect. 7.2, p. 257.

applies to only a very small percentage of asylum seekers. It seems to be clear that the Eurodac scheme for exchange of asylum seekers' fingerprints has not changed the situation considerably.

7.3 The Problems of the Dublin II Regulation

Let us rely on some recent statistics as regards the problems of the Dublin system. The Commission has reported to the European Parliament and to the Council on the evaluation of the Dublin system in 2007.[15] First, the Commission states that the analysis of the statistics provided by the Member States is extremely difficult. One of the main problems is the mismatch between the number of requests and decisions that each Member State reports to have received from other Member States and the number of requests and decisions that each Member State reports to have sent to other Member States. The incoming and outgoing data do not match due to the different interpretations of the definitions for registration and the incompleteness of certain data. Additionally, one can suspect that the Eurodac system is inefficient. Peers has rightly pointed out that the national border officials do not take the fingerprints of all persons who irregularly cross the border, and some of them actually cross the border without being caught.[16] The effect might be the subsequent return of an asylum seeker to that State.[17] On the other hand, if the asylum seekers destruct their travel documents, it will inevitably cause administrative problems for the functioning of the Dublin system.[18]

Based on the outgoing national data, the Commission has been able to draft a statistical presentation on the application of the Dublin II Regulation from September 2003 to December 2005.[19] It tells us that 55,310 requests for transfer were sent out, which is 11.5% of the total sum of asylum applications (589,499) in all Member States for the same period. Of the requests 72% were accepted, so in 40,180 cases, another Member State accepted to take responsibility for an asylum applicant. However, only 16,842 asylum applicants were actually transferred by the Member States, which is only about 2.9% of the total number of asylum applicants. As stated before, in 1998–1999 only 1.7% of all asylum applications in the EU resulted in the transfer of the asylum seeker.[20]

---

[15] Report from the Commission to the European Parliament and the Council on the evaluation of the Dublin system, COM (2007) 299 final, 6 June 2007.

[16] Peers 2006, *supra* n. 10, Sect. 7.2, p. 324.

[17] Craig and de Burca, *supra* n. 11, Sect. 7.2, p. 257.

[18] Peers 2006, *supra* n. 10, Sect. 7.2, p. 322.

[19] COM (2007) 299 final, 6 June 2007, pp. 3–5.

[20] Peers 2006, *supra* n. 10, p. 319.

These statistics show significant inefficiency and pinpoint the need to have a commonly agreed statistical framework in the field of asylum and immigration.[21] However, I find that it is too provocative to label the Dublin system to be a very expensive waste of time,[22] although it seems to apply to a relatively small percentage of asylum applicants. In its own way, it makes the international cooperation between the Member States concrete and thus might pave the way to a more harmonised CEAS. In any case, the statistics reveal the main problem of the Dublin system, namely the fact that the responsibility ultimately seems to lie in the overwhelming majority of cases with the State where the application is first filed, i.e. the default Member State.[23]

The Commission holds that irrespective of its flaws the data from the automatic reports from the Eurodac Central Unit are more reliable. In the period from 2003 to 2005, the data on 657,753 asylum applicants were successfully sent. The number of such transactions has consistently decreased (2003: 238,325; 2004: 232,205 and 2005: 187,233), which is interesting when having in mind that from 1 May 2004 onwards, 10 New Member States started applying the Eurodac regulation. In the same reference period, the Eurodac Central Unit registered 48,657 third country nationals apprehended in connection with the irregular crossing of an external border and 101,884 third country nationals found illegally present on the territory of a Member State. It is important to note, however, that although the asylum applications fell during the period from 2003 to 2005, they started to rise again in 2007. The number of immigrants has since been constantly growing especially on the southern external border of the EU.[24]

7.4 The Proposals–Dublin III Regulation and Other Current Developments

It is obvious that some amendments to the current system are necessary. The Commission has clearly indicated its intention to make the Dublin system more effective. This becomes evident, for example, in the Policy Plan on

[21] See e.g. Proposal for a Regulation of the European Parliament and of the Council on Community statistics on migration and international protection, COM (2005) 375 final, 14 September 2005.

[22] Compare Peers 2006, *supra* n. 10, Sect. 7.2, p. 321. and Craig and de Burca, *supra* n. 11, p. 257.

[23] See the Reflection Note on the Evaluation of the Dublin System and on the Dublin III Proposal, European Parliament, Directorate General Internal Policies of the Union, March 2009, PE 410.690, p. 2.

[24] Communication from the Commission to the Council, the European Parliament, the European Economic and Social Committee and the Committee of the Regions, Justice, Freedom and Security in Europe since 2005: An Evaluation of the Hague Programme and Action Plan, COM (2009) 263 final, 10 June 2009, pp. 2–3.

Asylum,[25] which has been given by the Commission in 2008. The European Commission's Proposals to recast the Dublin Regulation (Dublin III Regulation),[26] Eurodac Regulation[27] and the Reception Conditions Directive[28] belong to the same package of proposals in order to ensure a higher degree of harmonisation and to make the CEAS more efficient.

In the Dublin III Proposal several modifications are proposed with the aim of ensuring that the responsibility determination procedure operates more smoothly, in particular:

- deadlines for submitting take-back requests are established and the deadline for replying to requests for information is reduced;
- the cessation of responsibility clauses have been clarified particularly in regard to the circumstances under which the cessation clauses should apply, the Member State which bears the burden of proof and the consequences of the cessation responsibility;
- the circumstances and procedures for applying the discretionary humanitarian and sovereignty clauses have been clarified;
- rules of transfers have been added, i.e. on erroneous transfers and costs for transfers;
- the existing dispute settlement mechanism has been extended in order to cover matters of dispute on the application of the entire Regulation, and not only the disputes concerning the application of the humanitarian clause;
- a provision on the organisation of a compulsory interview is inserted, which may increase the efficiency of the Dublin system and provide adequate safeguards for the applicants for international protection.[29]

In this context it is relevant to illuminate the background by referring to the Hague Programme[30] adopted in 2005, which has previously contributed to the development to regulate migration flows and control the external borders of the European Union. The Hague Programme was in a way EU's response to the need to tackle the problems of increasing migratory flows and the growing threat of organised crime and terrorist attacks, like the attacks on New York 2001 and

[25] Communication from the Commission to the European Parliament, the Council, the European Economic and Social Committee and the Committee of Regions on the 'Policy Plan on Asylum, an Integrated Approach to Protection Across the EU', COM (2008) 360 final, 17 June 2008.

[26] COM (2008) 820 final, 3 December 2008.

[27] COM (2008) 825 final, 3 December 2008.

[28] COM (2008) 815 final, 3 December 2008.

[29] See the Dublin III Proposal, COM (2008) 820 final, 3 December 2008, p. 7.

[30] The Hague Programme: strengthening freedom, security and justice in the European Union, OJ, C 53, 3.3.2005, p. 1 and the Council and Commission action plan implementing the Hague Programme on strengthening freedom, security and justice in the European Union, OJ, C 198, 12.8.2005, p. 1.

Madrid 2004. This development has paved the way to the current Policy Plan on Asylum and the Dublin III Regulation.[31]

During the French Presidency, the Brussels European Council adopted the European Pact on Immigration and Asylum[32] in October 2008. According to the Presidency Conclusions,[33] the Pact will form for both the EU and its Member States, the basis of a common immigration and asylum policy, guided by a spirit of solidarity between Member States and cooperation with third countries. The Commission has rightly emphasised that in an open European Union without internal borders no Member State can manage immigration on its own.[34] The fundamental principles set out in the Pact are reflected in a series of measures that will have to be implemented immediately. Moreover, these principles will have an impact on the next multiannual Programme, the Stockholm Programme,[35] which has been finalised during the Swedish Presidency in 2009.

One of the major issues in the Pact is the efficiency and solidarity of migration policy. Consequently, in February 2009 the Commission proposed to set up an European Asylum Support Office[36] with the task of facilitating the exchange of information, analyses and experience among Member States and developing practical cooperation between administrations in charge of examining asylum applications. Operational experience has consistently pointed out the need for such a practical cooperation. In the Pact, the European Council solemnly reiterated that any persecuted foreigner is entitled to obtain aid and protection on the territory of the European Union in application of the Geneva Refugee Convention. Thus, the idea is to establish an operational agency to coordinate and step up cooperation on asylum between Member States, which is in line with the Hague Programme.

The EU Asylum *acquis* is relatively rapidly being amended. This can be shown by referring to the recent developments in regard to the EU legislation, for example Directive 2003/86/EC[37] on the right to family reunification, and Directive 2003/9/EC[38] concerning the minimum standards for the reception of asylum

---

[31] COM (2009) 263 final, 10.6.2009, p. 2.

[32] Council Document 13440/08 and see also the Communication from the Commission to the European Parliament, the Council, the European Economic and Social Committee and the Committee of Regions on a Common Immigration Policy for Europe: Principles, actions and tools, COM (2008) 359 final, 17 June 2008.

[33] Council Document 14368/08, Concl 4, Brussels 16 October 2008.

[34] COM (2008) 359 final, 17 June 2008, p. 4.

[35] The Stockholm Programme—An open and secure Europe serving and protecting citizens, OJ, C 115, 4.5.2010, pp. 1–38.

[36] Proposal for a Regulation of the European Parliament and of the Council establishing a European Asylum Support Office, COM (2009) 66 final, 18 February 2009.

[37] Council Directive 2003/86/EC of 22 September 2003 on the right to family reunification, OJ, L 251, 3.10.2003, p. 12.

[38] Council Directive 2003/9/EC of 27 January 2003 laying down minimum standards for the reception of asylum seekers, OJ, L 31, 6.2.2003, p. 18.

seekers. Directive 2008/115/EC[39] on the common standards and procedures in Member States for returning illegally staying third country nationals was adopted in December 2008. This directive aims at safeguarding that the ending of illegal stay of third country nationals is carried out through a fair and transparent procedure. Directive 2009/52/EC[40] prohibits the employment of irregular immigrants in order to fight illegal migration. Additionally, the Commission is in the process of amending the Qualification Directive[41] and the Asylum Procedures Directive.[42] There is also progress in the integrated border management, namely entry–exit system[43] through automatic alerts where someone overstays his or her visa, a system for the surveillance of the EU's southern and eastern external borders (EUROSUR)[44] and the evaluation and future development of FRONTEX.[45]

On the other hand, legal immigration also requires efforts to be updated. The Commission's Policy Plan on Legal Migration[46] was drafted in 2005 and it set out the initiatives to be taken on legal migration between 2006 and 2009. The Commission has tried to guarantee a common set of rights to all third country workers lawfully residing in a Member State and not yet entitled to long-term residence status, and to introduce a single application procedure along with a single residence and work permit.[47] Perhaps the most prominent novelty is the Directive

---

[39] Directive 2008/115/EC of the European Parliament and of the Council of 16 December 2008 on common standards and procedures in Member States for returning illegally staying third country nationals, OJ, L 348, 24.12.2008, p. 98.

[40] Directive 2009/52/EC of the European Parliament and of the Council of 18 June 2009 providing for minimum standards on sanctions and measures against employers of illegally staying third-country nationals, OJ L168, 30.6.2009, pp. 24–32.

[41] Council Directive 2004/83/EC on minimum standards for the qualification and status of third country nationals and stateless persons as refugees or as persons who otherwise need international protection and the content of the protection granted, OJ, L 304, 30.9.2004, p. 12.

[42] Council Directive 2004/85/EC on minimum standards on procedures in Member States for granting and withdrawing refugee status, OJ L 326, 13.12.2005, p. 13.

[43] Communication from the Commission to the European Parliament, the Council, the European Economic and Social Committee and the Committee of Regions, 'Preparing the next steps in border management in the European Union', COM (2008) 69 final, 13 February 2008.

[44] Communication from the Commission to the European Parliament, the Council, the European Economic and Social Committee and the Committee of Regions, 'Examining the creation of a European border surveillance system (EUROSUR)', COM (2008) 68 final, 13 February 2008.

[45] Communication from the Commission to the European Parliament, the Council, the European Economic and Social Committee and the Committee of Regions, 'Report on the evaluation and future development of the FRONTEX Agency', COM (2008) 67 final, 13 February 2008.

[46] Communication from the Commission, 'Policy Plan on Legal Migration', COM (2005) 669 final, 21 December 2005.

[47] Proposal for a Council Directive on a single application procedure for a single permit for third country nationals to reside and work in the territory of a Member State and on a common set of rights for third country workers legally residing in a Member State, COM (2007) 638 final, 23 October 2007.

2009/50/EC Blue Card[48] (i.e. Blue European Labour Card) for skilled immigrants, which resembles the US Green Card. The Blue Card would allow suitably qualified people and their families to live and work within the European Union. This system has been criticised, since it might encourage brain drain from poorer nations. A counter-argument for this has been that the Blue Card might reverse the current trend under which skilled migrants, mostly from Asia, migrate to USA to find work. Even the Hague Programme recognised that legal migration plays an important role in enhancing the knowledge-based economy in Europe.

Maximising the economic benefit of legal migration has been accompanied by concerted efforts to combat illegal migration and those who profit from it. Human smuggling and trafficking is a problem in the Mediterranean Member States. Over the past decade thousands of immigrants have died while seeking to enter EU by the Mediterranean Sea, which is actually a genuine human rights problem.[49] Therefore, the Commission has in June 2009 publicly announced its concern on the matter, especially in regard to the severe situation in Greece, Italy and Spain. However, a concrete attempt to solve the situation is made with the new Directive 2009/52/EC providing for sanctions against employers of illegally staying third country nationals.[50] The scale of the illegal migration is difficult to quantify, but in the proposal it has been estimated that the number of third country nationals illegally staying in the EU varied between 4 and 5–8 million in 2007. Thus it is an up-to-date question, whether the responsibility to deal with the asylum problem could be more effectively shared between the Member States.

7.5 The Interpretation of the Qualification Directive 2004/83/EC and the Dublin System

According to the Commission's report on the evaluation of the Dublin system, the Dublin II Regulation provides a workable system for determining responsibility for the examination of asylum applications. However, consistency with EU asylum *acquis* is relevant in order to reach a satisfactory level of legal protection for the asylum seekers. Even the Commission has pointed out in its report[51] that the notion of an 'examination of an asylum application' as defined in the Dublin II Regulation

[48] Proposal for a Council Directive on the conditions of entry and residence of third country nationals for the purposes of highly qualified employment, COM (2007) 637 final, 23 October 2007, especially Chapter III and Council Directive 2009/50/EC of 25 May 2009 on the conditions of entry and residence of third-country nationals for the purposes of highly qualified employment, OJ, L 155, 18.6.2009, pp. 17–29.

[49] See more thoroughly Commission Staff Working Document. Third annual report on the development of a common policy on illegal immigration, smuggling and trafficking of human beings, external borders, and the return of illegal residents, SEC(2009) 320 final, 9 March 2009.

[50] OJ L 168, 30.6.2009, pp. 24–32.

[51] COM (2007) 299 final, 6 June 2007, p. 6.

should be interpreted as implying the assessment whether the applicant in question qualifies as a refugee in accordance with the Qualification Directive 2004/83/EC.[52]

Both the refugee status and the criteria to qualify for subsidiary protection are defined in the Directive 2004/83/EC. However, it is necessary that the European Court of Justice tries to clarify them. According to Article 2 c, 'Refugee' means a third country national (or a stateless person) who, owing to a well-founded fear of being persecuted for reasons of race, religion, nationality, political opinion or membership of a particular social group, is outside the country of nationality (origin) and is unable or unwilling to avail himself or herself of the protection of that country. As stated in Article 2 e, a 'Person eligible for subsidiary protection' does not qualify as a refugee, but if returned to his or her country of origin, would face a real risk of suffering serious harm.

From this perspective, the ruling in the *Elgafaji* case[53] is illuminating and important. The problem in this case is related to the interpretation of Article 15, according to which serious harm in the applicant's country of origin is defined in the context of qualification for subsidiary protection. Serious harm consists of death penalty or execution, torture or inhuman or degrading treatment or punishment, or serious and individual threat to a civilian's life or person by reason of indiscriminate violence in situations of international or internal armed conflict. Obviously, the third criterion seems to be somewhat obscure. What is meant by a 'serious and individual threat to a civilian's life or person' or 'indiscriminate violence' and last but not least, what is an 'armed conflict'?

Mr. and Mrs. Elgafaji submitted applications for temporary residence permits in the Netherlands. They were eventually able to prove a real risk of indiscriminate violence to which they would be exposed if they were expelled to their country of origin, Iraq. The Court stated that 'the existence of a serious and individual threat to a life or person of an applicant for subsidiary protection is not subject to the condition that that applicant adduce evidence that he is specifically targeted by reason of factors particular to his personal circumstances'. One could conclude from the Elgafaji case that when there is discriminatory violence at hand in the country of origin, less evidence for the subsidiary protection is needed, and when there is indiscriminate violence, strong evidence of the threat is needed. However, the Elgafaji case proves that the existence of such a threat can exceptionally be considered to be established where the degree of indiscriminate violence in the armed conflict is such that merely the applicant's presence on the territory of that region would lead to a situation in which the applicant faces a real risk of being subject to that threat. For the sake of clarity, one would need still more case laws on the Directive 2004/83/EC.[54] For example, one might still wonder, what is meant by an 'armed conflict'?

[52] OJ, L 304, 30.9.2004, p. 12.

[53] ECJ, Case C-465/07 *Meki Elgafaji, Noor Elgafaji v Staatssecretaris van Justitie* [2009] *ECR* I-00921.

[54] Another example of recent case law determining refugee status under Directive 2004/83/EC is *C-31/09 Nawras Bobol*, judgment of June 17, 2010 available from http://curia.europa.eu. Here the ECJ considered the refusal of the Hungarian authorities to grant refugee status to a stateless Palestinian.

While implementing the Qualification Directive 2004/83/EC, the Finnish Parliament debated whether a separate criterion for humanitarian protection as a national peculiarity should be maintained.[55] Based on the novel para 88a of the Finnish immigration law, the applicant can be granted a residence permit to stay in Finland on grounds of humanitarian protection. Such a permit of residence can be granted even on the basis of a catastrophe such as volcanic eruption, which illustrates risk for the whole population in that area. On the grounds of the Elgafaji case one might wonder whether the subsidiary protection should suffice, since Article 15 c seems to cover the humanitarian aspects to protect the applicant relatively efficiently. For the sake of coherence and clarity in the European Union's asylum *acquis*, it is important that the national legislation of the Member States contain identical definitions on refugee status and subsidiary protection. This, however, has been safeguarded by the novel legislation. For example, the new para 88 contains an identical definition of the subsidiary protection compared to the Qualification Directive. Based on the indirect effect of EU law the national legislation should be interpreted in the light of the EU asylum acquis, which includes the case law of the European Court of Justice.

7.6 Concluding Remarks

The need for harmonisation and common definitions has become evident in the context of the Dublin system as well. As stated before, the different interpretations of the definitions for registration will confuse the statistics and contribute to the malfunctioning of the Dublin system as a whole. Besides, even the Dublin system and Regulation (EC) No 343/2003 requires interpretation, which can be shown by referring to the recent Petrosian case.[56] To conclude, one can only hope that the Member States will succeed in making the Dublin system and the asylum *acquis* more effective, transparent and fair. Interpretations of the European Court of Justice, i.e. 'judge made law', will not be able to make the Dublin system more efficient alone. New unifying legislation is needed, both in the Member States and in the European Union.

However, the Commission seems to be well aware of the current problems in this area. For example, it is important that the Dublin III Proposal extends the scope of application of the Regulation in order to include applicants for subsidiary protection, which ensures consistency with the Qualifications Directive 2004/83/EC.[57] Thus, it is up to Member States to take the necessary steps forward in the field of EU asylum law. It remains to be seen whether the attempt to create an

---

[55] See Governmental Proposal 166/2007 vp and the Law to amend immigration law 323/2009.

[56] ECJ, Case C-19/08 *Migrationsverket v Edgar Petrosian and others* [2009] *ECR* I-00495.

[57] See e.g. the Dublin III Proposal, COM (2008) 820 final, 3 December 2008, p. 7.

efficient CEAS would face political obstacles based on the fear of certain Member States that it would strengthen the federal aspects of the European Union too much.

References

Craig P, de Burca G (2008) EU law. Oxford University Press, Oxford
Fabrice F (2009) Schengen/Dublin: the association agreements with Iceland, Norway and Switserland. In: Martenczuk B, van Thiel S (eds) Justice, liberty, security: new challenges for EU external relations. VUBPress, Brussel, pp 145–183
Peers S (2006) EU justice and home affairs law. Oxford University Press, Oxford
Peers S (2011) EU justice and home affairs law, 3rd Ed, Oxford University Press, Oxford

Chapter 8
Conditions and Criteria for Determining Asylum

Alessandra Ricci Ascoli

Contents

8.1 Introduction 125
8.2 The Application Procedure 127
8.2.1 Access to Procedures 127
8.2.2 Decision-Making Authority 127
8.2.3 Decision-Maker 128
8.2.4 Examination of Applications 128
8.2.5 Access to Legal Counsel 128
8.2.6 Access to Interpretation 129
8.2.7 Rights to Confidentiality 129
8.2.8 Reasonable Time to Prepare a Case 130
8.2.9 Benefit of the Doubt 130
8.2.10 Reasoned Decisions 130
8.2.11 Equality in Access to Evidence 131
8.2.12 Right to an Effective Appeal 131
8.3 Conclusions 132
References 132

8.1 Introduction

In this paper I will present some considerations about the criteria for determining asylum within the framework of the European Union in the second phase of the Hague Programme. I will especially refer to the asylum systems of Greece and Italy, which face a considerable amount of arrivals of asylum seekers. Often, these

As an Amnesty International employee and activist I will particularly refer to the positions of this organization, but the responsibility for what is written remains exclusively mine.

Alessandra Ricci Ascoli, policy officer at Amnesty International.

F. A. N. J. Goudappel and H. S. Raulus (eds.), *The future of asylum in the European Union*, DOI: 10.1007/978-90-6704-802-6_8,

people reach other EU Member States and from there, according to the Dublin II Regulation, they are transferred back to the countries where they first arrived in Europe. According to this Regulation, only one Member State is responsible for the examination of an asylum claim. Usually, this is the first Member State the asylum seeker first entered the EU (Norway, Iceland and Switzerland joined the club).

It is true that the Refugee Convention does not establish any criteria for determining the Refugee status, but in 1979 the UNHCR published a Handbook on Procedures and Criteria for Determining Refugee Status under the 1951 Convention and the 1967 Protocol relating to the Status of Refugees.[1] This Handbook was re-edited in 1992 and consists of 61 pages. Even if the Handbook is not mandatory like the Convention, it should be mandatory that the officials who deal with status determination receive adequate training on it.

The Handbook is a fundamental point of reference when discussing the conditions and criteria of determining the refugee status, but I strongly doubt if decision-making bodies in all the EU Member States refer to it when determining the refugee status.

Providing international protection is a very complex issue, as the situations all over the world are different and change with the time. We easily agree that the world which approved the Refugee Convention is not the same anymore. The idea that people should not be persecuted, however, does not change and the conditions and criteria to establish if one person is at risk of persecution should not be the object of subjective determination.

When states discuss the criteria for determining the refugee status over and over, in fact they bring their own capacity of protection under discussion instead of the risk of persecution of the victims. If criteria shift easily from repressive to generous towards the refugees, it is not the objective and subjective risk of the person concerned in the country of origin which is at stake, but the contingent one of the host state. The latter can change because of economic, social or political reasons, but this has nothing to do with personal history of those fleeing persecution.

It has been stated that "Despite recent efforts to harmonize RSD Procedures, notably in the European Union, there is still no single model for RSD and there remains a troubling variation in outcomes in similar cases. RSD, which is vital to the protection of so many asylum seekers worldwide, is at best an imperfect, haphazard and challenging process...".[2]

Amnesty International has elaborated a set of basic safeguards for states to apply when determining refugee status.[3]

---

1 UNHCR 1992.

2 Jones 2009 p. 53.

3 Amnesty International 2009.

8.2 The Application Procedure

8.2.1 Access to Procedures

Access to a fair and satisfactory/effective asylum procedure should be granted to all asylum seekers under the jurisdiction of a Member State, both within its territory and at its borders. This includes insuring that immigration officials present all asylum applications to the competent central authority.

Before raising the issue of the criteria for determining asylum, it should be noted that the right to access to fair and efficient asylum procedures is undermined every day in Europe as the access to the territory is often denied. Especially EU Member States at the external border, like Greece, Spain, Italy and Malta, which face a considerable number of arrivals of aliens at their frontiers, do not have proper asylum systems (even if they formally implemented the EU legislation on this matter). Italy, for instance, has intercepted people in international waters and returned them to Libya, the country from where they tried to reach Europe after very dangerous journeys. By doing so, Italy has put the lives of those intercepted in serious danger, as Libya has not ratified the Geneva Convention on Refugee Status and the lives of foreigners is seriously at risk of ill-treatment or refoulement to their countries of origin.

It is also reported that Greek law enforcement officials forcibly return foreigners to Turkey at Evros. They also send back foreigners when they try to reach the Greek islands by making holes in their dinghies.[4] Those who escaped dangerous situations are not given the possibility even to apply for asylum and are put again in situations in which their life is at serious risk.

8.2.2 Decision-Making Authority

The asylum claims should be determined by a decision-making body which is independent and specialized, and provided with objective, independent and relevant information on the countries of origin, or any countries where the applicants might be sent.

In Greece, the determining authority is the police, the same authority which is in charge of arresting and expelling foreigners who do not have the right to stay on the territory of the state. Often the police do not make the distinction between asylum seekers and irregular migrants and push back to Turkey those who have the

[4] See among others Human Rights Watch 2008 and Pro-Asyl and Group of Lawyers for the Rights of Refugees and Migrants 2007.

right to wait for a decision on their asylum claim. Once in Turkey, these people are at risk of being refouled to their country of origin. Also, if people reach a Greek island, they are put in detention and they often do not have the possibility to apply for asylum.

8.2.3 Decision-Maker

Every asylum claim, whether submitted on arrival or after entry into the country, should be carried out by a fully qualified official of the responsible body, who should interview the applicant personally. Applicants should be interviewed by a person of the same gender if they so wish.

In Greece, when asylum seekers get the opportunity to have an interview for their application, they are not informed that they should explain the reasons for their application. Often, they are only asked about their name, nationality and date of birth, not knowing that a decision will be taken on the grounds of that information.

8.2.4 Examination of Applications

Every asylum application should be examined thoroughly and individually on all the circumstances of the case. The applicants should be able to present their case, and submit evidence, in a personal appearance before the decision-maker.

The first report on asylum procedures in Italy shows that the deciding authority deals unprofessionally when interviewing asylum seekers[5]: an interview lasts no more than 30 minutes in almost all the cases. During the interview, the most frequently asked questions are the following: how much did you pay for the journey? Which countries did you cross before you arrived to Italy? Why did you flee? Did you work in your country? Did you come to Italy to find a job? Is your intention to bring your family to Italy? Do you consider returning to your country? How do you earn your living? Who helps you? Where are you accommodated? [*sic*!]

8.2.5 Access to Legal Counsel

Asylum seekers should have access to effective legal counsel, UNHCR and appropriate NGOs, and should be made aware of this rights.

---

[5] Consorzio Italiano di Solidarietà 2005.

In several EU Member States, it is very difficult for asylum seekers to receive legal counsel. The organizations providing for it do not have the capacity to assist all those in need. As a consequence, many asylum seekers do not know their rights. Not only asylum seekers do not know them, but also often the relevant authorities have no clue. For instance, hospitals refuse to treat asylum seekers because the physicians think they are not allowed to receive medical care. Often, they do not get jobs because employers think they are not allowed to work. In Italy, a young asylum seeker who applied for international protection in February 2008, got the appointment for his interview with the relevant authority in October 2010. He had no other papers than the invitation to the interview. He did not know that he has the right to get a residence permit while waiting for the decision on his application and that he is allowed to work in the meantime. Nobody wants to offer him a job, while the law explicitly states that if the decision on the asylum claims is not adopted within six months from its presentation and the delay is not due to the asylum seeker, the asylum seeker is allowed to work until the procedure is concluded.

8.2.6 Access to Interpretation

Applicants should have access to a competent, qualified and impartial interpreter throughout all stages of the asylum procedure. They should have access to an interpreter of the same gender if they so wish.

In Greece, if asylum seekers get the opportunity to apply for international protection, they are not necessarily interviewed in a language they know. Interviews take place in Greek or English as there is not an interpreter present at the interview. Being interviewed by an official of the same gender does not happen in practice, even if the national legislation, which implements the EU directives, states so.

8.2.7 Rights to Confidentiality

An applicant has the right to confidentiality at all stages of the asylum process, including the fact that the application for asylum has been made.

Sometimes, asylum seekers are approached by consular authorities from their country of origin in order to assess their nationality. By definition, an asylum seeker is a person who seeks international protection and therefore the authorities of his countries should not be informed that he applied for asylum. In some countries, the fact that a citizen has applied for asylum abroad is seen as a crime and the rejected asylum seekers, when returned, are at risk of their lives and integrity for the only reason that they applied for asylum.

8.2.8 Reasonable Time to Prepare a Case

Taking into account the proof required in making an asylum claim, applicants should be given a reasonable amount of time to prepare their case and seek legal and other advice.

Some EU Member States apply fast track asylum procedures. While it can be stated that there are cases where an asylum claim can be examined within a short time (for instance, a person can be recognized as a *prima facie* refugee, or there are vulnerable people like traumatized people who should not wait too long for a decision), it is worrying that in some countries, fast track procedure lasts such a short time that asylum seekers are not given opportunity to prepare their case or the opportunity to present the necessary evidence. Also, in some cases, a person needs time to recover from the events or a trauma and is not in state to respond within the short time given. Some fast track procedures last only hours and are applied in the majority of the cases (for instance, at the borders).

8.2.9 Benefit of the Doubt

It is not always possible for asylum seekers to prove every part of their case with supporting evidence and so it is often necessary to give the applicant the benefit of the doubt.

The UNHCR Handbook on Procedures and Criteria for Determining Refugee Status states that "in most cases a person fleeing from persecution will have arrived with the barest necessities and very frequently even without personal documents". Where there are "statements that are not susceptible of proof… if the applicant's account appears credible, he should, unless there are good reasons to the contrary, be given the benefit of the doubt."[6]

8.2.10 Reasoned Decisions

Where a first instance asylum claim is rejected, applicants should be provided with clear and comprehensive reasons for the decision, which are fully in-line with procedural safeguards for fair and due process and which allow the applicants to effectively exercise their right to appeal to its full extent.

A reasoned motivation is a guarantee for the asylum seeker to exercise correctly his right to appeal. Decisions should explain in writing, in a language that the asylum seeker understands, how in his individual case the decision-maker assessed

[6] See *supra* n. 2, Sect. 8.1, para 196.

the evidence, took into consideration the relevant law and facts also referring to the situation in the country of origin.

According to the first report on asylum in Italy,[7] the determining authority justifies its decisions with standard sentences, with reference to a general situation in the country of origin instead of the personal history of the asylum seeker. In many cases the asylum seeker was asked if he was looking for work in Italy. When he replied positively to this question (because he wanted to work and did not want to be a burden for the state) this was interpreted in a way that the person concerned fled his country only to find a better living abroad. The asylum claim was thus rejected.

8.2.11 *Equality in Access to Evidence*

Providing an asylum seeker the full right to argue his/her case for asylum in a fair hearing requires the applicant to be able to rebut any evidence used against him/her:

- as a general rule, applicants should have access to copies of all documents used to decide their asylum claim;
- where an individual assessment of a risk of danger posed by disclosure reveals a security concern, alternatives to disclosure must be considered before using evidence withheld from an applicant where this would result in a negative decision;
- if the risk is to the applicant him/herself, the applicant should be informed of the situation and the extent of the risk, and then be allowed to choose;
- if the risk is to the RSD authority and other third parties, then anonymous disclosure should be the first option;
- if anonymity would not abate the security threat, as assessed on a case-by-case basis by a qualified and expert authority, then the RSD authority should consider not using the evidence in making its decision. Without the applicant's ability to rebut and respond to the evidence, the quality and legitimacy of the information is put into question. Refugees come from an oppressive situation where they face an individual risk, so their explanations and evidence could easily be unique to any official or outside understanding.

8.2.12 *Right to an Effective Appeal*

Every applicant should be given reasonable time to appeal his/her asylum decision before a competent and independent authority and should be given the right to stay

---

[7] See *supra* n. 5, Sect. 8.2.4, p. 70.

during the appeal procedure. In order to fulfill the requirements of fairness and avoid a breach of non-refoulement, the asylum procedures should guarantee that:

- the appeal is conducted by an independent body different from that which made the initial decision and which is either a judicial authority or a higher-administrative authority;
- appellants have a personal interview to allow an in-person opportunity to present their case and for the authority to make a personal assessment;
- the appeal procedure should include an examination of the merits of the individual case and all the relevant facts, including new relevant facts may come to light;
- the appeal authority provides clear and comprehensive reasons for the decision in case of a negative decision.

In May 2008, a new Presidential Decree was proposed in Greece. It would abolish the second stage of asylum procedures, leaving asylum seekers with no recourse to a substantial appeal. If the changes are adopted, asylum seekers whose applications have been rejected at the first stage would only have access to a review by the Council of State, which does not cover the substance of the request, but only examines procedural aspects. It has to be stressed that in Greece the recognition rate in first instances in 2008 was 0.05%. It is clear that the proposed amendment constitutes a serious danger for the international protection of those in need.

8.3 Conclusions

The criteria elaborated above by Amnesty International are fundamental in order to deal respectfully and professionally with those who apply for asylum. However, it appears that not all the EU Member States consider them as such. States should not be afraid to use the RSD Handbook as a tool when exercising their obligations. There is no provision that states that those who are not eligible for international protection have to be recognized as refugees. It is a tool for the officials to better understand what his or her tasks are and whom he or she is dealing with.

References

Amnesty International (2009) Stranded: refugee in Turkey denied protection. http://www.amnesty.org/en/library/info/EUR44/001/2009/en. Accessed 25 May 2010

Consorzio Italiano di Solidarietà (2005) Primo Rapporto sul diritto d'asilo in Italia. Rifugiati in Italia: La protezione negata. http://www.meltingpot.org/articolo5049.html. Accessed 25 May 2010

Human Rights Watch (2008) Stuck in a revolving door, Greece/Turkey. Iraqis and other asylum seekers and migrants at the Greece/Turkey entrance to the European Union. http://www.hrw.org/en/reports/2008/11/26/stuck-revolving-door-0) Accessed 25 May 2010

Jones M (2009) Refugee status determination: three challenges. 32 Forced Migration Review pp 53–54

Pro-Asyl and Group of Lawyers for the Rights of Refugees and Migrants (2007) The truth may be bitter, but must be told, the situation of Refugees in the Aegean and the practice of the Greek Coast guard. http://www.proasyl.de/fileadmin/proasyl/fm_redakteure/Englisch/Griechenland bericht_Engl.pdf. Accessed 25 May 2010

UN High Commissioner for Refugees (1992) Handbook on Procedures and Criteria for Determining Refugee Status under the 1951 Convention and the 1967 Protocol Relating to the Status of Refugees. http://www.unhcr.org/refworld/docid/3ae6b3314.html. Accessed 25 May 2010

Chapter 9
The Future of Asylum in Europe? A View from the European Council on Refugees and Exiles

Bjarte Vandvik

The European Union (EU) has been in the process of developing a Common European Asylum System (CEAS) for almost ten years. ECRE, a pan-European alliance of 69 refugee assisting non-governmental organizations in 30 European countries, promotes the protection and integration of asylum seekers and refugees based on the values of human dignity, human rights and an ethic of solidarity. ECRE, supports the creation of a CEAS if it leads to good standards of protection that are in line with international and European refugee and human rights law. It does not support harmonisation for its own sake. However, a genuine CEAS, which guarantees that refugees have an equal chance of being granted asylum, no matter where their asylum application is processed, is still far from reality. Without a CEAS which leads to better and more similar laws, policies and practices in all Member States as well as the political will to implement them, ECRE will continue to struggle with the negative impact of the large differences between Member States. These are the differences in the way one's application is treated, differences in the chance of receiving a refugee status or another form of protection, differences in reception conditions, differences in special policies for asylum seekers from certain countries, differences in integration measures and so on.

The lack of a level playing field in the area of asylum is drawn into sharp focus by one of the fundamental flaws of the Dublin Regulation,[1] this is the requirement that individuals must claim asylum in the first Member State they reach, premise being here that there are equal protection standards across the EU. As well as being unfair, the Dublin system is both resource-intensive and inefficient, and shifts

Bjarte Vandvik, Secretary General of the European Council of Refugees and Exiles

[1] Council Regulation (EC) No 343/2003 of 18 February 2003 establishing the criteria and mechanisms for determining the Member State responsible for examining an asylum application lodged in one of the Member States by a third-country national, Official Journal L 50 of 25 February 2003.

F. A. N. J. Goudappel and H. S. Raulus (eds.), *The future of asylum in the European Union*, DOI: 10.1007/978-90-6704-802-6_9,

additional burden to certain Member States experiencing particular pressures due to their geographical position.[2] The European Commission has adopted a proposal for amending the Dublin Regulation.[3] which recognizes that these factors require a mechanism enabling the temporary suspension of transfers to States that are experiencing particular pressures or failing to adhere to necessary reception and protection standards. However, such suspensions should be conditional on measures to address the failings of the State concerned through effective monitoring and resource allocation. This cannot be stressed enough: Member States are legally bound to meet their obligations under the EU asylum *aquis.* The European Commission, primarily, but also UNHCR and the European Asylum Support Office,[4] need to be empowered to ensure compliance through the systematic oversight of Member States' asylum systems.

Another instrument that is being reformed is the Reception Conditions Directive.[5] ECRE believes that, if adopted, the amendments proposed by the European Commission would constitute a considerable step forward towards the objective of providing dignified and comparable living standards for asylum seekers in the EU. Foremost among these amendments is the proposal to allow asylum seekers to work after six months. This would enable individuals to become more self-sufficient and be better prepared for both possible outcomes of the asylum procedure, namely return to the country of origin or integration into the host community. Similarly, the proposed amendment to ensure the identification of persons with special needs, such as children, victims of torture or persons who have suffered other forms of physical, psychological or sexual violence, will not only protect the rights of these particularly vulnerable individuals but will also produce cost savings for States by reducing the number of subsequent applications and spiraling medical costs which can result from failing to properly treat illnesses or conditions before they become more acute.

We all want a CEAS with the highest possible protection standards. However, the very notion of a CEAS risk becomes meaningless if asylum seekers continue to be systematically denied access to protection. There were in 2008 fewer than 240,000 asylum applications in the 27 Member States[6]; by contrast, in 1992, some 700,000 asylum claims were lodged in the then 15 EU countries. While the number of asylum applications in Europe rose in 2007 and 2008, this followed the 20-year

---

[2] See ECRE 2007 and ECRE 2008a.

[3] European Commission, *Proposal for a Regulation of the European Parliament and of the Council establishing an application for international protection lodged in one of the Member States by a third-country national or a stateless person (Recast)*, COM (2008) 0243 final, 3 December 2008.

[4] See ECRE 2008b.

[5] European Commission, *Proposal for a Directive of the European Parliament and of the Council laying down minimum standards for the reception of asylum seekers*, COM (2008) 815 final/2, 9.12.2008.

[6] UNHCR, As*ylum Levels and Trends in Industrialized Countries 2008: Statistical Overview of Asylum Applications Lodged in Europe and Selected Non-European Countries*, 24 March 2009.

low which was reached in 2006.[7] When these trends are observed in the light of Member States' continuous tightening of their border controls, it seems evident that refugees are finding it ever harder to find a safe haven in Europe.

Refugees have no more means to legally travel to the EU than any other category of persons, despite the right to seek asylum enshrined in Article 14 of the Universal Declaration of Human Rights. Persons fleeing persecution are therefore also forced into irregular channels thus creating so-called "mixed flows". In its recent Policy Plan on Asylum, the European Commission stated that "disorderly movements are a significant route to safety in the EU, with human smugglers acting as important facilitators for entry. The EU should therefore make an effort to ensure an orderly access of asylum seekers."[8] However, instead of facilitating legal ways for refugees to travel safely, Europe increasingly expects its neighbours to prevent people from reaching its borders, leaving many people in a state of limbo. While the Member States have the right to control their borders, security imperatives should not override the human rights commitments which are the founding principles of the EU.

The efforts of European governments to prevent migrants from reaching the EU has meant that border management activities are no longer confined to the physical frontiers of the Member States or to the external borders of the EU; instead, their scope has been extended well beyond these, to the high seas and into the territory of third countries, sometimes in cooperation with those countries' authorities. The externalization of border controls makes it extremely difficult to monitor what happens at the crucial moment when people in need of international protection come into contact with the authorities of the would-be asylum country for the first time, and allows people to be pushed back without anybody in Europe ever knowing about them. ECRE has consistently stressed that refugee and human rights obligations do not stop at national borders. Notwithstanding how convenient a presumption of irresponsibility may be to policy-makers keen to rid themselves of their legal duties, the obligation of non-*refoulement*, which prohibits returning refugees to countries where they may face persecution, does not arise only when a refugee is within or at the borders of a state, but also when a refugee is under its effective or *de facto* jurisdiction, albeit outside its territory.

When adopting the European Plan on Migration and Asylum in October 2008, the Member States expressed their commitment "that the necessary strengthening of European border controls should not prevent access to protection systems by those people entitled to benefit under them."[9] In the meantime, however, migrants are still suffering horrendous human rights violations and losing their lives on their

[7] Relevant statistical series are available at http://www.unhcr.org/pages/49c3646c4d6.html.

[8] European Commission, *Policy Plan on Asylum: An Integrated Approach to Protection across the EU* , COM(2008) 360 final, 17 June 2008, pp. 10–11.

[9] Council of the European Union, *European Pact on Immigration and Asylum*, ASIM 72, 24 September 2008, p. 11. Available at: http://register.consilium.europa.eu/pdf/en/08/st13/st13440.en08.pdf.

way to Europe.[10] Refugees are undoubtedly paying a high prize in their desperate attempt to reach the EU, but questions regarding asylum policy do not only concern their individual fates: they are also a reflection of the kind of society that the EU is building and the approach it is projecting to third countries. We are at a crossroads now as regards the future of asylum in Europe. We have the choice between building an open, inclusive society which upholds and promotes human rights and fosters positive cooperation with the rest or the world, or building a closed society, the so-called Fortress Europe. For Europe to go along the first route, the values of solidarity, integration and dialogue must be at the core of EU asylum policies.

References

ECRE (2007) The Dublin Regulation: Twenty Voices–Twenty Reasons for Change. http://www.ecre.org/topics/areas-of-work/protection-in-europe/136.html

ECRE (2008a) ECRE Comments on EU plans to establish a European Asylum Support Office (EASO). http://www.ecre.org/topics/areas-of-work/protection-in-europe/129.html

ECRE (2008b) Sharing responsibility for Refugee Protection in Europe: Dublin Reconsidered. http://www.ecre.org/topics/areas-of-work/protection-in-europe/134.html

[10] ECRE has collected a number of refugee stories highlighting the negative impact that obstacles in access to protection have on the rights of refugees. Available at: http://www.ecre.org/topics/areas-of-work/access-to-europe/89-access-to-europe-case-studies-qrefugee-storiesq.html.

Chapter 10
Conditions and Criteria for Determining Asylum

Jens Vedsted-Hansen

Contents

10.1 Introduction: The Quality of EU Asylum Standards 139
10.2 Formal Minimum Harmonisation? 141
10.3 Harmonised Interpretation of EU Norms? 145
10.4 Application of Substantive Provisions 147
10.5 The Criteria for Subsidiary Protection—Dynamic Interpretation or Restrictive Application? 148
10.5.1 Non-refoulement in Accordance with the European Convention on Human Rights 148
10.5.2 Protection Against Refoulement in the Context of Indiscriminate Violence 149
10.6 Conditions for Determining Asylum in the Future Common European Asylum System 151
10.6.1 Regulatory Factors Impeding Harmonisation 151
10.6.2 The Recast Directive Proposals and the Future Common European Asylum System 153
10.6.3 Concluding Remarks on the Stockholm Programme 154
References 155

10.1 Introduction: The Quality of EU Asylum Standards

The conditions and criteria for determining asylum are reflected in the totality of procedural and substantive aspects of the standards governing the examination of asylum applications, including the definition of beneficiaries of international protection. In the context of European asylum law and practice, the quality of these asylum standards can be meaningfully assessed by reference to three parameters,

J. Vedsted-Hansen (✉)
Aarhus University School of Law, Aarhus, Denmark
e-mail: jvh@jura.au.dk

F. A. N. J. Goudappel and H. S. Raulus (eds.), *The future of asylum in the European Union*, DOI: 10.1007/978-90-6704-802-6_10,

all of which are somewhat hypothetical but nonetheless relevant for the sake of comparison of asylum practices across Member States, and thereby indirectly indicating the level and efficiency of the EU harmonisation in this policy area:

- The likelihood that asylum applicants with comparable case background will receive *identical decisions* on their application in different Member States, given the absence of any right to choose the country of examination and potential asylum under the prevailing Dublin system; consequently, the degree to which it is immaterial to the outcome of the status determination procedure in which the Member State application has been submitted or by which it is examined, so that differences in legal framework will not in themselves cause secondary movements;
- The effective fulfilment across Member States of the *minimum standards* for the identification and protection of refugees and beneficiaries of subsidiary protection, laid down in the Qualification Directive,[1] as well as the reception standards for asylum seekers[2] and the procedural guarantees for asylum applications[3];
- The *conformity* of these general EU standards and the concrete decisions implementing them with Member States' existing, and potentially evolving, obligations under international refugee and human rights law.

The above-mentioned quality parameters provide a suitable basis for identifying the challenges to be met during the future stages of the EU harmonisation process. Implicitly, these challenges and the way in which they will be met are also among the main determining factors to the future of asylum—perceived as a complex of legal norms and institutions, political commitments and moral perceptions—in the European Union. In this connection it should be noted, however, that the future of asylum is critically dependent on an additional factor that is not going to be elaborated upon in the following discussion; the *accessibility* to the European Union—in terms of the territories of its Member States as well as the procedural arrangements for examining asylum applications—is the precondition *sine qua non* to the protection of persons fleeing risk of persecution and other human rights violations, and hence, to the effective fulfilment of international obligations towards such persons.[4]

How is it then possible to assess the EU harmonisation process along these parameters? I would suggest three different aspects of the interpretation and application of asylum norms that seem to be decisive to the success in harmonising asylum policy and practice, thereby also influencing the legal quality of asylum harmonisation: First, the degree of formal minimum harmonisation of substantive and procedural standards applicable to asylum seekers and refugees (Sect. 10.2, *infra*). Second, the Member States' interpretation of EU norms, and the issue of

---

[1] Council Directive 2004/83 of 29 April 2004 (OJ L 304/12 of 30 September 2004).

[2] Council Directive 2003/9 of 27 January 2004 (OJ L 31/18 of 6 February 2003).

[3] Council Directive 2005/85 of 1 December 2005 (OJ L 326/13 of 13 December 2005).

[4] Cf., Gammeltoft-Hansen 2011 pp. 28–31. Notably, the broader meaning of the 'quality of protection' is here defined as the cumulative effect of the certainty, the scope and the level of rights afforded to refugees.

whether such domestic interpretations are being effectively scrutinised by the EU Court of Justice (Sect. 10.3). Third, the concrete application of the substantive provisions of the EU asylum measures, in particular as regards the crucial issues of law and fact in the application of definitional provisions (Sect. 10.4). Following a general discussion of these regulatory aspects, the interpretation and application of EU asylum norms shall be illustrated by more concrete analysis of the criteria for subsidiary protection as defined in Article 15 of the Qualification Directive, based on the interpretation by the EU Court of Justice (Sect. 10.5). Against this background, the possible future developments of the Common European Asylum System will be discussed, setting out some general reflections on regulatory factors that may ultimately impede or undermine harmonisation, despite official ambitions to promote it; after which some observations will be given on the proposed recasts of the Qualification Directive and the Asylum Procedures Directive tabled by the Commission in October 2009, and their potential for remedying the failures of the first phase EU asylum *acquis*; the concluding remarks will also comment on the Stockholm Programme that was adopted by the European Council in December 2009 (Sect. 10.6).

10.2 Formal Minimum Harmonisation?

It is hardly controversial to suggest that the legal measures adopted during the first phase of EU legislation under the Amsterdam Treaty (1999–2004/5) are a far cry from effectively harmonising the substantive and procedural standards for the examination of asylum applications. Neither does such a conclusion necessitate extensive documentation, inasmuch as the state of legal affairs in this area is well known. The failure of the EU legislator to provide genuine minimum harmonisation of the standards governing Member States' asylum procedures and substantive protection performance is widely recognised, even though some observers would argue that anything else would have been surprising, given the combination of the Treaty basis and the political controversies surrounding the regulatory activities in this area.[5]

Against this background, a few significant examples would seem to suffice in order to illustrate the points here made. First, as far as *reception conditions* are concerned, the scope of asylum applicants' freedom of movement is surprisingly unclear, given the standard allowing Member States to 'confine an applicant to a particular place' in accordance with national law when it 'proves necessary, for example for legal reasons or reasons of public order'; as a consequence, there is no standard with effective impact on the crucial issue of *detention* of asylum

[5] For early warnings in this respect, see Guild 2001; Hathaway 2003. See generally Battjes 2006 Chaps. 5, 6 and 8; on the Qualification Directive, McAdam 2007; on the Asylum Procedures Directive, Costello 2005.

applicants.[6] Similarly, in respect of socio-economic rights for this group of persons, the EU standards are based on deference to Member States regarding the access of asylum applicants to *employment*, by way of the possibility to 'determine a period of time' during which they shall not have access to the labour market; to 'decide the conditions for granting access to the labour market' if a first instance decision has not been taken within one year after the presentation of the application; and the 'reasons of labour market policies' for which Member States may give priority to EU citizens and legally resident third-country nationals.[7]

As regards the *definition of beneficiaries* of international protection, the Qualification Directive apparently resulted in a significant degree of harmonisation of the interpretation of the Convention refugee definition, as well as the criteria for granting subsidiary protection in accordance with human rights obligations.[8] Nonetheless, the Directive allows for certain optional mechanisms that may deviate from the general standards. Most importantly, Member States are given the option to exclude persons falling within the harmonised Convention refugee definition from being 'granted' EU refugee status under security-related criteria which constitute *de facto* exclusion grounds in addition to, and therefore at variance with, the Refugee Convention.[9] Other examples of definitional ambiguities would be the standards for assessment of facts that leave quite some room for domestic variations,[10] and the provision governing the recognition of refugees *sur place* which is far from eliminating possible differences of interpretation and application across Member States.[11]

In addition, the Qualification Directive contains important optional provisions concerning the *protection standards* for persons who have been granted protection under the Directive. Firstly, it allows for the *reduction of standards* for those refugees and subsidiary protection beneficiaries whose status is deemed to have been obtained on the basis of activities engaged in 'for the sole or main purpose of creating the necessary conditions for being recognised' as a refugee or a person eligible for subsidiary protection; the proviso that such reduction must be kept within the limits set by the Refugee Convention and other international obligations does not change the fact that the Directive has deferred important aspects of the issue to Member States.[12]

Secondly, there is also significant deference to Member States regarding the introduction of *differential standards* for subsidiary protection beneficiaries, as

6 See *supra* n. 2, Sect. 10.1, Article 7.

7 Ibid., Article 11.

8 See *supra* n. 1, Sect. 10.1, Articles 4–8 with general standards, and Articles 9–14 and Articles 15–19, respectively.

9 Ibid., Article 14 (4) and (5); the formal exclusion grounds have been laid down in the Qualification Directive Article 12, largely yet not entirely in accordance with Article 1 E, F and D of the Refugee Convention.

10 Ibid., Article 4.

11 Ibid., Article 5 (2) and (3).

12 Ibid., Article 20 (6) and (7), respectively.

compared to Convention refugees. A striking example is the standard concerning access to employment; while refugees shall be authorised to engage in employed or self-employed activities immediately after their refugee status has been 'granted',[13] that right is significantly qualified for beneficiaries of subsidiary protection in that the 'situation of the labour market' may be taken into account, including for 'possible prioritisation of access to employment for a limited period of time' which is to be determined in accordance with national law; and subsidiary protection beneficiaries must have access to a post for which they have received an offer 'in accordance with national rules on prioritisation in the labour market'.[14] Further differentiation is permitted on the right of subsidiary protection beneficiaries to social welfare and health care, both of which may be limited to 'core benefits' that will then have to be provided at the same levels and under the same eligibility conditions as nationals.[15]

Perhaps most notably, the Asylum Procedures Directive leaves Member States several options to derogate from the 'basic' *procedural principles and guarantees* for asylum applicants in 'specific procedures',[16] including procedures dealing with the notion of so-called 'European safe third countries'.[17] Derogations are also permitted in procedures at the border or in transit zones where asylum applications may, under national law, be considered either unfounded or inadmissible[18]; thus, in such border procedures asylum applicants may be rejected not only on formal grounds of inadmissibility, but also on the basis of a substantive examination not complying with the basic principles and guarantees otherwise laid down in the Directive.

In the same Directive, there is a striking absence of automatic *suspensive effect of appeals* against negative asylum decisions. This essentially leaves it up to Member States to decide the extent to which the required 'effective remedy' shall be in compliance with international standards, notwithstanding the fact that these very international standards undoubtedly require States to grant suspensive effect in circumstances such as those prevailing in many cases dealt with by the Asylum Procedures Directive.[19]

---

13 Ibid., Article 26 (1). The unfortunate notion of 'granting' refugee status pursuant to Article 13 is structurally linked to the *de facto* exclusion mechanism under Article 14; see critical remarks above.

14 Ibid., Article 26 (3).

15 Ibid., Articles 28 (2) and 29 (2); according to recital 34 of the Qualification Directive preamble the somewhat unclear notion of 'core benefits' is to be understood to cover 'at least minimum income support, assistance in case of illness, pregnancy and parental assistance, in so far as they are granted to nationals according to the Member State's legislation.

16 See *supra* n. 3, Sect. 10.1, Article 23, taken together with Articles 36 and 35, respectively.

17 Ibid., Article 36; due to the ECJ annulment of Article 36 (3), this provision cannot be implemented by Member States.

18 Ibid., Article 35 (2) and (3).

19 Ibid., Article 39 (3) (a) and (b).

The problems and flaws inherent in such harmonisation measures have already been acknowledged by the European Commission. In its 2007 *Green Paper* on the future Common European Asylum System, the Commission pointed out the large degree of flexibility in the Asylum Procedures Directive, such as the provisions on accelerated procedures, border procedures, and inadmissible applications; and it invited for reassessment of the content and added value of certain procedural devices such as the concepts of 'safe countries of origin', 'safe third-countries' and 'European safe third countries'.[20] For the Reception Conditions Directive, the Commission stated quite straightforwardly that the wide margin of discretion left to Member States by several key provisions results in negating the desired harmonisation effect.[21] Similarly, in response to the call of the Hague Programme for uniformity of protection, the Commission suggested to clarify concepts pertaining to the eligibility criteria for refugee and subsidiary protection status so as to minimise the margin for divergent interpretation and application in different Member States which is currently allowed by the provisions of the Qualification Directive; for the protection standards, it was suggested that a higher degree of harmonisation would mean reducing the flexibility allowed by the current legal framework regarding the content and duration of the rights to be granted as well as the possibility to limit or refuse access to certain rights.[22]

In the same vein, the Commission's *2008 Policy Plan on Asylum* is concerned with the different results produced by diverse procedural arrangements and qualified safeguards, arguing that such features of the Asylum Procedures Directive can damage the very objective of ensuring access to protection under equivalent conditions across the EU.[23] The significant variations across Member States in recognition of similar protection needs are said to be to some extent rooted in the wording of certain provisions of the Qualification Directive.[24] Similarly, a number of problematic issues identified in the Reception Conditions Directive are held to be largely due to the amount of discretion allowed to Member States in a number of key areas, so that the future amended Directive should contribute to achieving a higher degree of harmonisation and improved standards of reception.[25]

The amendments proposed by the Commission of the three aforementioned Directives—the recast Reception Conditions Directive,[26] Asylum Procedures

---

[20] Document COM 2007 301 final of 6 June 2007, Green Paper on the future Common European Asylum System, presented by the Commission, pp. 3–4.

[21] Ibid., pp. 4–5.

[22] Ibid., p. 6.

[23] Document COM(2008) 360/3 of 17 June 2008, Policy Plan on Asylum. An integrated approach to protection across the EU, Communication from the Commission, p. 5.

[24] Ibid., p. 5.

[25] Ibid., p. 4.

[26] Document COM(2008) 815 final of 3 December 2008, Proposal for a Directive of the European Parliament and of the Council laying down minimum standards for the reception of asylum seekers.

Directive[27] and Qualification Directive[28]—have the potential of considerably remedying many of these problems. While the proposal for a recast Qualification Directive shall be discussed briefly below in Sect. 10.6, it should be noted already at this stage that experience from the negotiations of the first generation of Directives might suggest that there is a very real possibility that numerous, and quite important, changes may be introduced during the negotiation process, with the result of weakening the amendments proposed by the Commission.

10.3 Harmonised Interpretation of EU Norms?

Some of the problems discussed above, in particular those pertaining to certain concepts and structural issues in the Qualification Directive, may have more or less significant impact on Member States' asylum practices, depending on the extent to which the political, administrative and judicial authorities avail themselves of the optional elements and the ambiguities of the various Directive provisions. As regards the latter, preliminary ruling references from domestic courts to the EU Court of Justice must be considered decisive to the settlement of interpretation divergences, and thereby indirectly to the full harmonisation of asylum law.

Notably, however, the applicable criteria for requesting such rulings within the area of immigration and asylum law may have been counterproductive to the effective harmonisation of the interpretation of Directives and other legislative acts. There seems to be no doubt that the modifications of the general criteria for submitting requests for preliminary rulings, as adopted by the Amsterdam Treaty,[29] may have reduced the likelihood that relevant issues of interpretation of the asylum Directives would find their way to clarification and, consequently, to a harmonised legal practice across Member States. Conversely, the abandonment of that modification by the Lisbon Treaty should be an important step towards more genuine harmonisation of the interpretation, since under the new TFEU system domestic courts shall request preliminary rulings of asylum Directives under the ordinary criteria for such references.[30]

Nonetheless, even under the ordinary system for domestic courts' referral of cases for preliminary rulings it may be a cause for trouble, at least in some

[27] Document COM(2009) 554 final of 21 October 2009, Proposal for a Directive of the European Parliament and of the Council on minimum standards on procedures in Member States for granting and withdrawing international protection.

[28] Document COM(2009) 551 final of 21 October 2009, Proposal for a Directive of the European Parliament and of the Council on minimum standards for the qualification and status of third country nationals or stateless persons as beneficiaries of international protection and the content of the protection granted.

[29] Article 68 TEC, as contrasted with the general criteria for preliminary rulings under Article 234 TEC. See, for a critical account, Noll and Vedsted-Hansen 1999, p. 373.

[30] Article 267 TFEU.

Member States, that this may occur less frequently than one would consider ideal for the sake of harmonisation and clarification of interpretation issues pertaining to the various legislative acts. As long as this problem remains unsolved as a general feature of EU law, it may affect the full harmonisation of asylum practices; even more so due to the fact that this is still a relatively new and underdeveloped area of EU law. Furthermore, it is still to be seen which interpretive approach the EU Court of Justice is going to take to the legislative acts concerning asylum and third-country immigration; it is not self-evident that the emphasis put on EU integration and on individual rights in the area of intra-EU migration will be fully upheld in the context of these new legislative competences vis-à-vis non-EU citizens. Other mechanisms for supervision and quality control of Member States' interpretation and application of the asylum Directives, such as those lying with the Commission and possibly with the forthcoming European Asylum Support Office, may therefore be of particular importance in this area.[31]

In any event, domestic courts will still have rather significant influence on the actual presentation of requests for preliminary rulings to the EU Court of Justice, as well as on the subsequent application of the Court's interpretation to the concrete cases. As an example of less than ideal domestic impact in that respect, the first case concerning a preliminary ruling on issues of substantive asylum law is worthwhile mentioning.[32] Here the conduct of the Dutch Council of State both before and after the EU Court proceedings may appear a bit confusing from the perspective of harmonisation of EU law. In its order for reference to the European Court of Justice, the Dutch Council of State indicated a questionable understanding of the scope of protection for asylum applicants according to ECHR Article 3; an early judgment of the European Court of Human Rights concerning *non-refoulement* under Article 3 was subjected to a narrow reading, whereas a recent judgment dissociating itself from that narrow understanding of ECHR Article 3 was held not to have abandoned the more narrow interpretation that had allegedly been adopted in the former case.[33] While this interpretation was indeed neither binding on the EU Court of Justice nor decisive to the specific question of EU law raised before it, the domestic court's indication might be seen as an undue attempt to narrow the interpretation of the Qualification Directive.

In the Dutch authorities' subsequent decision of the case, the Council of State seems to have insisted on its previous legal position concerning the relationship

[31] Document COM (2009) 66 final of 18 February 2009, Proposal for a Regulation of the European Parliament and of the Council establishing a European Asylum Support Office. See also para 6.2.1 of the Stockholm Programme – An open and secure Europe serving and protecting the citizens, adopted by the European Council 10-11 December 2009, OJ 2010 C 115/01.

[32] ECJ, Case C-465/07 of 17 February 2009 in *Elgafaji* [2009] *ECR* I-921. The judgment is discussed in some detail in Sect. 10.5.2, *infra*.

[33] Dutch Council of State, order for reference of 12 October 2007 in the case of *Elgafaji and Elgafaji v. State Secretary for Justice* (quoted in the Council of State judgment of 25 May 2009, no. 200702174/2/V2, para 2.3.4 – unofficial translation).

between Article 15 (c) of the Qualification Directive and ECHR Article 3 that had essentially been turned down by the EU Court of Justice[34]; here again, the Dutch Council of State advanced a narrow and ambiguous understanding of the Strasbourg case law on ECHR Article 3, apparently basing itself on a highly selective reading of the judgment of the EU Court of Justice.[35] The interpretive approach taken by the Dutch authorities in this case cannot be seen as affirmative to the harmonising impact of preliminary rulings of the EU Court of Justice. Rather, the Dutch Council of State might seem to have made itself part of a legal-political game, not so much between the European Court of Human Rights and the EU Court of Justice as between these two European courts and the domestic lawmakers and decision makers at the administrative or judicial level in Member States.

10.4 Application of Substantive Provisions

The third aspect of the interpretation and application of EU asylum norms that can be decisive to the full and effective harmonisation of Member States' asylum practices, thereby also determining the quality of asylum in its regulatory meaning, shall only be briefly outlined here. The concrete application of the substantive norms in the EU asylum Directives, in particular the definitional provisions, may differ due to other circumstances than formal exceptions and derogations from the general standards of the Directives, or the lack of genuine harmonisation of the interpretation of the substantive provisions. It is well known among asylum practitioners that the assessment of evidence and facts is often crucial to the possibility of positive results for asylum applicants. Furthermore, it is widely recognised that the approach to *evidentiary issues* may vary considerably among authorities and individual decision makers; in addition, it is sometimes difficult or even impossible to obtain effective judicial review of administrative decisions concerning such issues.[36]

Let me mention just two aspects of the assessment of facts and evidence in order to illustrate the point that it takes more than legislative and interpretive efforts to secure harmonisation of asylum practice across Member States. First, the collection, assessment and application of country of origin information are often *de facto* decisive to the outcome of potentially large numbers of asylum applications; high professional standards are required of those collecting and assessing the information, and a high level of procedural safeguards in this regard is indispensable, not least in terms of transparency towards the applicants and their

[34] See *supra* n. 32, Sect. 10.3.

[35] Dutch Council of State, judgment of 25 May 2009 in case 200702174/2/V2, para 2.3.8 (unofficial translation).

[36] See generally, Noll 2005.

legal representatives.[37] Second, an important issue in asylum cases is the distinction between *law and facts* in the application of the provisions defining the beneficiaries of international protection; there is an often complex dialectical interaction between these two aspects of the examination of asylum applications.[38] The abstract interpretation of the definitional provisions may delimitate the general and individual facts that will be subject to examination in the concrete cases, just as the presentation of facts may be a major determinant for the actual scope and application of the law as it has been generally interpreted.

These matters cannot be dealt with merely on the basis of positive legislation, if the principled aim is that comparable asylum applications are to be given the same outcome across Member States. Additional attention must be given to *practical*, *organisational* and *cultural* factors influencing asylum practice at the domestic level.[39] Against that background, the prospective establishment of the European Asylum Support Office may prove useful.[40] It is also to be welcomed that the Stockholm Programme foresees the further development of the European Asylum Curriculum and emphasises the enhancement of convergence and quality of asylum decisions with a view to reducing disparities.[41] Given the nature of these issues, the efforts will have to go beyond domestic institutional arrangements. Here again, the *legislative framework* governing the harmonisation process is important, and the complex interaction between such specific legal developments on the one hand, and the organisational arrangements and cultural factors on the other, should be kept in mind.

10.5 The Criteria for Subsidiary Protection—Dynamic Interpretation or Restrictive Application?

10.5.1 Non-refoulement in Accordance with the European Convention on Human Rights

As mentioned above in Sect. 10.2, an element of the EU harmonisation of asylum law has been the adoption of common standards in the Qualification Directive for the recognition of Convention refugee status as well as for the granting of subsidiary protection to third country nationals in need of international protection beyond the scope of the Refugee Convention. The eligibility

[37] Cf., Gyulai 2007.

[38] Cf., Vedsted-Hansen 2005b.

[39] Cf., Lambert 2009 and Lambert 2010.

[40] Document COM(2009) 66 final of 18 February 2009, Proposal for a Regulation of the European Parliament and of the Council establishing a European Asylum Support Office.

[41] Section 6.2.1 of the Stockholm Programme—An open and secure Europe serving and protecting the citizens, adopted by the European Council 10–11 December 2009, *supra* n. 31.

criteria for subsidiary protection beneficiaries are partly based on Member States' existing *non-refoulement* obligations under international human rights law, in particular the ECHR.[42] Whereas the Qualification Directive generally requires applicants for subsidiary protection to be facing a real risk of suffering serious harm,[43] the Directive specifically defines such serious harm as (a) death penalty or execution; or (b) torture or inhuman or degrading treatment of punishment of an applicant in the country of origin; or (c) serious and individual threat to a civilian's life or person by reason of indiscriminate violence in situations of international or internal armed conflict.[44]

The first two types of harm have obviously been defined in accordance with ECHR Protocol 6 Article 1 as well as Protocol 13, and Article 3, respectively. Thus, the interpretation of the two provisions in Article 15 (a) and (b) of the Qualification Directive will in all likelihood be directly guided by the relevant case law of the European Court of Human Rights under these ECHR provisions. This seems to follow not only from general tendencies towards harmonised interpretation of the ECHR and similar norms in EU law; interpretive correspondence is particularly warranted within the area of EU asylum law, and the already existing tendency can be expected to be reinforced by the Lisbon Treaty, given that the EU Charter of Fundamental Rights has now achieved binding status with the same legal value as the Treaties.[45]

10.5.2 Protection Against Refoulement in the Context of Indiscriminate Violence

Article 15 (c) of the Qualification Directive has no textual parallel in the ECHR, and both the wording and the structure of Article 15 seem to indicate that Article 15 (c) is meant to extend the scope of subsidiary protection beyond the ECHR obligations reflected in Article 15 (a) and (b). This understanding was confirmed by the EU Court of Justice in a preliminary ruling that clarified the distinction between the ECHR sources of the Qualification Directive and the specific EU criterion for subsidiary protection that has been laid down in Article 15 (c) of the

---

[42] Cf., recital 25 of the Qualification Directive preamble: 'It is necessary to introduce criteria on the basis of which applicants for international protection are to be recognised as eligible for subsidiary protection. Those criteria should be drawn from international obligations under human rights instruments and practices existing in Member States.'

[43] See *supra* n. 1, Sect. 10.1, Article 2 (e).

[44] Ibid., Article 15, cf. Article 2 (e).

[45] TEU Article 6 (1), cf., Articles 19 and 53 of the EU Charter of Fundamental Rights. Needless to say, the possible future accession by the EU to the ECHR according to TEU Article 6 (2) will further bring the interpretation of EU legal acts in line with the ECHR and the case law of the European Court of Human Rights.

Directive. Given that the content of Article 15 (c) is different from ECHR Article 3, this Directive provision must be interpreted independently from Article 15 (a) and (b).[46]

As an implicit effect of its interpretation of Article 15 (c) of the Qualification Directive, the EU Court of Justice may potentially have informed the more general understanding of the requirement of 'individualised risk' that may also be relevant to the interpretation of ECHR Article 3. Thus, in its interpretation of Article 15 (c), the Court discussed whether the existence of a serious and individual threat to the life or person of the applicant for subsidiary protection is subject to the condition that the applicant can adduce evidence that he is *specifically* targeted by reason of factors *particular* to his circumstances. By comparing the various types of serious harm as defined in Article 15 of the Directive, the Court considered Article 15 (a) and (b) as covering situations in which the applicant is 'specifically exposed to the risk of a particular type of harm'.[47] This may suggest two different aspects or meanings of 'individualisation': one implying *particularised risk* due to circumstances particular to the individual applicant; the other aspect referring to the *particular form* of serious harm such as that defined in Article 15 (a) and (b).

As regards Article 15 (c) of the Directive, the EU Court of Justice concluded that the word 'individual' must be understood as covering harm to civilians *irrespective of their identity* where the degree of indiscriminate violence characterising the armed conflict taking place reaches such a high level that substantial grounds are shown for believing that a civilian would, *solely* on account of his presence on the territory of that country or region, face a real risk of being subject to the serious threat referred to in Article 15 (c).[48] While this interpretation is likely to ensure that the provision has its own field of application, the Court also stated that the objective finding of such a risk linked to the *general* situation is not, as a rule, sufficient to establish that the conditions in Article 15 (c) have been met in respect of a specific person. The Directive was, nonetheless, held to allow for the possibility of an *exceptional* situation which would be characterised by such a high degree of risk that substantial grounds would be shown for believing that that person would be subject *individually* to the risk in question.[49]

The Court's observations on 'individualisation' are formally irrelevant to the discussion of the criteria for *non-refoulement* under ECHR Article 3, since the judgment made it clear that Article 15 (c) of the Directive differs from the ECHR and must therefore be interpreted independently. Importantly in this connection, the independent meaning of Article 15 (c) of the Directive cannot be considered weakened, and the interpretation to that effect was not contradicted, by the Court's remark in the judgment, stating that the interpretation of Article 15 (c) thus pronounced by the Court is fully compatible with the ECHR, including the case law of

---

[46] See *supra* n. 32, Sect. 10.3, para 28.

[47] Ibid., paras 30–32.

[48] Ibid., para 35.

[49] Ibid., para 37.

the European Court of Human Rights relating to ECHR Article 3[50]; this final remark must rather be seen as a pure and simple expression of the Court's systematic check of the compatibility of its interpretation of the Directive with the ECHR.[51]

On the other hand, the EU Court of Justice clearly alludes to interpretation of the ECHR by considering the 'broad logic' of Article 15 of the Directive; in that connection the Court stated that the harm defined in Article 15 (a) and (b) requires a 'clear degree of individualisation'.[52] This might be discarded as reflecting an incorrect understanding of the interpretation of ECHR Article 3 in the case law of the European Court of Human Rights. In the light of the passages of the judgment quoted above it is not entirely clear to which form of 'individualisation' the EU Court of Justice was actually referring. Again, this term may be understood as referring either to particular *forms of harm*, or to the *assessment of evidence* pertaining to the individual's exposure to risk.

Further clarification of these concepts may still be needed, as was illustrated by the domestic court's subsequent application of the interpretation given in the preliminary ruling by the EU Court of Justice to the concrete case.[53] In any event, it can be concluded that there is no basis for the assertion that the EU Court of Justice has implicitly reintroduced a substantive 'individualisation' requirement into the interpretation of ECHR Article 3 that would be hard to reconcile with the interpretation of Article 3 as it has been clarified in recent judgments of the European Court of Human Rights.[54]

10.6 Conditions for Determining Asylum in the Future Common European Asylum System

10.6.1 Regulatory Factors Impeding Harmonisation

The exceptions and optional mechanisms discussed above in Sect. 10.2 may be considered as being at variance with the requirement of minimum standards in Article 63 TEC which was the legislative basis of these asylum measures. From a

---

[50] Ibid., para 44.

[51] This reading of para 44 of the judgment is supported by the Court's express statement that the fundamental right guaranteed under ECHR Article 3 forms part of the general principles of Community law, observance of which is ensured by the Court, ibid., para 28.

[52] Ibid., para 38.

[53] Dutch Council of State, judgment of 25 May 2009 in case 200702174/2/V2. For further details, see Sect. 10.3, *supra*.

[54] See, in particular, *Salah Sheekh v. Netherlands*, ECtHR judgment of 11 January 2007; *NA. v. United Kingdom*, ECtHR judgment of 17 July 2008. For an account of this development of the ECtHR case law, and further discussion of the ECJ ruling in *Elgafaji*, see Vedsted-Hansen 2010.

different perspective, they may also be seen as a rather logical consequence of the unanimity requirement initially laid down in Article 67 TEC; every single Member State was in a position to insist on such deference to domestic law, effectively allowing them to uphold particular arrangements, due to the mere possibility of laying down a veto against the Directive proposals. Since there is no longer a requirement of unanimity when amending the Directives, it should in principle become easier to disregard such particularities in the upcoming negotiations of the proposed amendments of the asylum Directives.

By going beyond this explanatory approach, however, it may be possible to identify certain risks or potentials of differentiation between the various regulatory areas that are the subject matter of these Directives. It is in fact quite remarkable how much the degree of formal harmonisation brought about by the asylum Directives varies. Thus, Member States agreed on relatively high and firm protection standards in the Directive on Temporary Protection[55]; admittedly, this Directive is in itself optional in the specific sense that it will only be implemented after a specific Council decision establishing the existence of a mass influx situation and consequently activating the temporary protection mechanisms under the Directive.[56] More importantly, the Qualification Directive may be considered as potentially capable of ensuring effective harmonisation of some of the core definitional issues, as well as certain protection standards that are quite well in line with the Refugee Convention and the human rights obligations underlying subsidiary protection. Member States apparently tend to accept a higher degree of harmonisation in some regulatory areas, while they insist on the deference to domestic law in other areas such as the standards for asylum procedures, thereby in effect undermining the minimum standard harmonisation that was stipulated by Article 63 TEC.

A pragmatic, yet complex combination of *regulatory tradition* and *calculated evasion* might be part of the explanation of this tendency.[57] As regards the definitional provisions, implementation in domestic law occurs indirectly and often opaquely by Member States' asylum authorities, whether administrative or judicial. Thus, the interpretation of the Qualification Directive will often be interacting with the assessment of individual cases in which evidentiary issues play a major role; this is likely to reduce transparency in the application of the Directive insofar as a considerable amount of issues will hardly be apparent as general problems of interpretation. In addition to the interaction between interpretive and evidentiary elements of the decisions, domestic limitations of judicial review may exacerbate the problem of transparency. As a result, it may become difficult to prove if Member States—indirectly, unintentionally or *de facto*—deviate from the minimum definitional standards laid down in the Qualification Directive. Expected *lack of transparency* in the implementation of the Directive might therefore have been

[55] Council Directive 2001/55 of 20 July 2001 (OJ L 212/12 of 7 August 2001).

[56] Ibid., Article 5 (1) and (3).

[57] Cf., Vedsted-Hansen 2005a.

one of the reasons why a relatively high degree of formal harmonisation was accepted in this area which, in any event, to a large extent concerns Member States' already existing international obligations.

To the contrary, the Asylum Procedures Directive governs administrative and procedural matters for which the international obligations appear unspecific or less firm; at the same time, and perhaps more importantly, it will be much more transparent and controllable to which extent the stipulated minimum standards on procedural issues have been implemented at the domestic level. Member States do not have the same *de facto* possibility to evade common standards in this regard, because any administrative or procedural arrangement at variance with the Asylum Procedures Directive will be readily discovered both by the affected individuals and by the EU mechanisms supervising the implementation of EU law. This might explain why Member States insisted on exceptions and optional provisions in order to ensure the possibility of maintaining domestic particularities, by implicit use of the right of veto that was inherent in the unanimity requirement.

10.6.2 The Recast Directive Proposals and the Future Common European Asylum System

To sum up by reference to the three harmonisation parameters suggested in Sect. 10.1, it may be concluded that the likelihood of identical outcomes of comparable asylum applications in different Member States is low, given the significant variations in recognition practices.[58] Fulfilment of genuine minimum protection standards is limited, primarily due to the significant exceptions and derogations permitted by the Qualification Directive, the Reception Conditions Directive and in particular the Asylum Procedures Directive. For much the same reason, the conformity of EU standards and Member States' practices with the obligations under international refugee and human rights law is disputable, not least as regards the inherent differentiation between the various protection categories that may be at variance with international prohibitions of discrimination.

The fact that the requirement of unanimity has been abandoned—initially by Article 67 (5) TEC when amending the asylum Directives, and more generally since the entry into force of the Lisbon Treaty on 1 December 2009—should in principle make it easier to disregard such domestic particularities in the upcoming negotiations of the proposed amendments of the asylum Directives that are going to constitute the second phase of the EU asylum *acquis*. It is now going to become demonstrated in practice whether the formal changes of legislative competences will lead to more effective harmonisation through the adoption of the three recast

[58] Cf., UN High Commissioner for Refugees, Asylum in the European Union. A Study of the Implementation of the Qualification Directive 2007 available at http://www.unhcr.org/refworld/docid/473050632.html (accessed 19 May 2010).

Directives proposed by the Commission: the Reception Conditions Directive,[59] the Asylum Procedures Directive[60] and the Qualification Directive.[61]

As regards the two latter Directives, negotiations are still at the very early stage. Thus, the scope and nature of the amendments of these Directives, so essential to the conditions and criteria for determining asylum in the future Common European Asylum System, cannot yet be meaningfully predicted. Based on the Commission proposals, however, it can be generally posited that the EU legislator has been provided a basis for significantly remedying the failures of harmonisation of asylum procedures by adopting more genuine minimum standards in this area.

In the proposed recast of the Qualification Directive, the Commission has focused primarily on the improvement of protection standards, aiming to remove all the limitations of such standards for subsidiary protection beneficiaries as compared to Convention refugees; as stated in the explanatory memorandum, such an approximation of rights is necessary to ensure full respect of the principle of non-discrimination, and it further corresponds to the call of the Hague Programme for the creation of a uniform status of protection.[62] Indeed, there are also important amendments proposed for some of the definitional provisions of the Qualification Directive; yet the weaknesses in this context, mentioned above in Sect. 10.2—most crucially the *de facto* exclusion grounds at variance with the Refugee Convention—are not affected by the recast Directive proposal; the Commission may have had the reasonable calculation that modification of these provisions would most likely become an unsuccessful undertaking.

10.6.3 Concluding Remarks on the Stockholm Programme

Whatever the impact of the new formal legislative competences, the commitment of Member States to achieve fuller harmonisation will ultimately prove decisive to the outcome of the negotiations on the proposed recast asylum Directives. In that context there is a quite remarkable absence of specific policy directions for the future developments in this regulatory area in the recently adopted Stockholm

---

59 Document COM (2008) 815 final of 3 December 2008, Proposal for a Directive of the European Parliament and of the Council laying down minimum standards for the reception of asylum seekers.

60 Document COM (2009) 554 final of 21 October 2009, Proposal for a Directive of the European Parliament and of the Council on minimum standards on procedures in Member States for granting and withdrawing international protection.

61 Document COM(2009) 551 final of 21 October 2009, Proposal for a Directive of the European Parliament and of the Council on minimum standards for the qualification and status of third country nationals or stateless persons as beneficiaries of international protection and the content of the protection granted.

62 Ibid., p. 8.

Programme setting out the general EU policy objectives pertaining to Area of Freedom, Security and Justice.[63]

The Programme recognises that there are still significant differences between national provisions and their application, and the establishment of a Common European Asylum System is designated as a 'key policy objective' for the EU in order to achieve a higher degree of harmonisation; in that connection it is stated that both common rules and a better and more coherent application of them should prevent or reduce secondary movements within the EU, and increase mutual trust between Member States.[64] The Dublin System is said to remain the 'cornerstone in building the CEAS' as it clearly allocates responsibility for the examination of asylum applications.[65] Thus, the perspectives of the individual asylum seeker, refugee and subsidiary protection beneficiary are not the main focus of the Programme.[66]

In line with this overall policy approach, the Programme contains no concrete provision for the evaluation of *de jure* and *de facto* approximation of Member States' criteria for determining asylum. Similarly, no specific mechanism is stipulated for quality assurance across asylum systems, apart from the reference to 'convergence and ongoing quality' with a view to reducing disparities of asylum decisions as 'another important task' for the future European Asylum Support Office.[67] More generally, the Council and the European Parliament are invited to intensify the efforts to establish a common asylum procedure and a uniform status in accordance with Article 78 TFEU; yet no specific directions are given as to which level, degree and quality of harmonisation should result from this, despite the thorough groundwork tabled by the Commission well in advance of the adoption of the Stockholm Programme.

References

Battjes H (2006) European asylum law and international law. Martinus Nijhoff Publishers, Leiden

Costello C (2005) The asylum procedures directive and the proliferation of safe country practices: deterrence, deflection and the dismantling of international protection? Eur J Migr L 7(1):35–70

Gammeltoft-Hansen T (2011) Access to asylum. International Refugee Law and Globalisation of Migration Control, Cambridge University Press, Cambridge

[63] Stockholm Programme—An open and secure Europe serving and protecting the citizens, adopted by the European Council 10–11 December 2009, *supra* n. 31.

[64] Ibid., Section 6.2.1, p. 69.

[65] Ibid., p. 70.

[66] Importantly, however, the Stockholm Programme, *supra* n. 31, restates the Tampere Conclusion objective of a 'full and inclusive application' of the Refugee Convention, and other relevant international treaties, ibid., p. 69.

[67] Ibid., Section 62.1, p. 70.

Guild E (2001) Between persecution and protection. In: Dashwood A et al (eds) The Cambridge yearbook of European legal studies vol 3. Hart Publishing, Oxford., pp 169–197
Gyulai G (2007) Country information in asylum procedures. Quality as a legal requirement in the EU. http://www.unhcr.org/cgi-bin/texis/vtx/refworld/rwmain?docid=479074032&page=search
Hathaway JC (2003) What's in a label? Eur J Migr L 5(1):1–21
Lambert H (2009) Transnational judicial dialogue, harmonization and the Common European Asylum System. Int Comp L Q 58(3):519–543
Lambert H (2010) The limits of transnational law. Refugee law, policy harmonization and judicial dialogue in the European Union. Cambridge University Press, Cambridge
McAdam J (2007) The qualification directive: an overview. In: Zwaan K (ed) The qualification directive: central themes problem issues, and implementation in selected member states. Wolf Legal Publishers, Nijmegen, pp 7–29
Noll G (ed) (2005) Proof, evidentiary assessment and credibility in asylum procedures. Martinus Nijhoff Publishers, Leiden
Noll G, Vedsted-Hansen J (1999) Non-communitarians: Refugee and asylum policies. In: Alston P (ed) The EU and human rights. Oxford University Press, Oxford, pp 359–408
UN High Commissioner for Refugees (2007) Asylum in the European Union. A study of the implementation of the Qualification Directive. http://www.unhcr.org/refworld/docid/473050632.html. (accessed 19 May 2010)
Vedsted-Hansen J (2005a) Common EU standards on asylum–Optional harmonisation and exclusive procedures? Eur J Migr L 7(4):369–376
Vedsted-Hansen J (2005b) The borderline between questions of fact and questions of law. In: Noll G (ed) Proof, evidentiary assessment and credibility in asylum procedures. Martinus Nijhoff Publishers, Leiden, pp. 57–65
Vedsted-Hansen J (2010) European non-Refoulement revisited. Scand Stud L 55:275–282

Annex 1

32003L0009

Council Directive 2003/9/EC of 27 January 2003 laying down minimum standards for the reception of asylum seekers

Official Journal L 031, 06/02/2003 p. 0018–0025

Council Directive 2003/9/EC

of 27 January 2003

laying down minimum standards for the reception of asylum seekers

THE COUNCIL OF THE EUROPEAN UNION,

Having regard to the Treaty establishing the European Community, and in particular point (1)(b) of the first subparagraph of Article 63 thereof,

Having regard to the proposal from the Commission (1),

Having regard to the opinion of the European Parliament (2),

Having regard to the opinion of the Economic and Social Committee (3),

Having regard to the opinion of the Committee of the Regions (4),

Whereas:

(1) A common policy on asylum, including a Common European Asylum System, is a constituent part of the European Union's objective of progressively establishing an area of freedom, security and justice open to those who, forced by circumstances, legitimately seek protection in the Community.

(2) At its special meeting in Tampere on 15 and 16 October 1999, the European Council agreed to work towards establishing a Common European Asylum System, based on the full and inclusive application of the Geneva Convention relating to the Status of Refugees of 28 July 1951, as supplemented by the New York Protocol of 31 January 1967, thus maintaining the principle of non-refoulement.

(3) The Tampere Conclusions provide that a Common European Asylum System should include, in the short term, common minimum conditions of reception of asylum seekers.

F. A. N. J. Goudappel and H. S. Raulus (eds.), *The future of asylum in the European Union*, DOI: 10.1007/978-90-6704-802-6,

(4) The establishment of minimum standards for the reception of asylum seekers is a further step towards a European asylum policy.

(5) This Directive respects the fundamental rights and observes the principles recognised in particular by the Charter of Fundamental Rights of the European Union. In particular, this Directive seeks to ensure full respect for human dignity and to promote the application of Articles 1 and 18 of the said Charter.

(6) With respect to the treatment of persons falling within the scope of this Directive, Member States are bound by obligations under instruments of international law to which they are party and which prohibit discrimination.

(7) Minimum standards for the reception of asylum seekers that will normally suffice to ensure them a dignified standard of living and comparable living conditions in all Member States should be laid down.

(8) The harmonisation of conditions for the reception of asylum seekers should help to limit the secondary movements of asylum seekers influenced by the variety of conditions for their reception.

(9) Reception of groups with special needs should be specifically designed to meet those needs.

(10) Reception of applicants who are in detention should be specifically designed to meet their needs in that situation.

(11) In order to ensure compliance with the minimum procedural guarantees consisting in the opportunity to contact organisations or groups of persons that provide legal assistance, information should be provided on such organisations and groups of persons.

(12) The possibility of abuse of the reception system should be restricted by laying down cases for the reduction or withdrawal of reception conditions for asylum seekers.

(13) The efficiency of national reception systems and cooperation among Member States in the field of reception of asylum seekers should be secured.

(14) Appropriate coordination should be encouraged between the competent authorities as regards the reception of asylum seekers, and harmonious relationships between local communities and accommodation centres should therefore be promoted.

(15) It is in the very nature of minimum standards that Member States have the power to introduce or maintain more favourable provisions for third country nationals and stateless persons who ask for international protection from a Member State.

(16) In this spirit, Member States are also invited to apply the provisions of this Directive in connection with procedures for deciding on applications for forms of protection other than that emanating from the Geneva Convention for third country nationals and stateless persons.

(17) The implementation of this Directive should be evaluated at regular intervals.

(18) Since the objectives of the proposed action, namely to establish minimum standards on the reception of asylum seekers in Member States, cannot be sufficiently achieved by the Member States and can therefore, by reason of the scale and effects of the proposed action, be better achieved by the Community, the Community may adopt measures in accordance with the principles of subsidiarity as set out in Article 5 of the Treaty. In accordance with the principle of proportionality, as set out in that Article, this Directive does not go beyond what is necessary in order to achieve those objectives.

(19) In accordance with Article 3 of the Protocol on the position of the United Kingdom and Ireland, annexed to the Treaty on European Union and to the Treaty establishing the European Community, the United Kingdom gave notice, by letter of 18 August 2001, of its wish to take part in the adoption and application of this Directive.

(20) In accordance with Article 1 of the said Protocol, Ireland is not participating in the adoption of this Directive. Consequently, and without prejudice to Article 4 of the aforementioned Protocol, the provisions of this Directive do not apply to Ireland.

(21) In accordance with Articles 1 and 2 of the Protocol on the position of Denmark, annexed to the Treaty on European Union and to the Treaty establishing the European Community, Denmark is not participating in the adoption of this Directive and is therefore neither bound by it nor subject to its application,

HAS ADOPTED THIS DIRECTIVE:

CHAPTER I

PURPOSE, DEFINITIONS AND SCOPE

Article 1

Purpose
The purpose of this Directive is to lay down minimum standards for the reception of asylum seekers in Member States.

Article 2

Definitions
For the purposes of this Directive:

(a) "Geneva Convention" shall mean the Convention of 28 July 1951 relating to the status of refugees, as amended by the New York Protocol of 31 January 1967;
(b) "application for asylum" shall mean the application made by a third-country national or a stateless person which can be understood as a request for international protection from a Member State, under the Geneva Convention. Any application for international protection is presumed to be an application for asylum unless a third-country national or a stateless person explicitly requests another kind of protection that can be applied for separately;
(c) "applicant" or "asylum seeker" shall mean a third country national or a stateless person who has made an application for asylum in respect of which a final decision has not yet been taken;
(d) "family members" shall mean, in so far as the family already existed in the country of origin, the following members of the applicant's family who are present in the same Member State in relation to the application for asylum:

  (i) the spouse of the asylum seeker or his or her unmarried partner in a stable relationship, where the legislation or practice of the Member State concerned treats unmarried couples in a way comparable to married couples under its law relating to aliens;
  (ii) the minor children of the couple referred to in point (i) or of the applicant, on condition that they are unmarried and dependent and regardless of whether they were born in or out of wedlock or adopted as defined under the national law;

(e) "refugee" shall mean a person who fulfils the requirements of Article 1(A) of the Geneva Convention;
(f) "refugee status" shall mean the status granted by a Member State to a person who is a refugee and is admitted as such to the territory of that Member State;
(g) "procedures" and "appeals", shall mean the procedures and appeals established by Member States in their national law;
(h) "unaccompanied minors" shall mean persons below the age of eighteen who arrive in the territory of the Member States unaccompanied by an adult responsible for them whether by law or by custom, and for as long as they are not effectively taken into the care of such a person; it shall include minors who are left unaccompanied after they have entered the territory of Member States;
(i) "reception conditions" shall mean the full set of measures that Member States grant to asylum seekers in accordance with this Directive;
(j) "material reception conditions" shall mean the reception conditions that include housing, food and clothing, provided in kind, or as financial allowances or in vouchers, and a daily expenses allowance;

(k) "detention" shall mean confinement of an asylum seeker by a Member State within a particular place, where the applicant is deprived of his or her freedom of movement;
(l) "accommodation centre" shall mean any place used for collective housing of asylum seekers.

Article 3

Scope

1. This Directive shall apply to all third country nationals and stateless persons who make an application for asylum at the border or in the territory of a Member State as long as they are allowed to remain on the territory as asylum seekers, as well as to family members, if they are covered by such application for asylum according to the national law.
2. This Directive shall not apply in cases of requests for diplomatic or territorial asylum submitted to representations of Member States.
3. This Directive shall not apply when the provisions of Council Directive 2001/55/EC of 20 July 2001 on minimum standards for giving temporary protection in the event of a mass influx of displaced persons and on measures promoting a balance of efforts between Member States in receiving such persons and bearing the consequences thereof (5) are applied.
4. Member States may decide to apply this Directive in connection with procedures for deciding on applications for kinds of protection other than that emanating from the Geneva Convention for third-country nationals or stateless persons who are found not to be refugees.

Article 4

More favourable provisions
Member States may introduce or retain more favourable provisions in the field of reception conditions for asylum seekers and other close relatives of the applicant who are present in the same Member State when they are dependent on him or for humanitarian reasons insofar as these provisions are compatible with this Directive.

CHAPTER II

GENERAL PROVISIONS ON RECEPTION CONDITIONS

Article 5

Information

1. Member States shall inform asylum seekers, within a reasonable time not exceeding fifteen days after they have lodged their application for asylum with the competent authority, of at least any established benefits and of the obligations with which they must comply relating to reception conditions.

   Member States shall ensure that applicants are provided with information on organisations or groups of persons that provide specific legal assistance and organisations that might be able to help or inform them concerning the available reception conditions, including health care.

2. Member States shall ensure that the information referred to in para 1 is in writing and, as far as possible, in a language that the applicants may reasonably be supposed to understand. Where appropriate, this information may also be supplied orally.

Article 6

Documentation

1. Member States shall ensure that, within three days after an application is lodged with the competent authority, the applicant is provided with a document issued in his or her own name certifying his or her status as an asylum seeker or testifying that he or she is allowed to stay in the territory of the Member State while his or her application is pending or being examined.

   If the holder is not free to move within all or a part of the territory of the Member State, the document shall also certify this fact.

2. Member States may exclude application of this Article when the asylum seeker is in detention and during the examination of an application for asylum made at the border or within the context of a procedure to decide on the right of the applicant legally to enter the territory of a Member State. In specific cases, during the examination of an application for asylum, Member States may provide applicants with other evidence equivalent to the document referred to in para 1.
3. The document referred to in para 1 need not certify the identity of the asylum seeker.
4. Member States shall adopt the necessary measures to provide asylum seekers with the document referred to in para 1, which must be valid for as long as they are authorised to remain in the territory of the Member State concerned or at the border thereof.
5. Member States may provide asylum seekers with a travel document when serious humanitarian reasons arise that require their presence in another State.

Article 7

Residence and freedom of movement

1. Asylum seekers may move freely within the territory of the host Member State or within an area assigned to them by that Member State. The assigned area shall not affect the unalienable sphere of private life and shall allow sufficient scope for guaranteeing access to all benefits under this Directive.
2. Member States may decide on the residence of the asylum seeker for reasons of public interest, public order or, when necessary, for the swift processing and effective monitoring of his or her application.
3. When it proves necessary, for example for legal reasons or reasons of public order, Member States may confine an applicant to a particular place in accordance with their national law.
4. Member States may make provision of the material reception conditions subject to actual residence by the applicants in a specific place, to be determined by the Member States. Such a decision, which may be of a general nature, shall be taken individually and established by national legislation.
5. Member States shall provide for the possibility of granting applicants temporary permission to leave the place of residence mentioned in paras 2 and 4 and/or the assigned area mentioned in para 1. Decisions shall be taken individually, objectively and impartially and reasons shall be given if they are negative.

   The applicant shall not require permission to keep appointments with authorities and courts if his or her appearance is necessary.

6. Member States shall require applicants to inform the competent authorities of their current address and notify any change of address to such authorities as soon as possible.

Article 8

Families
Member States shall take appropriate measures to maintain as far as possible family unity as present within their territory, if applicants are provided with housing by the Member State concerned. Such measures shall be implemented with the asylum seeker's agreement.

Article 9

Medical screening
Member States may require medical screening for applicants on public health grounds.

Article 10

Schooling and education of minors

1. Member States shall grant to minor children of asylum seekers and to asylum seekers who are minors access to the education system under similar conditions as nationals of the host Member State for so long as an expulsion measure against them or their parents is not actually enforced. Such education may be provided in accommodation centres.

   The Member State concerned may stipulate that such access must be confined to the State education system.
   Minors shall be younger than the age of legal majority in the Member State in which the application for asylum was lodged or is being examined. Member States shall not withdraw secondary education for the sole reason that the minor has reached the age of majority.

2. Access to the education system shall not be postponed for more than three months from the date the application for asylum was lodged by the minor or the minor's parents. This period may be extended to one year where specific education is provided in order to facilitate access to the education system.
3. Where access to the education system as set out in para 1 is not possible due to the specific situation of the minor, the Member State may offer other education arrangements.

Article 11

Employment

1. Member States shall determine a period of time, starting from the date on which an application for asylum was lodged, during which an applicant shall not have access to the labour market.
2. If a decision at first instance has not been taken within one year of the presentation of an application for asylum and this delay cannot be attributed to the applicant, Member States shall decide the conditions for granting access to the labour market for the applicant.
3. Access to the labour market shall not be withdrawn during appeals procedures, where an appeal against a negative decision in a regular procedure has suspensive effect, until such time as a negative decision on the appeal is notified.

4. For reasons of labour market policies, Member States may give priority to EU citizens and nationals of States parties to the Agreement on the European Economic Area and also to legally resident third-country nationals.

Article 12

Vocational training

Member States may allow asylum seekers access to vocational training irrespective of whether they have access to the labour market.

Access to vocational training relating to an employment contract shall depend on the extent to which the applicant has access to the labour market in accordance with Article 11.

Article 13

General rules on material reception conditions and health care

1. Member States shall ensure that material reception conditions are available to applicants when they make their application for asylum.
2. Member States shall make provisions on material reception conditions to ensure a standard of living adequate for the health of applicants and capable of ensuring their subsistence.
   Member States shall ensure that that standard of living is met in the specific situation of persons who have special needs, in accordance with Article 17, as well as in relation to the situation of persons who are in detention.
3. Member States may make the provision of all or some of the material reception conditions and health care subject to the condition that applicants do not have sufficient means to have a standard of living adequate for their health and to enable their subsistence.
4. Member States may require applicants to cover or contribute to the cost of the material reception conditions and of the health care provided for in this Directive, pursuant to the provision of para 3, if the applicants have sufficient resources, for example if they have been working for a reasonable period of time.

   If it transpires that an applicant had sufficient means to cover material reception conditions and health care at the time when these basic needs were being covered, Member States may ask the asylum seeker for a refund.

5. Material reception conditions may be provided in kind, or in the form of financial allowances or vouchers or in a combination of these provisions.

   Where Member States provide material reception conditions in the form of financial allowances or vouchers, the amount thereof shall be determined in accordance with the principles set out in this Article.

Article 14

Modalities for material reception conditions

1. Where housing is provided in kind, it should take one or a combination of the following forms:

   a. premises used for the purpose of housing applicants during the examination of an application for asylum lodged at the border;

b. accommodation centres which guarantee an adequate standard of living;
c. private houses, flats, hotels or other premises adapted for housing applicants.

2. Member States shall ensure that applicants provided with the housing referred to in para 1(a), (b) and (c) are assured:

   a. protection of their family life;
   b. the possibility of communicating with relatives, legal advisers and representatives of the United Nations High Commissioner for Refugees (UNHCR) and non-governmental organisations (NGOs) recognised by Member States.

   Member States shall pay particular attention to the prevention of assault within the premises and accommodation centres referred to in para 1(a) and (b).

3. Member States shall ensure, if appropriate, that minor children of applicants or applicants who are minors are lodged with their parents or with the adult family member responsible for them whether by law or by custom.
4. Member States shall ensure that transfers of applicants from one housing facility to another take place only when necessary. Member States shall provide for the possibility for applicants to inform their legal advisers of the transfer and of their new address.
5. Persons working in accommodation centres shall be adequately trained and shall be bound by the confidentiality principle as defined in the national law in relation to any information they obtain in the course of their work.
6. Member States may involve applicants in managing the material resources and non-material aspects of life in the centre through an advisory board or council representing residents.
7. Legal advisors or counsellors of asylum seekers and representatives of the United Nations High Commissioner for Refugees or non-governmental organisations designated by the latter and recognised by the Member State concerned shall be granted access to accommodation centres and other housing facilities in order to assist the said asylum seekers. Limits on such access may be imposed only on grounds relating to the security of the centres and facilities and of the asylum seekers.
8. Member States may exceptionally set modalities for material reception conditions different from those provided for in this Article, for a reasonable period which shall be as short as possible, when:

   - an initial assessment of the specific needs of the applicant is required,
   - material reception conditions, as provided for in this Article, are not available in a certain geographical area,
   - housing capacities normally available are temporarily exhausted,
   - the asylum seeker is in detention or confined to border posts.

   These different conditions shall cover in any case basic needs.

Article 15

Health care

1. Member States shall ensure that applicants receive the necessary health care which shall include, at least, emergency care and essential treatment of illness.
2. Member States shall provide necessary medical or other assistance to applicants who have special needs.

CHAPTER III

REDUCTION OR WITHDRAWAL OF RECEPTION CONDITIONS

Article 16

Reduction or withdrawal of reception conditions

1. Member States may reduce or withdraw reception conditions in the following cases:

   a. where an asylum seeker:

      - abandons the place of residence determined by the competent authority without informing it or, if requested, without permission, or
      - does not comply with reporting duties or with requests to provide information or to appear for personal interviews concerning the asylum procedure during a reasonable period laid down in national law, or
      - has already lodged an application in the same Member State.

      When the applicant is traced or voluntarily reports to the competent authority, a duly motivated decision, based on the reasons for the disappearance, shall be taken on the reinstallation of the grant of some or all of the reception conditions;

   b. where an applicant has concealed financial resources and has therefore unduly benefited from material reception conditions.

   If it transpires that an applicant had sufficient means to cover material reception conditions and health care at the time when these basic needs were being covered, Member States may ask the asylum seeker for a refund.

2. Member States may refuse conditions in cases where an asylum seeker has failed to demonstrate that the asylum claim was made as soon as reasonably practicable after arrival in that Member State.
3. Member States may determine sanctions applicable to serious breaching of the rules of the accommodation centres as well as to seriously violent behaviour.
4. Decisions for reduction, withdrawal or refusal of reception conditions or sanc-tions referred to in paras 1, 2 and 3 shall be taken individually, objectively and impartially and reasons shall be given. Decisions shall be based on the particular situation of the person concerned, especially with regard to persons covered by Article 17, taking into account the principle of proportionality. Member States shall under all circumstances ensure access to emergency health care.
5. Member States shall ensure that material reception conditions are not withdrawn or reduced before a negative decision is taken.

CHAPTER IV

PROVISIONS FOR PERSONS WITH SPECIAL NEEDS

Article 17

General principle

1. Member States shall take into account the specific situation of vulnerable persons such as minors, unaccompanied minors, disabled people, elderly people, pregnant women, single parents with minor children and persons who have been subjected to torture, rape or other serious forms of psychological, physical or sexual violence, in the national legislation implementing the provisions of Chapter II relating to material reception conditions and health care.
2. Paragraph 1 shall apply only to persons found to have special needs after an individual evaluation of their situation.

Article 18

Minors

1. The best interests of the child shall be a primary consideration for Member States when implementing the provisions of this Directive that involve minors.
2. Member States shall ensure access to rehabilitation services for minors who have been victims of any form of abuse, neglect, exploitation, torture or cruel, inhuman and degrading treatment, or who have suffered from armed conflicts, and ensure that appropriate mental health care is developed and qualified counselling is provided when needed.

Article 19

Unaccompanied minors

1. Member States shall as soon as possible take measures to ensure the necessary representation of unaccompanied minors by legal guardianship or, where necessary, representation by an organisation which is responsible for the care and well-being of minors, or by any other appropriate representation. Regular assessments shall be made by the appropriate authorities.
2. Unaccompanied minors who make an application for asylum shall, from the moment they are admitted to the territory to the moment they are obliged to leave the host Member State in which the application for asylum was made or is being examined, be placed:

   a. with adult relatives;
   b. with a foster-family;
   c. in accommodation centres with special provisions for minors;
   d. in other accommodation suitable for minors.

   Member States may place unaccompanied minors aged 16 or over in accommodation centres for adult asylum seekers.
   As far as possible, siblings shall be kept together, taking into account the best interests of the minor concerned and, in particular, his or her age and degree of maturity. Changes of residence of unaccompanied minors shall be limited to a minimum.

3. Member States, protecting the unaccompanied minor's best interests, shall endeavour to trace the members of his or her family as soon as possible. In cases where there may be a threat to the life or integrity of the minor or his or her close relatives, particularly if they have remained in the country of origin, care must be taken to ensure that the collection, processing and circulation of information concerning those persons is undertaken on a confidential basis, so as to avoid jeopardising their safety.
4. Those working with unaccompanied minors shall have had or receive appropriate training concerning their needs, and shall be bound by the confidentiality principle as defined in the national law, in relation to any information they obtain in the course of their work.

Article 20

Victims of torture and violence
Member States shall ensure that, if necessary, persons who have been subjected to torture, rape or other serious acts of violence receive the necessary treatment of damages caused by the aforementioned acts.

CHAPTER V

APPEALS

Article 21

Appeals

1. Member States shall ensure that negative decisions relating to the granting of benefits under this Directive or decisions taken under Article 7 which individually affect asylum seekers may be the subject of an appeal within the procedures laid down in the national law. At least in the last instance the possibility of an appeal or a review before a judicial body shall be granted.
2. Procedures for access to legal assistance in such cases shall be laid down in national law.

CHAPTER VI

ACTIONS TO IMPROVE THE EFFICIENCY OF THE RECEPTION SYSTEM

Article 22

Cooperation
Member States shall regularly inform the Commission on the data concerning the number of persons, broken down by sex and age, covered by reception conditions and provide full information on the type, name and format of the documents provided for by Article 6.

Article 23

Guidance, monitoring and control system
Member States shall, with due respect to their constitutional structure, ensure that appropriate guidance, monitoring and control of the level of reception conditions are established.

Article 24

Staff and resources

1. Member States shall take appropriate measures to ensure that authorities and other organisations implementing this Directive have received the necessary basic training with respect to the needs of both male and female applicants.
2. Member States shall allocate the necessary resources in connection with the national provisions enacted to implement this Directive.

CHAPTER VII

FINAL PROVISIONS

Article 25

Reports
By 6 August 2006, the Commission shall report to the European Parliament and the Council on the application of this Directive and shall propose any amendments that are necessary.

Member States shall send the Commission all the information that is appropriate for drawing up the report, including the statistical data provided for by Article 22 by 6 February 2006.
After presenting the report, the Commission shall report to the European Parliament and the Council on the application of this Directive at least every five years.

Article 26

Transposition

1. Member States shall bring into force the laws, regulations and administrative provisions necessary to comply with this Directive by 6 February 2005. They shall forthwith inform the Commission thereof.

   When the Member States adopt these measures, they shall contain a reference to this Directive or shall be accompanied by such a reference on the occasion of their official publication. Member States shall determine how such a reference is to be made.

2. Member States shall communicate to the Commission the text of the provisions of national law which they adopt in the field relating to the enforcement of this Directive.

Article 27

Entry into force
This Directive shall enter into force on the day of its publication in the Official Journal of the European Union.

Article 28

Addressees
This Directive is addressed to the Member States in accordance with the Treaty establishing the European Union.

Done at Brussels, 27 January 2003.
For the Council
The President
G. Papandreou

1. OJ C 213 E, 31.7.2001, p. 286.
2. Opinion delivered on 25 April 2002 (not yet published in the Official Journal).
3. OJ C 48, 21.2.2002, p. 63.
4. OJ C 107, 3.5.2002, p. 85.
5. OJ L 212, 7.8.2001, p. 12.

Annex 2

32004L0083

Council Directive 2004/83/EC of 29 April 2004 on minimum standards for the qualification and status of third country nationals or stateless persons as refugees or as persons who otherwise need international protection and the content of the protection granted

Official Journal L 304, 30/09/2004 p. 0012–0023

Council Directive 2004/83/EC of 29 April 2004 on minimum standards for the qualification and status of third country nationals or stateless persons as refugees or as persons who otherwise need international protection and the content of the protection granted

THE COUNCIL OF THE EUROPEAN UNION,

Having regard to the Treaty establishing the European Community, and in particular points 1(c), 2(a) and 3(a) of Article 63 thereof,
Having regard to the proposal from the Commission (1),

Having regard to the opinion of the European Parliament (2),

Having regard to the opinion of the European Economic and Social Committee (3),

Having regard to the opinion of the Committee of the Regions (4),

Whereas:

1. A common policy on asylum, including a Common European Asylum System, is a constituent part of the European Union's objective of progressively establishing an area of freedom, security and justice open to those who, forced by circumstances, legitimately seek protection in the Community.
2. The European Council at its special meeting in Tampere on 15 and 16 October 1999 agreed to work towards establishing a Common European Asylum System, based on the full and inclusive application of the Geneva Convention relating to the Status of Refugees of 28 July 1951 (Geneva Convention), as supplemented by the New York Protocol of 31 January 1967 (Protocol), thus affirming the principle of non-refoulement and ensuring that nobody is sent back to persecution.
3. The Geneva Convention and Protocol provide the cornerstone of the international legal regime for the protection of refugees.
4. The Tampere conclusions provide that a Common European Asylum System should include, in the short term, the approximation of rules on the recognition of refugees and the content of refugee status.

F. A. N. J. Goudappel and H. S. Raulus (eds.), *The future of asylum in the European Union*, DOI: 10.1007/978-90-6704-802-6,

5. The Tampere conclusions also provide that rules regarding refugee status should be complemented by measures on subsidiary forms of protection, offering an appropriate status to any person in need of such protection.
6. The main objective of this Directive is, on the one hand, to ensure that Member States apply common criteria for the identification of persons genuinely in need of international protection, and, on the other hand, to ensure that a minimum level of benefits is available for these persons in all Member States.
7. The approximation of rules on the recognition and content of refugee and subsidiary protection status should help to limit the secondary movements of applicants for asylum between Member States, where such movement is purely caused by differences in legal frameworks.
8. It is in the very nature of minimum standards that Member States should have the power to introduce or maintain more favourable provisions for third country nationals or stateless persons who request international protection from a Member State, where such a request is understood to be on the grounds that the person concerned is either a refugee within the meaning of Article 1(A) of the Geneva Convention, or a person who otherwise needs international protection.
9. Those third country nationals or stateless persons, who are allowed to remain in the territories of the Member States for reasons not due to a need for international protection but on a discretionary basis on compassionate or humanitarian grounds, fall outside the scope of this Directive.
10. This Directive respects the fundamental rights and observes the principles recognised in particular by the Charter of Fundamental Rights of the European Union. In particular this Directive seeks to ensure full respect for human dignity and the right to asylum of applicants for asylum and their accompanying family members.
11. With respect to the treatment of persons falling within the scope of this Directive, Member States are bound by obligations under instruments of international law to which they are party and which prohibit discrimination.
12. The "best interests of the child" should be a primary consideration of Member States when implementing this Directive.
13. This Directive is without prejudice to the Protocol on asylum for nationals of Member States of the European Union as annexed to the Treaty Establishing the European Community.
14. The recognition of refugee status is a declaratory act.
15. Consultations with the United Nations High Commissioner for Refugees may provide valuable guidance for Member States when determining refugee status according to Article 1 of the Geneva Convention.
16. Minimum standards for the definition and content of refugee status should be laid down to guide the competent national bodies of Member States in the application of the Geneva Convention.
17. It is necessary to introduce common criteria for recognising applicants for asylum as refugees within the meaning of Article 1 of the Geneva Convention.
18. In particular, it is necessary to introduce common concepts of protection needs arising sur place; sources of harm and protection; internal protection; and persecution, including the reasons for persecution.
19. Protection can be provided not only by the State but also by parties or organisations, including international organisations, meeting the conditions of this Directive, which control a region or a larger area within the territory of the State.
20. It is necessary, when assessing applications from minors for international protection, that Member States should have regard to child-specific forms of persecution.
21. It is equally necessary to introduce a common concept of the persecution ground "membership of a particular social group".
22. Acts contrary to the purposes and principles of the United Nations are set out in the Preamble and Articles 1 and 2 of the Charter of the United Nations and are, amongst others, embodied in the United Nations Resolutions relating to measures combating terrorism, which declare that "acts, methods and practices of terrorism are contrary to the purposes and principles of the United Nations" and that "knowingly financing, planning and inciting terrorist acts are also contrary to the purposes and principles of the United Nations".

23. As referred to in Article 14, "status" can also include refugee status.
24. Minimum standards for the definition and content of subsidiary protection status should also be laid down. Subsidiary protection should be complementary and additional to the refugee protection enshrined in the Geneva Convention.
25. It is necessary to introduce criteria on the basis of which applicants for international protection are to be recognised as eligible for subsidiary protection. Those criteria should be drawn from international obligations under human rights instruments and practices existing in Member States.
26. Risks to which a population of a country or a section of the population is generally exposed do normally not create in themselves an individual threat which would qualify as serious harm.
27. Family members, merely due to their relation to the refugee, will normally be vulnerable to acts of persecution in such a manner that could be the basis for refugee status.
28. The notion of national security and public order also covers cases in which a third country national belongs to an association which supports international terrorism or supports such an association.
29. While the benefits provided to family members of beneficiaries of subsidiary protection status do not necessarily have to be the same as those provided to the qualifying beneficiary, they need to be fair in comparison to those enjoyed by beneficiaries of subsidiary protection status.
30. Within the limits set out by international obligations, Member States may lay down that the granting of benefits with regard to access to employment, social welfare, health care and access to integration facilities requires the prior issue of a residence permit.
31. This Directive does not apply to financial benefits from the Member States which are granted to promote education and training.
32. The practical difficulties encountered by beneficiaries of refugee or subsidiary protection status concerning the authentication of their foreign diplomas, certificates or other evidence of formal qualification should be taken into account.
33. Especially to avoid social hardship, it is appropriate, for beneficiaries of refugee or subsidiary protection status, to provide without discrimination in the context of social assistance the adequate social welfare and means of subsistence.
34. With regard to social assistance and health care, the modalities and detail of the provision of core benefits to beneficiaries of subsidiary protection status should be determined by national law. The possibility of limiting the benefits for beneficiaries of subsidiary protection status to core benefits is to be understood in the sense that this notion covers at least minimum income support, assistance in case of illness, pregnancy and parental assistance, in so far as they are granted to nationals according to the legislation of the Member State concerned.
35. Access to health care, including both physical and mental health care, should be ensured to beneficiaries of refugee or subsidiary protection status.
36. The implementation of this Directive should be evaluated at regular intervals, taking into consideration in particular the evolution of the international obligations of Member States regarding non-refoulement, the evolution of the labour markets in the Member States as well as the development of common basic principles for integration.
37. Since the objectives of the proposed Directive, namely to establish minimum standards for the granting of international protection to third country nationals and stateless persons by Member States and the content of the protection granted, cannot be sufficiently achieved by the Member States and can therefore, by reason of the scale and effects of the Directive, be better achieved at Community level, the Community may adopt measures, in accordance with the principle of subsidiarity as set out in Article 5 of the Treaty. In accordance with the principle of proportionality, as set out in that Article, this Directive does not go beyond what is necessary in order to achieve those objectives.
38. In accordance with Article 3 of the Protocol on the position of the United Kingdom and Ireland, annexed to the Treaty on European Union and to the Treaty establishing the European Community, the United Kingdom has notified, by letter of 28 January 2002, its wish to take part in the adoption and application of this Directive.

39. In accordance with Article 3 of the Protocol on the position of the United Kingdom and Ireland, annexed to the Treaty on European Union and to the Treaty establishing the European Community, Ireland has notified, by letter of 13 February 2002, its wish to take part in the adoption and application of this Directive.
40. In accordance with Articles 1 and 2 of the Protocol on the position of Denmark, annexed to the Treaty on European Union and to the Treaty establishing the European Community, Denmark is not taking part in the adoption of this Directive and is not bound by it or subject to its application,

HAS ADOPTED THIS DIRECTIVE,

CHAPTER I

GENERAL PROVISIONS

Article 1

Subject matter and scope
The purpose of this Directive is to lay down minimum standards for the qualification of third country nationals or stateless persons as refugees or as persons who otherwise need international protection and the content of the protection granted.

Article 2

Definitions
For the purposes of this Directive:

(a) "international protection" means the refugee and subsidiary protection status as defined in (d) and (f);
(b) "Geneva Convention" means the Convention relating to the status of refugees done at Geneva on 28 July 1951, as amended by the New York Protocol of 31 January 1967;
(c) "refugee" means a third country national who, owing to a well-founded fear of being persecuted for reasons of race, religion, nationality, political opinion or membership of a particular social group, is outside the country of nationality and is unable or, owing to such fear, is unwilling to avail himself or herself of the protection of that country, or a stateless person, who, being outside of the country of former habitual residence for the same reasons as mentioned above, is unable or, owing to such fear, unwilling to return to it, and to whom Article 12 does not apply;
(d) "refugee status" means the recognition by a Member State of a third country national or a stateless person as a refugee;
(e) "person eligible for subsidiary protection" means a third country national or a stateless person who does not qualify as a refugee but in respect of whom substantial grounds have been shown for believing that the person concerned, if returned to his or her country of origin, or in the case of a stateless person, to his or her country of former habitual residence, would face a real risk of suffering serious harm as defined in Article 15, and to whom Article 17(1) and (2) do not apply, and is unable, or, owing to such risk, unwilling to avail himself or herself of the protection of that country;
(f) "subsidiary protection status" means the recognition by a Member State of a third country national or a stateless person as a person eligible for subsidiary protection;
(g) "application for international protection" means a request made by a third country national or a stateless person for protection from a Member State, who can be understood to seek refugee status or subsidiary protection status, and who does not explicitly request another kind of protection, outside the scope of this Directive, that can be applied for separately;

(h) "family members" means, insofar as the family already existed in the country of origin, the following members of the family of the beneficiary of refugee or subsidiary protection status who are present in the same Member State in relation to the application for international protection:

the spouse of the beneficiary of refugee or subsidiary protection status or his or her unmarried partner in a stable relationship, where the legislation or practice of the Member State concerned treats unmarried couples in a way comparable to married couples under its law relating to aliens, the minor children of the couple referred to in the first indent or of the beneficiary of refugee or subsidiary protection status, on condition that they are unmarried and dependent and regardless of whether they were born in or out of wedlock or adopted as defined under the national law;

(i) "unaccompanied minors" means third-country nationals or stateless persons below the age of 18, who arrive on the territory of the Member States unaccompanied by an adult responsible for them whether by law or custom, and for as long as they are not effectively taken into the care of such a person; it includes minors who are left unaccompanied after they have entered the territory of the Member States;

(j) "residence permit" means any permit or authorisation issued by the authorities of a Member State, in the form provided for under that State's legislation, allowing a third country national or stateless person to reside on its territory;

(k) "country of origin" means the country or countries of nationality or, for stateless persons, of former habitual residence.

Article 3

More favourable standards

Member States may introduce or retain more favourable standards for determining who qualifies as a refugee or as a person eligible for subsidiary protection, and for determining the content of international protection, in so far as those standards are compatible with this Directive.

CHAPTER II

ASSESSMENT OF APPLICATIONS FOR INTERNATIONAL PROTECTION

Article 4

Assessment of facts and circumstances

1. Member States may consider it the duty of the applicant to submit as soon as possible all elements needed to substantiate the application for international protection. In cooperation with the applicant it is the duty of the Member State to assess the relevant elements of the application.
2. The elements referred to in of para 1 consist of the applicant's statements and all documentation at the applicants disposal regarding the applicant's age, background, including that of relevant relatives, identity, nationality(ies), country(ies) and place(s) of previous residence, previous asylum applications, travel routes, identity and travel documents and the reasons for applying for international protection.
3. The assessment of an application for international protection is to be carried out on an individual basis and includes taking into account:

   (a) all relevant facts as they relate to the country of origin at the time of taking a decision on the application; including laws and regulations of the country of origin and the manner in which they are applied;
   (b) the relevant statements and documentation presented by the applicant including information on whether the applicant has been or may be subject to persecution or serious harm;

(c) the individual position and personal circumstances of the applicant, including factors such as background, gender and age, so as to assess whether, on the basis of the applicant's personal circumstances, the acts to which the applicant has been or could be exposed would amount to persecution or serious harm;
(d) whether the applicant's activities since leaving the country of origin were engaged in for the sole or main purpose of creating the necessary conditions for applying for international protection, so as to assess whether these activities will expose the applicant to persecution or serious harm if returned to that country;
(e) whether the applicant could reasonably be expected to avail himself of the protection of another country where he could assert citizenship.

4. The fact that an applicant has already been subject to persecution or serious harm or to direct threats of such persecution or such harm, is a serious indication of the applicant's well-founded fear of persecution or real risk of suffering serious harm, unless there are good reasons to consider that such persecution or serious harm will not be repeated.
5. Where Member States apply the principle according to which it is the duty of the applicant to substantiate the application for international protection and where aspects of the applicant's statements are not supported by documentary or other evidence, those aspects shall not need confirmation, when the following conditions are met:

(a) the applicant has made a genuine effort to substantiate his application;
(b) all relevant elements, at the applicant's disposal, have been submitted, and a satisfactory explanation regarding any lack of other relevant elements has been given;
(c) the applicant's statements are found to be coherent and plausible and do not run counter to available specific and general information relevant to the applicant's case;
(d) the applicant has applied for international protection at the earliest possible time, unless the applicant can demonstrate good reason for not having done so; and
(e) the general credibility of the applicant has been established.

Article 5

International protection needs arising sur place

1. A well-founded fear of being persecuted or a real risk of suffering serious harm may be based on events which have taken place since the applicant left the country of origin.
2. A well-founded fear of being persecuted or a real risk of suffering serious harm may be based on activities which have been engaged in by the applicant since he left the country of origin, in particular where it is established that the activities relied upon constitute the expression and continuation of convictions or orientations held in the country of origin.
3. Without prejudice to the Geneva Convention, Member States may determine that an applicant who files a subsequent application shall normally not be granted refugee status, if the risk of persecution is based on circumstances which the applicant has created by his own decision since leaving the country of origin.

Article 6

Actors of persecution or serious harm
Actors of persecution or serious harm include:

(a) the State;
(b) parties or organisations controlling the State or a substantial part of the territory of the State;

(c) non-State actors, if it can be demonstrated that the actors mentioned in (a) and (b), including international organisations, are unable or unwilling to provide protection against persecution or serious harm as defined in Article 7.

Article 7

Actors of protection

1. Protection can be provided by:

   (a) the State; or
   (b) parties or organisations, including international organisations, controlling the State or a substantial
   part of the territory of the State.

2. Protection is generally provided when the actors mentioned in para 1 take reasonable steps to prevent the persecution or suffering of serious harm, inter alia, by operating an effective legal system for the detection, prosecution and punishment of acts constituting persecution or serious harm, and the applicant has access to such protection.
3. When assessing whether an international organisation controls a State or a substantial part of its territory and provides protection as described in para 2, Member States shall take into account any guidance which may be provided in relevant Council acts.

Article 8

Internal protection

1. As part of the assessment of the application for international protection, Member States may determine that an applicant is not in need of international protection if in a part of the country of origin there is no well-founded fear of being persecuted or no real risk of suffering serious harm and the applicant can reasonably be expected to stay in that part of the country.
2. In examining whether a part of the country of origin is in accordance with para 1, Member States shall at the time of taking the decision on the application have regard to the general circumstances prevailing in that part of the country and to the personal circumstances of the applicant.
3. Paragraph 1 may apply notwithstanding technical obstacles to return to the country of origin.

CHAPTER III

QUALIFICATION FOR BEING A REFUGEE

Article 9

Acts of persecution

1. Acts of persecution within the meaning of article 1 A of the Geneva Convention must:

   (a) be sufficiently serious by their nature or repetition as to constitute a severe violation of basic human rights, in particular the rights from which derogation cannot be made under Article 15(2) of the European Convention for the Protection of Human Rights and Fundamental Freedoms; or
   (b) be an accumulation of various measures, including violations of human rights which is sufficiently severe as to affect an individual in a similar manner as mentioned in (a).

2. Acts of persecution as qualified in para 1, can, inter alia, take the form of:

   (a) acts of physical or mental violence, including acts of sexual violence;
   (b) legal, administrative, police, and/or judicial measures which are in them-selves discriminatory or which are implemented in a discriminatory manner;
   (c) prosecution or punishment, which is disproportionate or discriminatory;
   (d) denial of judicial redress resulting in a disproportionate or discriminatory punishment;
   (e) prosecution or punishment for refusal to perform military service in a conflict, where performing military service would include crimes or acts falling under the exclusion clauses as set out in Article 12(2);
   (f) acts of a gender-specific or child-specific nature.

3. In accordance with Article 2(c), there must be a connection between the reasons mentioned in Article 10 and the acts of persecution as qualified in para 1.

Article 10

Reasons for persecution

1. Member States shall take the following elements into account when assessing the reasons for persecution:

   (a) the concept of race shall in particular include considerations of colour, descent, or membership of a particular ethnic group;
   (b) the concept of religion shall in particular include the holding of theistic, non-theistic and atheistic beliefs, the participation in, or abstention from, formal worship in private or in public, either alone or in community with others, other religious acts or expressions of view, or forms of personal or communal conduct based on or mandated by any religious belief;
   (c) the concept of nationality shall not be confined to citizenship or lack thereof but shall in particular include membership of a group determined by its cultural, ethnic, or linguistic identity, common geographical or political origins or its relationship with the population of another State;
   (d) a group shall be considered to form a particular social group where in particular:

   members of that group share an innate characteristic, or a common background that cannot be changed, or share a characteristic or belief that is so fundamental to identity or conscience that a person should not be forced to renounce it, and
   that group has a distinct identity in the relevant country, because it is perceived as being different by the surrounding society;
   depending on the circumstances in the country of origin, a particular social group might include a group based on a common characteristic of sexual orientation. Sexual orientation cannot be understood to include acts considered to be criminal in accordance with national law of the Member States: Gender related aspects might be considered, without by themselves alone creating a presumption for the applicability of this Article;

   (e) the concept of political opinion shall in particular include the holding of an opinion, thought or belief on a matter related to the potential actors of persecution mentioned in Article 6 and to their policies or methods, whether or not that opinion, thought or belief has been acted upon by the applicant.

2. When assessing if an applicant has a well-founded fear of being persecuted it is immaterial whether the applicant actually possesses the racial, religious, national, social or political characteristic which attracts the persecution, provided that such a characteristic is attributed to the applicant by the actor of persecution.

Article 11

Cessation

1. A third country national or a stateless person shall cease to be a refugee, if he or she:

(a) has voluntarily re-availed himself or herself of the protection of the country of nationality; or
(b) having lost his or her nationality, has voluntarily re-acquired it; or
(c) has acquired a new nationality, and enjoys the protection of the country of his or her new nationality; or
(d) has voluntarily re-established himself or herself in the country which he or she left or outside which he or she remained owing to fear of persecution; or
(e) can no longer, because the circumstances in connection with which he or she has been recognised as a refugee have ceased to exist, continue to refuse to avail himself or herself of the protection of the country of nationality;
(f) being a stateless person with no nationality, he or she is able, because the circumstances in connection with which he or she has been recognised as a refugee have ceased to exist, to return to the country of former habitual residence.

2. In considering points (e) and (f) of para 1, Member States shall have regard to whether the change of circumstances is of such a significant and non-temporary nature that the refugee's fear of persecution can no longer be regarded as well-founded.

Article 12

Exclusion

1. A third country national or a stateless person is excluded from being a refugee, if:

(a) he or she falls within the scope of Article 1 D of the Geneva Convention, relating to protection or assistance from organs or agencies of the United Nations other than the United Nations High Commissioner for Refugees. When such protection or assistance has ceased for any reason, without the position of such persons being definitely settled in accordance with the relevant resolutions adopted by the General Assembly of the United Nations, these persons shall ipso facto be entitled to the benefits of this Directive;
(b) he or she is recognised by the competent authorities of the country in which he or she has taken residence as having the rights and obligations which are attached to the possession of the nationality of that country; or rights and obligations equivalent to those.

2. A third country national or a stateless person is excluded from being a refugee where there are serious reasons for considering that:

(a) he or she has committed a crime against peace, a war crime, or a crime against humanity, as defined in the international instruments drawn up to make provision in respect of such crimes;
(b) he or she has committed a serious non-political crime outside the country of refuge prior to his or her admission as a refugee; which means the time of issuing a residence permit based on the granting of refugee status; particularly cruel actions, even if committed with an allegedly political objective, may be classified as serious non-political crimes;
(c) he or she has been guilty of acts contrary to the purposes and principles of the United Nations as set out in the Preamble and Articles 1 and 2 of the Charter of the United Nations.

3. Paragraph 2 applies to persons who instigate or otherwise participate in the commission of the crimes or acts mentioned therein.

CHAPTER IV

REFUGEE STATUS

Article 13

Granting of refugee status
Member States shall grant refugee status to a third country national or a stateless person, who qualifies as a refugee in accordance with Chapters II and III.

Article 14

Revocation of, ending of or refusal to renew refugee status

1. Concerning applications for international protection filed after the entry into force of this Directive, Member States shall revoke, end or refuse to renew the refugee status of a third country national or a stateless person granted by a governmental, administrative, judicial or quasi-judicial body, if he or she has ceased to be a refugee in accordance with Article 11.
2. Without prejudice to the duty of the refugee in accordance with Article 4(1) to disclose all relevant facts and provide all relevant documentation at his/her disposal, the Member State, which has granted refugee status, shall on an individual basis demonstrate that the person concerned has ceased to be or has never been a refugee in accordance with para 1 of this Article.
3. Member States shall revoke, end or refuse to renew the refugee status of a third country national or a stateless person, if, after he or she has been granted refugee status, it is established by the Member State concerned that:

   (a) he or she should have been or is excluded from being a refugee in accordance with Article 12;
   (b) his or her misrepresentation or omission of facts, including the use of false documents, were decisive for the granting of refugee status.

4. Member States may revoke, end or refuse to renew the status granted to a refugee by a governmental, administrative, judicial or quasi-judicial body, when:

   (a) there are reasonable grounds for regarding him or her as a danger to the security of the Member State in which he or she is present;
   (b) he or she, having been convicted by a final judgement of a particularly serious crime, constitutes a danger to the community of that Member State.

5. In situations described in para 4, Member States may decide not to grant status to a refugee, where such a decision has not yet been taken.
6. Persons to whom paras 4 or 5 apply are entitled to rights set out in or similar to those set out in Articles 3, 4, 16, 22, 31 and 32 and 33 of the Geneva Convention in so far as they are present in the Member State.

CHAPTER V

QUALIFICATION FOR SUBSIDIARY PROTECTION

Article 15

Serious harm

Serious harm consists of:

(a) death penalty or execution; or
(b) torture or inhuman or degrading treatment or punishment of an applicant in the country of origin; or
(c) serious and individual threat to a civilian's life or person by reason of indiscriminate violence in situations of international or internal armed conflict.

Article 16

Cessation

1. A third country national or a stateless person shall cease to be eligible for subsidiary protection when the circumstances which led to the granting of subsidiary protection status have ceased to exist or have changed to such a degree that protection is no longer required.
2. In applying para 1, Member States shall have regard to whether the change of circumstances is of such a significant and non-temporary nature that the person eligible for subsidiary protection no longer faces a real risk of serious harm.

Article 17

Exclusion

1. A third country national or a stateless person is excluded from being eligible for subsidiary protection where there are serious reasons for considering that:

   (a) he or she has committed a crime against peace, a war crime, or a crime against humanity, as defined in the international instruments drawn up to make provision in respect of such crimes;
   (b) he or she has committed a serious crime;
   (c) he or she has been guilty of acts contrary to the purposes and principles of the United Nations as set out in the Preamble and Articles 1 and 2 of the Charter of the United Nations;
   (d) he or she constitutes a danger to the community or to the security of the Member State in which he or she is present.

2. Paragraph 1 applies to persons who instigate or otherwise participate in the commission of the crimes or acts mentioned therein.
3. Member States may exclude a third country national or a stateless person from being eligible for subsidiary protection, if he or she prior to his or her admission to the Member State has committed one or more crimes, outside the scope of para 1, which would be punishable by imprisonment, had they been committed in the Member State concerned, and if he or she left his or her country of origin solely in order to avoid sanctions resulting from these crimes.

CHAPTER VI

SUBSIDIARY PROTECTION STATUS

Article 18

Granting of subsidiary protection status
Member States shall grant subsidiary protection status to a third country national or a stateless person eligible for subsidiary protection in accordance with Chapters II and V.

Article 19

Revocation of, ending of or refusal to renew subsidiary protection status

1. Concerning applications for international protection filed after the entry into force of this Directive, Member States shall revoke, end or refuse to renew the subsidiary protection status of a third country national or a stateless person granted by a governmental, administrative, judicial or quasi-judicial body, if he or she has ceased to be eligible for subsidiary protection in accordance with Article 16.
2. Member States may revoke, end or refuse to renew the subsidiary protection status of a third country national or a stateless person granted by a governmental, administrative, judicial or quasi-judicial body, if after having been granted subsidiary protection status, he or she should have been excluded from being eligible for subsidiary protection in accordance with Article 17(3).
3. Member States shall revoke, end or refuse to renew the subsidiary protection status of a third country national or a stateless person, if:

   (a) he or she, after having been granted subsidiary protection status, should have been or is excluded from being eligible for subsidiary protection in accordance with Article 17(1) and (2);
   (b) his or her misrepresentation or omission of facts, including the use of false documents, were decisive for the granting of subsidiary protection status.

4. Without prejudice to the duty of the third country national or stateless person in accordance with Article 4(1) to disclose all relevant facts and provide all relevant documentation at his/her disposal, the Member State, which has granted the subsidiary protection status, shall on an individual basis demonstrate that the person concerned has ceased to be or is not eligible for subsidiary protection in accordance with paras 1, 2 and 3 of this Article.

CHAPTER VII

CONTENT OF INTERNATIONAL PROTECTION

Article 20

General rules

1. This Chapter shall be without prejudice to the rights laid down in the Geneva Convention.
2. This Chapter shall apply both to refugees and persons eligible for subsidiary protection unless otherwise indicated.
3. When implementing this Chapter, Member States shall take into account the specific situation of vulnerable persons such as minors, unaccompanied minors, disabled people, elderly people, pregnant women, single parents with minor children and persons who have been subjected to torture, rape or other serious forms of psychological, physical or sexual violence.
4. Paragraph 3 shall apply only to persons found to have special needs after an individual evaluation of their situation.

5. The best interest of the child shall be a primary consideration for Member States when implementing the provisions of this Chapter that involve minors.
6. Within the limits set out by the Geneva Convention, Member States may reduce the benefits of this Chapter, granted to a refugee whose refugee status has been obtained on the basis of activities engaged in for the sole or main purpose of creating the necessary conditions for being recognised as a refugee.
7. Within the limits set out by international obligations of Member States, Member States may reduce the benefits of this Chapter, granted to a person eligible for subsidiary protection, whose subsidiary protection status has been obtained on the basis of activities engaged in for the sole or main purpose of creating the necessary conditions for being recognised as a person eligible for subsidiary protection.

Article 21

Protection from refoulement

1. Member States shall respect the principle of non-refoulement in accordance with their international obligations.
2. Where not prohibited by the international obligations mentioned in para 1, Member States may refoule a refugee, whether formally recognised or not, when:

   (a) there are reasonable grounds for considering him or her as a danger to the security of the Member State in which he or she is present; or
   (b) he or she, having been convicted by a final judgement of a particularly serious crime, constitutes a danger to the community of that Member State.

3. Member States may revoke, end or refuse to renew or to grant the residence permit of (or to) a refugee to whom para 2 applies.

Article 22

Information

Member States shall provide persons recognised as being in need of international protection, as soon as possible after the respective protection status has been granted, with access to information, in a language likely to be understood by them, on the rights and obligations relating to that status.

Article 23

Maintaining family unity

1. Member States shall ensure that family unity can be maintained.
2. Member States shall ensure that family members of the beneficiary of refugee or subsidiary protection status, who do not individually qualify for such status, are entitled to claim the benefits referred to in Articles 24 to 34, in accordance with national procedures and as far as it is compatible with the personal legal status of the family member.

In so far as the family members of beneficiaries of subsidiary protection status are concerned, Member States may define the conditions applicable to such benefits.
In these cases, Member States shall ensure that any benefits provided guarantee an adequate standard of living.

3. Paragraphs 1 and 2 are not applicable where the family member is or would be excluded from refugee or subsidiary protection status pursuant to Chapters III and V.
4. Notwithstanding paras 1 and 2, Member States may refuse, reduce or withdraw the benefits referred therein for reasons of national security or public order.
5. Member States may decide that this Article also applies to other close relatives who lived together as part of the family at the time of leaving the country of origin, and who were wholly or mainly dependent on the beneficiary of refugee or subsidiary protection status at that time.

Article 24

Residence permits

1. As soon as possible after their status has been granted, Member States shall issue to beneficiaries of refugee status a residence permit which must be valid for at least three years and renewable unless compelling reasons of national security or public order otherwise require, and without prejudice to Article 21(3).

   Without prejudice to Article 23(1), the residence permit to be issued to the family members of the beneficiaries of refugee status may be valid for less than three years and renewable.

2. As soon as possible after the status has been granted, Member States shall issue to beneficiaries of subsidiary protection status a residence permit which must be valid for at least one year and renewable, unless compelling reasons of national security or public order otherwise require.

Article 25

Travel document

1. Member States shall issue to beneficiaries of refugee status travel documents in the form set out in the Schedule to the Geneva Convention, for the purpose of travel outside their territory unless compelling reasons of national security or public order otherwise require.
2. Member States shall issue to beneficiaries of subsidiary protection status who are unable to obtain a national passport, documents which enable them to travel, at least when serious humanitarian reasons arise that require their presence in another State, unless compelling reasons of national security or public order otherwise require.

Article 26

Access to employment

1. Member States shall authorise beneficiaries of refugee status to engage in employed or self-employed activities subject to rules generally applicable to the profession and to the public service, immediately after the refugee status has been granted.

2. Member States shall ensure that activities such as employment-related education opportunities for adults, vocational training and practical workplace experience are offered to beneficiaries of refugee status, under equivalent conditions as nationals.
3. Member States shall authorise beneficiaries of subsidiary protection status to engage in employed or self-employed activities subject to rules generally applicable to the profession and to the public service immediately after the subsidiary protection status has been granted. The situation of the labour market in the Member States may be taken into account, including for possible prioritisation of access to employment for a limited period of time to be determined in accordance with national law. Member States shall ensure that the beneficiary of subsidiary protection status has access to a post for which the beneficiary has received an offer in accordance with national rules on prioritisation in the labour market.
4. Member States shall ensure that beneficiaries of subsidiary protection status have access to activities such as employment-related education opportunities for adults, vocational training and practical workplace experience, under conditions to be decided by the Member States.
5. The law in force in the Member States applicable to remuneration, access to social security systems relating to employed or self-employed activities and other conditions of employment shall apply.

Article 27

Access to education

1. Member States shall grant full access to the education system to all minors granted refugee or subsidiary protection status, under the same conditions as nationals.
2. Member States shall allow adults granted refugee or subsidiary protection status access to the general education system, further training or retraining, under the same conditions as third country nationals legally resident.
3. Member States shall ensure equal treatment between beneficiaries of refugee or subsidiary protection status and nationals in the context of the existing recognition procedures for foreign diplomas, certificates and other evidence of formal qualifications.

Article 28

Social welfare

1. Member States shall ensure that beneficiaries of refugee or subsidiary protection status receive, in the Member State that has granted such statuses, the necessary social assistance, as provided to nationals of that Member State.
2. By exception to the general rule laid down in para 1, Member States may limit social assistance granted to beneficiaries of subsidiary protection status to core benefits which will then be provided at the same levels and under the same eligibility conditions as nationals.

Article 29

Health care

1. Member States shall ensure that beneficiaries of refugee or subsidiary protection status have access to health care under the same eligibility conditions as nationals of the Member State that has granted such statuses.
2. By exception to the general rule laid down in para 1, Member States may limit health care granted to beneficiaries of subsidiary protection to core benefits which will then be provided at the same levels and under the same eligibility conditions as nationals.

3. Member States shall provide, under the same eligibility conditions as nationals of the Member State that has granted the status, adequate health care to beneficiaries of refugee or subsidiary protection status who have special needs, such as pregnant women, disabled people, persons who have undergone torture, rape or other serious forms of psychological, physical or sexual violence or minors who have been victims of any form of abuse, neglect, exploitation, torture, cruel, inhuman and degrading treatment or who have suffered from armed conflict.

Article 30

Unaccompanied minors

1. As soon as possible after the granting of refugee or subsidiary protection status Member States shall take the necessary measures, to ensure the representation of unaccompanied minors by legal guardianship or, where necessary, by an organisation responsible for the care and well-being of minors, or by any other appropriate representation including that based on legislation or Court order.
2. Member States shall ensure that the minor's needs are duly met in the implementation of this Directive by the appointed guardian or representative. The appropriate authorities shall make regular assessments.
3. Member States shall ensure that unaccompanied minors are placed either:

   (a) with adult relatives; or
   (b) with a foster family; or
   (c) in centres specialised in accommodation for minors; or
   (d) in other accommodation suitable for minors.

   In this context, the views of the child shall be taken into account in accordance with his or her age and degree of maturity.

4. As far as possible, siblings shall be kept together, taking into account the best interests of the minor concerned and, in particular, his or her age and degree of maturity. Changes of residence of unaccompanied minors shall be limited to a minimum.
5. Member States, protecting the unaccompanied minor's best interests, shall endeavour to trace the members of the minor's family as soon as possible. In cases where there may be a threat to the life or integrity of the minor or his or her close relatives, particularly if they have remained in the country of origin, care must be taken to ensure that the collection, processing and circulation of information concerning those persons is undertaken on a confidential basis.
6. Those working with unaccompanied minors shall have had or receive appropriate training concerning their needs.

Article 31

Access to accommodation

The Member States shall ensure that beneficiaries of refugee or subsidiary protection status have access to accommodation under equivalent conditions as other third country nationals legally resident in their territories.

Article 32

Freedom of movement within the Member State

Member States shall allow freedom of movement within their territory to beneficiaries of refugee or subsidiary protection status, under the same conditions and restrictions as those provided for other third country nationals legally resident in their territories.

Article 33

Access to integration facilities

1. In order to facilitate the integration of refugees into society, Member States shall make provision for integration programmes which they consider to be appropriate or create pre-conditions which guarantee access to such programmes.
2. Where it is considered appropriate by Member States, beneficiaries of subsidiary protection status shall be granted access to integration programmes.

Article 34

Repatriation
Member States may provide assistance to beneficiaries of refugee or subsidiary protection status who wish to repatriate.

CHAPTER VIII

ADMINISTRATIVE COOPERATION

Article 35

Cooperation
Member States shall each appoint a national contact point, whose address they shall communicate to the Commission, which shall communicate it to the other Member States.
Member States shall, in liaison with the Commission, take all appropriate measures to establish direct cooperation and an exchange of information between the competent authorities.

Article 36

Staff
Member States shall ensure that authorities and other organisations implementing this Directive have received the necessary training and shall be bound by the confidentiality principle, as defined in the national law, in relation to any information they obtain in the course of their work.

CHAPTER IX

FINAL PROVISIONS

Article 37

Reports

1. By 10 April 2008, the Commission shall report to the European Parliament and the Council on the application of this Directive and shall propose any amendments that are necessary. These proposals for amendments shall be made by way of priority in relation to Articles 15, 26 and 33. Member States shall send the Commission all the information that is appropriate for drawing up that report by 10 October 2007.
2. After presenting the report, the Commission shall report to the European Parliament and the Council on the application of this Directive at least every five years.

Article 38

Transposition

1. The Member States shall bring into force the laws, regulations and administrative provisions necessary to comply with this Directive before 10 October 2006 . They shall forthwith inform the Commission thereof.

   When the Member States adopt those measures, they shall contain a reference to this Directive or shall be accompanied by such a reference on the occasion of their official publication. The methods of making such reference shall be laid down by Member States.

2. Member States shall communicate to the Commission the text of the provisions of national law which they adopt in the field covered by this Directive.

Article 39

Entry into force
This Directive shall enter into force on the twentieth day following that of its publication in the Official Journal of the European Union.

Article 40

Addressees
This Directive is addressed to the Member States in accordance with the Treaty establishing the European Community.

Done at Luxembourg, 29 April 2004.
For the Council
The President
M. Mc Dowell

(1) OJ C 51 E, 26.2.2002, p. 325.
(2) OJ C 300 E, 11.12.2003, p. 25.
(3) OJ C 221, 17.9.2002, p. 43.
(4) OJ C 278, 14.11.2002, p. 44.

Annex 3

Council Directive 2005/85/EC of 1 December 2005 on minimum standards on procedures in Member States for granting and withdrawing refugee status

Official Journal L 326, 13/12/2005 p. 0013–0034

Council Directive 2005/85/EC

of 1 December 2005

on minimum standards on procedures in Member States for granting and withdrawing refugee status

THE COUNCIL OF THE EUROPEAN UNION,

Having regard to the Treaty establishing the European Community, and in particular point (1)(d) of the first para of Article 63 thereof,

Having regard to the proposal from the Commission [1],

Having regard to the opinion of the European Parliament [2],

Having regard to the opinion of the European Economic and Social Committee [3],

Whereas:

(1) A common policy on asylum, including a Common European Asylum System, is a constituent part of the European Union's objective of establishing progressively an area of freedom, security and justice open to those who, forced by circumstances, legitimately seek protection in the Community.
(2) The European Council, at its special meeting in Tampere on 15 and 16 October 1999, agreed to work towards establishing a Common European Asylum System, based on the full and inclusive application of the Geneva Convention of 28 July 1951 relating to the status of refugees, as amended by the New York Protocol of 31 January 1967 (Geneva Convention), thus affirming the principle of non-refoulement and ensuring that nobody is sent back to persecution.
(3) The Tampere Conclusions provide that a Common European Asylum System should include, in the short term, common standards for fair and efficient asylum procedures in the Member States and, in the longer term, Community rules leading to a common asylum procedure in the European Community.
(4) The minimum standards laid down in this Directive on procedures in Member States for granting or withdrawing refugee status are therefore a first measure on asylum procedures.
(5) The main objective of this Directive is to introduce a minimum framework in the Community on procedures for granting and withdrawing refugee status.

F. A. N. J. Goudappel and H. S. Raulus (eds.), *The future of asylum in the European Union*, DOI: 10.1007/978-90-6704-802-6,

(6) The approximation of rules on the procedures for granting and withdrawing refugee status should help to limit the secondary movements of applicants for asylum between Member States, where such movement would be caused by differences in legal frameworks.
(7) It is in the very nature of minimum standards that Member States should have the power to introduce or maintain more favourable provisions for third country nationals or stateless persons who ask for international protection from a Member State, where such a request is understood to be on the grounds that the person concerned is a refugee within the meaning of Article 1(A) of the Geneva Convention.
(8) This Directive respects the fundamental rights and observes the principles recognised in particular by the Charter of Fundamental Rights of the European Union.
(9) With respect to the treatment of persons falling within the scope of this Directive, Member States are bound by obligations under instruments of international law to which they are party and which prohibit discrimination.
(10) It is essential that decisions on all applications for asylum be taken on the basis of the facts and, in the first instance, by authorities whose personnel has the appropriate knowledge or receives the necessary training in the field of asylum and refugee matters.
(11) It is in the interest of both Member States and applicants for asylum to decide as soon as possible on applications for asylum. The organisation of the processing of applications for asylum should be left to the discretion of Member States, so that they may, in accordance with their national needs, prioritise or accelerate the processing of any application, taking into account the standards in this Directive.
(12) The notion of public order may cover a conviction for committing a serious crime.
(13) In the interests of a correct recognition of those persons in need of protection as refugees within the meaning of Article 1 of the Geneva Convention, every applicant should, subject to certain exceptions, have an effective access to procedures, the opportunity to cooperate and properly communicate with the competent authorities so as to present the relevant facts of his/her case and sufficient procedural guarantees to pursue his/her case throughout all stages of the procedure. Moreover, the procedure in which an application for asylum is examined should normally provide an applicant at least with the right to stay pending a decision by the determining authority, access to the services of an interpreter for submitting his/her case if interviewed by the authorities, the opportunity to communicate with a representative of the United Nations High Commissioner for Refugees (UNHCR) or with any organisation working on its behalf, the right to appropriate notification of a decision, a motivation of that decision in fact and in law, the opportunity to consult a legal adviser or other counsellor, and the right to be informed of his/her legal position at decisive moments in the course of the procedure, in a language he/she can reasonably be supposed to understand.
(14) In addition, specific procedural guarantees for unaccompanied minors should be laid down on account of their vulnerability. In this context, the best interests of the child should be a primary consideration of Member States.
(15) Where an applicant makes a subsequent application without presenting new evidence or arguments, it would be disproportionate to oblige Member States to carry out a new full examination procedure. In these cases, Member States should have a choice of procedure involving exceptions to the guarantees normally enjoyed by the applicant.
(16) Many asylum applications are made at the border or in a transit zone of a Member State prior to a decision on the entry of the applicant. Member States should be able to keep existing procedures adapted to the specific situation of these applicants at the border. Common rules should be defined on possible exceptions made in these circumstances to the guarantees normally enjoyed by applicants. Border procedures should mainly apply to those applicants who do not meet the conditions for entry into the territory of the Member States.
(17) A key consideration for the well-foundedness of an asylum application is the safety of the applicant in his/her country of origin. Where a third country can be regarded as a safe country of origin, Member States should be able to designate it as safe and presume its safety for a particular applicant, unless he/she presents serious counter-indications.

(18) Given the level of harmonisation achieved on the qualification of third country nationals and stateless persons as refugees, common criteria for designating third countries as safe countries of origin should be established.

(19) Where the Council has satisfied itself that those criteria are met in relation to a particular country of origin, and has consequently included it in the minimum common list of safe countries of origin to be adopted pursuant to this Directive, Member States should be obliged to consider applications of persons with the nationality of that country, or of stateless persons formerly habitually resident in that country, on the basis of the rebuttable presumption of the safety of that country. In the light of the political importance of the designation of safe countries of origin, in particular in view of the implications of an assessment of the human rights situation in a country of origin and its implications for the policies of the European Union in the field of external relations, the Council should take any decisions on the establishment or amendment of the list, after consultation of the European Parliament.

(20) It results from the status of Bulgaria and Romania as candidate countries for accession to the European Union and the progress made by these countries towards membership that they should be regarded as constituting safe countries of origin for the purposes of this Directive until the date of their accession to the European Union.

(21) The designation of a third country as a safe country of origin for the purposes of this Directive cannot establish an absolute guarantee of safety for nationals of that country. By its very nature, the assessment underlying the designation can only take into account the general civil, legal and political circumstances in that country and whether actors of persecution, torture or inhuman or degrading treatment or punishment are subject to sanction in practice when found liable in the country concerned. For this reason, it is important that, where an applicant shows that there are serious reasons to consider the country not to be safe in his/her particular circumstances, the designation of the country as safe can no longer be considered relevant for him/her.

(22) Member States should examine all applications on the substance, i.e. assess whether the applicant in question qualifies as a refugee in accordance with Council Directive 2004/83/EC of 29 April 2004 on minimum standards for the qualification and status of third country nationals or stateless persons as refugees or as persons who otherwise need international protection and the content of the protection granted [4], except where the present Directive provides otherwise, in particular where it can be reasonably assumed that another country would do the examination or provide sufficient protection. In particular, Member States should not be obliged to assess the substance of an asylum application where a first country of asylum has granted the applicant refugee status or otherwise sufficient protection and the applicant will be readmitted to this country.

(23) Member States should also not be obliged to assess the substance of an asylum application where the applicant, due to a connection to a third country as defined by national law, can reasonably be expected to seek protection in that third country. Member States should only proceed on this basis where this particular applicant would be safe in the third country concerned. In order to avoid secondary movements of applicants, common principles for the consideration or designation by Member States of third countries as safe should be established.

(24) Furthermore, with respect to certain European third countries, which observe particularly high human rights and refugee protection standards, Member States should be allowed to not carry out, or not to carry out full examination of asylum applications regarding applicants who enter their territory from such European third countries. Given the potential consequences for the applicant of a restricted or omitted examination, this application of the safe third country concept should be restricted to cases involving third countries with respect to which the Council has satisfied itself that the high standards for the safety of the third country concerned, as set out in this Directive, are fulfilled. The Council should take decisions in this matter after consultation of the European Parliament.

(25) It follows from the nature of the common standards concerning both safe third country concepts as set out in this Directive, that the practical effect of the concepts depends on whether the third country in question permits the applicant in question to enter its territory.

(26) With respect to the withdrawal of refugee status, Member States should ensure that persons benefiting from refugee status are duly informed of a possible reconsideration of their status and have the opportunity to submit their point of view before the authorities can take a motivated decision to withdraw their status. However, dispensing with these guarantees should be allowed where the reasons for the cessation of the refugee status is not related to a change of the conditions on which the recognition was based.

(27) It reflects a basic principle of Community law that the decisions taken on an application for asylum and on the withdrawal of refugee status are subject to an effective remedy before a court or tribunal within the meaning of Article 234 of the Treaty. The effectiveness of the remedy, also with regard to the examination of the relevant facts, depends on the administrative and judicial system of each Member State seen as a whole.

(28) In accordance with Article 64 of the Treaty, this Directive does not affect the exercise of the responsibilities incumbent upon Member States with regard to the maintenance of law and order and the safeguarding of internal security.

(29) This Directive does not deal with procedures governed by Council Regulation (EC) No 343/2003 of 18 February 2003 establishing the criteria and mechanisms for determining the Member State responsible for examining an asylum application lodged in one of the Member States by a third-country national [5].

(30) The implementation of this Directive should be evaluated at regular intervals not exceeding two years.

(31) Since the objective of this Directive, namely to establish minimum standards on procedures in Member States for granting and withdrawing refugee status cannot be sufficiently attained by the Member States and can therefore, by reason of the scale and effects of the action, be better achieved at Community level, the Community may adopt measures, in accordance with the principle of subsidiarity as set out in Article 5 of the Treaty. In accordance with the principle of proportionality, as set out in that Article, this Directive does not go beyond what is necessary in order to achieve this objective.

(32) In accordance with Article 3 of the Protocol on the position of the United Kingdom and Ireland, annexed to the Treaty on European Union and to the Treaty establishing the European Community, the United Kingdom has notified, by letter of 24 January 2001, its wish to take part in the adoption and application of this Directive.

(33) In accordance with Article 3 of the Protocol on the position of the United Kingdom and Ireland, annexed to the Treaty on European Union and to the Treaty establishing the European Community, Ireland has notified, by letter of 14 February 2001, its wish to take part in the adoption and application of this Directive.

(34) In accordance with Articles 1 and 2 of the Protocol on the position of Denmark, annexed to the Treaty on European Union and to the Treaty establishing the European Community, Denmark does not take part in the adoption of this Directive and is not bound by it or subject to its application,

HAS ADOPTED THIS DIRECTIVE:

CHAPTER I

GENERAL PROVISIONS

Article 1

Purpose

The purpose of this Directive is to establish minimum standards on procedures in Member States for granting and withdrawing refugee status.

Article 2

Definitions

For the purposes of this Directive:

(a) "Geneva Convention" means the Convention of 28 July 1951 relating to the status of refugees, as amended by the New York Protocol of 31 January 1967;
(b) "application" or "application for asylum" means an application made by a third country national or stateless person which can be understood as a request for international protection from a Member State under the Geneva Convention. Any application for international protection is presumed to be an application for asylum, unless the person concerned explicitly requests another kind of protection that can be applied for separately;
(c) "applicant" or "applicant for asylum" means a third country national or stateless person who has made an application for asylum in respect of which a final decision has not yet been taken;
(d) "final decision" means a decision on whether the third country national or stateless person be granted refugee status by virtue of Directive 2004/83/EC and which is no longer subject to a remedy within the framework of Chapter V of this Directive irrespective of whether such remedy has the effect of allowing applicants to remain in the Member States concerned pending its outcome, subject to Annex III to this Directive;
(e) "determining authority" means any quasi-judicial or administrative body in a Member State responsible for examining applications for asylum and competent to take decisions at first instance in such cases, subject to Annex I;
(f) "refugee" means a third country national or a stateless person who fulfils the requirements of Article 1 of the Geneva Convention as set out in Directive 2004/83/EC;
(g) "refugee status" means the recognition by a Member State of a third country national or stateless person as a refugee;
(h) "unaccompanied minor" means a person below the age of 18 who arrives in the territory of the Member States unaccompanied by an adult responsible for him/her whether by law or by custom, and for as long as he/she is not effectively taken into the care of such a person; it includes a minor who is left unaccompanied after he/she has entered the territory of the Member States;
(i) "representative" means a person acting on behalf of an organisation representing an unaccompanied minor as legal guardian, a person acting on behalf of a national organisation which is responsible for the care and well-being of minors, or any other appropriate representation appointed to ensure his/her best interests;
(j) "withdrawal of refugee status" means the decision by a competent authority to revoke, end or refuse to renew the refugee status of a person in accordance with Directive 2004/83/EC;
(k) "remain in the Member State" means to remain in the territory, including at the border or in transit zones, of the Member State in which the application for asylum has been made or is being examined.

Article 3

Scope

1. This Directive shall apply to all applications for asylum made in the territory, including at the border or in the transit zones of the Member States, and to the withdrawal of refugee status.
2. This Directive shall not apply in cases of requests for diplomatic or territorial asylum submitted to representations of Member States.
3. Where Member States employ or introduce a procedure in which asylum applications are examined both as applications on the basis of the Geneva Convention and as applications for other kinds of international protection given under the circumstances defined by Article 15 of Directive 2004/83/EC, they shall apply this Directive throughout their procedure.

4. Moreover, Member States may decide to apply this Directive in procedures for deciding on applications for any kind of international protection.

Article 4

Responsible authorities

1. Member States shall designate for all procedures a determining authority which will be responsible for an appropriate examination of the applications in accordance with this Directive, in particular Articles 8(2) and 9.

   In accordance with Article 4(4) of Regulation (EC) No 343/2003, applications for asylum made in a Member State to the authorities of another Member State carrying out immigration controls there shall be dealt with by the Member State in whose territory the application is made.

2. However, Member States may provide that another authority is responsible for the purposes of:

   (a) processing cases in which it is considered to transfer the applicant to another State according to the rules establishing criteria and mechanisms for determining which State is responsible for considering an application for asylum, until the transfer takes place or the requested State has refused to take charge of or take back the applicant;
   (b) taking a decision on the application in the light of national security provisions, provided the determining authority is consulted prior to this decision as to whether the applicant qualifies as a refugee by virtue of Directive 2004/83/EC;
   (c) conducting a preliminary examination pursuant to Article 32, provided this authority has access to the applicant's file regarding the previous application;
   (d) processing cases in the framework of the procedures provided for in Article 35(1);
   (e) refusing permission to enter in the framework of the procedure provided for in Article 35(2) to (5), subject to the conditions and as set out therein;
   (f) establishing that an applicant is seeking to enter or has entered into the Member State from a safe third country pursuant to Article 36, subject to the conditions and as set out in that Article.

3. Where authorities are designated in accordance with para 2, Member States shall ensure that the personnel of such authorities have the appropriate knowledge or receive the necessary training to fulfil their obligations when implementing this Directive.

Article 5

More favourable provisions
Member States may introduce or maintain more favourable standards on procedures for granting and withdrawing refugee status, insofar as those standards are compatible with this Directive.

CHAPTER II

BASIC PRINCIPLES AND GUARANTEES

Article 6

Access to the procedure

1. Member States may require that applications for asylum be made in person and/or at a designated place.
2. Member States shall ensure that each adult having legal capacity has the right to make an application for asylum on his/her own behalf.
3. Member States may provide that an application may be made by an applicant on behalf of his/her dependants. In such cases Member States shall ensure that dependant adults consent to the lodging of the application on their behalf, failing which they shall have an opportunity to make an application on their own behalf.

   Consent shall be requested at the time the application is lodged or, at the latest, when the personal interview with the dependant adult is conducted.

4. Member States may determine in national legislation:

   (a) the cases in which a minor can make an application on his/her own behalf;
   (b) the cases in which the application of an unaccompanied minor has to be lodged by a representative as provided for in Article 17(1)(a);
   (c) the cases in which the lodging of an application for asylum is deemed to constitute also the lodging of an application for asylum for any unmarried minor.

5. Member States shall ensure that authorities likely to be addressed by someone who wishes to make an application for asylum are able to advise that person how and where he/she may make such an application and/or may require these authorities to forward the application to the competent authority.

Article 7

Right to remain in the Member State pending the examination of the application

1. Applicants shall be allowed to remain in the Member State, for the sole purpose of the procedure, until the determining authority has made a decision in accordance with the procedures at first instance set out in Chapter III. This right to remain shall not constitute an entitlement to a residence permit.
2. Member States can make an exception only where, in accordance with Articles 32 and 34, a subsequent application will not be further examined or where they will surrender or extradite, as appropriate, a person either to another Member State pursuant to obligations in accordance with a European arrest warrant [6] or otherwise, or to a third country, or to international criminal courts or tribunals.

Article 8

Requirements for the examination of applications

1. Without prejudice to Article 23(4)(i), Member States shall ensure that applications for asylum are neither rejected nor excluded from examination on the sole ground that they have not been made as soon as possible.
2. Member States shall ensure that decisions by the determining authority on applications for asylum are taken after an appropriate examination. To that end, Member States shall ensure that:

   (a) applications are examined and decisions are taken individually, objectively and impartially;
   (b) precise and up-to-date information is obtained from various sources, such as the United Nations High Commissioner for Refugees (UNHCR), as to the general situation prevailing in the

countries of origin of applicants for asylum and, where necessary, in countries through which they have transited, and that such information is made available to the personnel responsible for examining applications and taking decisions;

(c) the personnel examining applications and taking decisions have the knowledge with respect to relevant standards applicable in the field of asylum and refugee law.

3. The authorities referred to in Chapter V shall, through the determining authority or the applicant or otherwise, have access to the general information referred to in para 2(b), necessary for the fulfilment of their task.
4. Member States may provide for rules concerning the translation of documents relevant for the examination of applications.

Article 9

Requirements for a decision by the determining authority

1. Member States shall ensure that decisions on applications for asylum are given in writing.
2. Member States shall also ensure that, where an application is rejected, the reasons in fact and in law are stated in the decision and information on how to challenge a negative decision is given in writing.

   Member States need not state the reasons for not granting refugee status in a decision where the applicant is granted a status which offers the same rights and benefits under national and Community law as the refugee status by virtue of Directive 2004/83/EC. In these cases, Member States shall ensure that the reasons for not granting refugee status are stated in the applicant's file and that the applicant has, upon request, access to his/her file.
   Moreover, Member States need not provide information on how to challenge a negative decision in writing in conjunction with a decision where the applicant has been provided with this information at an earlier stage either in writing or by electronic means accessible to the applicant.

3. For the purposes of Article 6(3), and whenever the application is based on the same grounds, Member States may take one single decision, covering all dependants.

Article 10

Guarantees for applicants for asylum

1. With respect to the procedures provided for in Chapter III, Member States shall ensure that all applicants for asylum enjoy the following guarantees:

   (a) they shall be informed in a language which they may reasonably be supposed to understand of the procedure to be followed and of their rights and obligations during the procedure and the possible consequences of not complying with their obligations and not cooperating with the authorities. They shall be informed of the time-frame, as well as the means at their disposal for fulfilling the obligation to submit the elements as referred to in Article 4 of Directive 2004/83/EC. This information shall be given in time to enable them to exercise the rights guaranteed in this Directive and to comply with the obligations described in Article 11;
   (b) they shall receive the services of an interpreter for submitting their case to the competent authorities whenever necessary. Member States shall consider it necessary to give these

services at least when the determining authority calls upon the applicant to be interviewed as referred to in Articles 12 and 13 and appropriate communication cannot be ensured without such services. In this case and in other cases where the competent authorities call upon the applicant, these services shall be paid for out of public funds;
(c) they shall not be denied the opportunity to communicate with the UNHCR or with any other organisation working on behalf of the UNHCR in the territory of the Member State pursuant to an agreement with that Member State;
(d) they shall be given notice in reasonable time of the decision by the determining authority on their application for asylum. If a legal adviser or other counsellor is legally representing the applicant, Member States may choose to give notice of the decision to him/her instead of to the applicant for asylum;
(e) they shall be informed of the result of the decision by the determining authority in a language that they may reasonably be supposed to understand when they are not assisted or represented by a legal adviser or other counsellor and when free legal assistance is not available. The information provided shall include information on how to challenge a negative decision in accordance with the provisions of Article 9(2).

2. With respect to the procedures provided for in Chapter V, Member States shall ensure that all applicants for asylum enjoy equivalent guarantees to the ones referred to in para 1(b), (c) and (d) of this Article.

Article 11

Obligations of the applicants for asylum

1. Member States may impose upon applicants for asylum obligations to cooperate with the competent authorities insofar as these obligations are necessary for the processing of the application.
2. In particular, Member States may provide that:

(a) applicants for asylum are required to report to the competent authorities or to appear before them in person, either without delay or at a specified time;
(b) applicants for asylum have to hand over documents in their possession relevant to the examination of the application, such as their passports;
(c) applicants for asylum are required to inform the competent authorities of their current place of residence or address and of any changes thereof as soon as possible. Member States may provide that the applicant shall have to accept any communication at the most recent place of residence or address which he/she indicated accordingly;
(d) the competent authorities may search the applicant and the items he/she carries with him/her;
(e) the competent authorities may take a photograph of the applicant; and
(f) the competent authorities may record the applicant's oral statements, provided he/she has previously been informed thereof.

Article 12

Personal interview

1. Before a decision is taken by the determining authority, the applicant for asylum shall be given the opportunity of a personal interview on his/her application for asylum with a person competent under national law to conduct such an interview.

Member States may also give the opportunity of a personal interview to each dependant adult referred to in Article 6(3).
Member States may determine in national legislation the cases in which a minor shall be given the opportunity of a personal interview.

2. The personal interview may be omitted where:

(a) the determining authority is able to take a positive decision on the basis of evidence available; or
(b) the competent authority has already had a meeting with the applicant for the purpose of assisting him/her with completing his/her application and submitting the essential information regarding the application, in terms of Article 4(2) of Directive 2004/83/EC; or
(c) the determining authority, on the basis of a complete examination of information provided by the applicant, considers the application to be unfounded in cases where the circumstances mentioned in Article 23(4)(a), (c), (g), (h) and (j) apply.

3. The personal interview may also be omitted where it is not reasonably practicable, in particular where the competent authority is of the opinion that the applicant is unfit or unable to be interviewed owing to enduring circumstances beyond his/her control. When in doubt, Member States may require a medical or psychological certificate.

Where the Member State does not provide the applicant with the opportunity for a personal interview pursuant to this para, or where applicable, to the dependant, reasonable efforts shall be made to allow the applicant or the dependant to submit further information.

4. The absence of a personal interview in accordance with this Article shall not prevent the determining authority from taking a decision on an application for asylum.
5. The absence of a personal interview pursuant to para 2(b) and (c) and para 3 shall not adversely affect the decision of the determining authority.
6. Irrespective of Article 20(1), Member States, when deciding on the application for asylum, may take into account the fact that the applicant failed to appear for the personal interview, unless he/she had good reasons for the failure to appear.

Article 13

Requirements for a personal interview

1. A personal interview shall normally take place without the presence of family members unless the determining authority considers it necessary for an appropriate examination to have other family members present.
2. A personal interview shall take place under conditions which ensure appropriate confidentiality.
3. Member States shall take appropriate steps to ensure that personal interviews are conducted under conditions which allow applicants to present the grounds for their applications in a comprehensive manner. To that end, Member States shall:

(a) ensure that the person who conducts the interview is sufficiently competent to take account of the personal or general circumstances surrounding the application, including the applicant's cultural origin or vulnerability, insofar as it is possible to do so; and
(b) select an interpreter who is able to ensure appropriate communication between the applicant and the person who conducts the interview. The communication need not necessarily take place in the language preferred by the applicant for asylum if there is another language which he/she may reasonably be supposed to understand and in which he/she is able to communicate.

4. Member States may provide for rules concerning the presence of third parties at a personal interview.
5. This Article is also applicable to the meeting referred to in Article 12(2)(b).

Article 14

Status of the report of a personal interview in the procedure

1. Member States shall ensure that a written report is made of every personal interview, containing at least the essential information regarding the application, as presented by the applicant, in terms of Article 4(2) of Directive 2004/83/EC.
2. Member States shall ensure that applicants have timely access to the report of the personal interview. Where access is only granted after the decision of the determining authority, Member States shall ensure that access is possible as soon as necessary for allowing an appeal to be prepared and lodged in due time.
3. Member States may request the applicant's approval of the contents of the report of the personal interview.

   Where an applicant refuses to approve the contents of the report, the reasons for this refusal shall be entered into the applicant's file.
   The refusal of an applicant to approve the contents of the report shall not prevent the determining authority from taking a decision on his/her application.

4. This Article is also applicable to the meeting referred to in Article 12(2)(b).

Article 15

Right to legal assistance and representation

1. Member States shall allow applicants for asylum the opportunity, at their own cost, to consult in an effective manner a legal adviser or other counsellor, admitted or permitted as such under national law, on matters relating to their asylum applications.
2. In the event of a negative decision by a determining authority, Member States shall ensure that free legal assistance and/or representation be granted on request, subject to the provisions of para 3.
3. Member States may provide in their national legislation that free legal assistance and/or representation is granted:

   (a) only for procedures before a court or tribunal in accordance with Chapter V and not for any onward appeals or reviews provided for under national law, including a rehearing of an appeal following an onward appeal or review; and/or
   (b) only to those who lack sufficient resources; and/or
   (c) only to legal advisers or other counsellors specifically designated by national law to assist and/or represent applicants for asylum; and/or
   (d) only if the appeal or review is likely to succeed.

4. Member States shall ensure that legal assistance and/or representation granted under point (d) is not arbitrarily restricted.
5. Rules concerning the modalities for filing and processing requests for legal assistance and/or representation may be provided by Member States.
6. Member States may also:

   (a) impose monetary and/or time-limits on the provision of free legal assistance and/or representation, provided that such limits do not arbitrarily restrict access to legal assistance and/or representation;
   (b) provide that, as regards fees and other costs, the treatment of applicants shall not be more favourable than the treatment generally accorded to their nationals in matters pertaining to legal assistance.

7. Member States may demand to be reimbursed wholly or partially for any expenses granted if and when the applicant's financial situation has improved considerably or if the decision to grant such benefits was taken on the basis of false information supplied by the applicant.

Article 16

Scope of legal assistance and representation

1. Member States shall ensure that a legal adviser or other counsellor admitted or permitted as such under national law, and who assists or represents an applicant for asylum under the terms of national law, shall enjoy access to such information in the applicant's file as is liable to be examined by the authorities referred to in Chapter V, insofar as the information is relevant to the examination of the application.

   Member States may make an exception where disclosure of information or sources would jeopardise national security, the security of the organisations or person(s) providing the information or the security of the person(s) to whom the information relates or where the investigative interests relating to the examination of applications of asylum by the competent authorities of the Member States or the international relations of the Member States would be compromised. In these cases, access to the information or sources in question shall be available to the authorities referred to in Chapter V, except where such access is precluded in cases of national security.

2. Member States shall ensure that the legal adviser or other counsellor who assists or represents an applicant for asylum has access to closed areas, such as detention facilities and transit zones, for the purpose of consulting that applicant. Member States may only limit the possibility of visiting applicants in closed areas where such limitation is, by virtue of national legislation, objectively necessary for the security, public order or administrative management of the area, or in order to ensure an efficient examination of the application, provided that access by the legal adviser or other counsellor is not thereby severely limited or rendered impossible.
3. Member States may provide rules covering the presence of legal advisers or other counsellors at all interviews in the procedure, without prejudice to this Article or to Article 17(1)(b).
4. Member States may provide that the applicant is allowed to bring with him/her to the personal interview a legal adviser or other counsellor admitted or permitted as such under national law.

   Member States may require the presence of the applicant at the personal interview, even if he/she is represented under the terms of national law by such a legal adviser or counsellor, and may require the applicant to respond in person to the questions asked.
   The absence of a legal adviser or other counsellor shall not prevent the competent authority from conducting the personal interview with the applicant.

Article 17

Guarantees for unaccompanied minors

1. With respect to all procedures provided for in this Directive and without prejudice to the provisions of Articles 12 and 14, Member States shall:

   a. as soon as possible take measures to ensure that a representative represents and/or assists the unaccompanied minor with respect to the examination of the application. This representative can also be the representative referred to in Article 19 of Directive 2003/9/EC of 27 January 2003 laying down minimum standards for the reception of asylum seekers [7];

b. ensure that the representative is given the opportunity to inform the unaccompanied minor about the meaning and possible consequences of the personal interview and, where appropriate, how to prepare himself/herself for the personal interview. Member States shall allow the representative to be present at that interview and to ask questions or make comments, within the framework set by the person who conducts the interview.

Member States may require the presence of the unaccompanied minor at the personal interview, even if the representative is present.

2. Member States may refrain from appointing a representative where the unaccompanied minor:

(a) will in all likelihood reach the age of maturity before a decision at first instance is taken; or
(b) can avail himself, free of charge, of a legal adviser or other counsellor, admitted as such under national law to fulfil the tasks assigned above to the representative; or
(c) is married or has been married.

3. Member States may, in accordance with the laws and regulations in force on 1 December 2005, also refrain from appointing a representative where the unaccompanied minor is 16 years old or older, unless he/she is unable to pursue his/her application without a representative.
4. Member States shall ensure that:
(a) if an unaccompanied minor has a personal interview on his/her application for asylum as referred to in Articles 12, 13 and 14, that interview is conducted by a person who has the necessary knowledge of the special needs of minors;
(b) an official with the necessary knowledge of the special needs of minors prepares the decision by the determining authority on the application of an unaccompanied minor.
5. Member States may use medical examinations to determine the age of unaccompanied minors within the framework of the examination of an application for asylum.

In cases where medical examinations are used, Member States shall ensure that:

(a) unaccompanied minors are informed prior to the examination of their application for asylum, and in a language which they may reasonably be supposed to understand, of the possibility that their age may be determined by medical examination. This shall include information on the method of examination and the possible consequences of the result of the medical examination for the examination of the application for asylum, as well as the consequences of refusal on the part of the unaccompanied minor to undergo the medical examination;
(b) unaccompanied minors and/or their representatives consent to carry out an examination to determine the age of the minors concerned; and
(c) the decision to reject an application for asylum from an unaccompanied minor who refused to undergo this medical examination shall not be based solely on that refusal.

The fact that an unaccompanied minor has refused to undergo such a medical examination shall not prevent the determining authority from taking a decision on the application for asylum.

6. The best interests of the child shall be a primary consideration for Member States when implementing this Article.

Article 18

Detention

1. Member States shall not hold a person in detention for the sole reason that he/she is an applicant for asylum.

2. Where an applicant for asylum is held in detention, Member States shall ensure that there is a possibility of speedy judicial review.

Article 19

Procedure in case of withdrawal of the application

1. Insofar as Member States provide for the possibility of explicit withdrawal of the application under national law, when an applicant for asylum explicitly withdraws his/her application for asylum, Member States shall ensure that the determining authority takes a decision to either discontinue the examination or reject the application.
2. Member States may also decide that the determining authority can decide to discontinue the examination without taking a decision. In this case, Member States shall ensure that the determining authority enters a notice in the applicant's file.

Article 20

Procedure in the case of implicit withdrawal or abandonment of the application

1. When there is reasonable cause to consider that an applicant for asylum has implicitly withdrawn or abandoned his/her application for asylum, Member States shall ensure that the determining authority takes a decision to either discontinue the examination or reject the application on the basis that the applicant has not established an entitlement to refugee status in accordance with Directive 2004/83/EC.

   Member States may assume that the applicant has implicitly withdrawn or abandoned his/her application for asylum in particular when it is ascertained that:

   (a) he/she has failed to respond to requests to provide information essential to his/her application in terms of Article 4 of Directive 2004/83/EC or has not appeared for a personal interview as provided for in Articles 12, 13 and 14, unless the applicant demonstrates within a reasonable time that his/her failure was due to circumstances beyond his control;
   (b) he/she has absconded or left without authorisation the place where he/she lived or was held, without contacting the competent authority within a reasonable time, or he/she has not within a reasonable time complied with reporting duties or other obligations to communicate.

   For the purposes of implementing these provisions, Member States may lay down time-limits or guidelines.

2. Member States shall ensure that the applicant who reports again to the competent authority after a decision to discontinue as referred to in para 1 of this Article is taken, is entitled to request that his/her case be reopened, unless the request is examined in accordance with Articles 32 and 34.

   Member States may provide for a time-limit after which the applicant's case can no longer be re-opened.
   Member States shall ensure that such a person is not removed contrary to the principle of non-refoulement.
   Member States may allow the determining authority to take up the examination at the stage where it was discontinued.

Article 21

The role of UNHCR

1. Member States shall allow the UNHCR:

    (a) to have access to applicants for asylum, including those in detention and in airport or port transit zones;
    (b) to have access to information on individual applications for asylum, on the course of the procedure and on the decisions taken, provided that the applicant for asylum agrees thereto;
    (c) to present its views, in the exercise of its supervisory responsibilities under Article 35 of the Geneva Convention, to any competent authorities regarding individual applications for asylum at any stage of the procedure.

2. Paragraph 1 shall also apply to an organisation which is working in the territory of the Member State concerned on behalf of the UNHCR pursuant to an agreement with that Member State.

Article 22

Collection of information on individual cases
For the purposes of examining individual cases, Member States shall not:

(a) directly disclose information regarding individual applications for asylum, or the fact that an application has been made, to the alleged actor(s) of persecution of the applicant for asylum;
(b) obtain any information from the alleged actor(s) of persecution in a manner that would result in such actor(s) being directly informed of the fact that an application has been made by the applicant in question, and would jeopardise the physical integrity of the applicant and his/her dependants, or the liberty and security of his/her family members still living in the country of origin.

CHAPTER III

PROCEDURES AT FIRST INSTANCE

SECTION I

Article 23

Examination procedure

1. Member States shall process applications for asylum in an examination procedure in accordance with the basic principles and guarantees of Chapter II.
2. Member States shall ensure that such a procedure is concluded as soon as possible, without prejudice to an adequate and complete examination.

    Member States shall ensure that, where a decision cannot be taken within six months, the applicant concerned shall either:

    (a) be informed of the delay; or

(b) receive, upon his/her request, information on the time-frame within which the decision on his/her application is to be expected. Such information shall not constitute an obligation for the Member State towards the applicant concerned to take a decision within that time-frame.

3. Member States may prioritise or accelerate any examination in accordance with the basic principles and guarantees of Chapter II, including where the application is likely to be well-founded or where the applicant has special needs.
4. Member States may also provide that an examination procedure in accordance with the basic principles and guarantees of Chapter II be prioritised or accelerated if:

(a) the applicant, in submitting his/her application and presenting the facts, has only raised issues that are not relevant or of minimal relevance to the examination of whether he/she qualifies as a refugee by virtue of Directive 2004/83/EC; or
(b) the applicant clearly does not qualify as a refugee or for refugee status in a Member State under Directive 2004/83/EC; or
(c) the application for asylum is considered to be unfounded:

i. because the applicant is from a safe country of origin within the meaning of Articles 29, 30 and 31, or
ii. because the country which is not a Member State, is considered to be a safe third country for the applicant, without prejudice to Article 28(1); or

(d) the applicant has misled the authorities by presenting false information or documents or by withholding relevant information or documents with respect to his/her identity and/or nationality that could have had a negative impact on the decision; or
(e) the applicant has filed another application for asylum stating other personal data; or
(f) the applicant has not produced information establishing with a reasonable degree of certainty his/her identity or nationality, or it is likely that, in bad faith, he/she has destroyed or disposed of an identity or travel document that would have helped establish his/her identity or nationality; or
(g) the applicant has made inconsistent, contradictory, improbable or insufficient representations which make his/her claim clearly unconvincing in relation to his/her having been the object of persecution referred to in Directive 2004/83/EC; or
(h) the applicant has submitted a subsequent application which does not raise any relevant new elements with respect to his/her particular circumstances or to the situation in his/her country of origin; or
(i) the applicant has failed without reasonable cause to make his/her application earlier, having had opportunity to do so; or
(j) the applicant is making an application merely in order to delay or frustrate the enforcement of an earlier or imminent decision which would result in his/her removal; or
(k) the applicant has failed without good reason to comply with obligations referred to in Article 4(1) and (2) of Directive 2004/83/EC or in Articles11(2)(a) and (b) and 20(1) of this Directive; or
(l) the applicant entered the territory of the Member State unlawfully or prolonged his/her stay unlawfully and, without good reason, has either not presented himself/herself to the authorities and/or filed an application for asylum as soon as possible, given the circumstances of his/her entry; or
(m) the applicant is a danger to the national security or public order of the Member State, or the applicant has been forcibly expelled for serious reasons of public security and public order under national law; or
(n) the applicant refuses to comply with an obligation to have his/her fingerprints taken in accordance with relevant Community and/or national legislation; or
(o) the application was made by an unmarried minor to whom Article 6(4)(c) applies, after the application of the parents or parent responsible for the minor has been rejected and no relevant new elements were raised with respect to his/her particular circumstances or to the situation in his/her country of origin.

Article 24

Specific procedures

1. Member States may provide for the following specific procedures derogating from the basic principles and guarantees of Chapter II:

   a. a preliminary examination for the purposes of processing cases considered within the framework set out in Section IV;
   b. procedures for the purposes of processing cases considered within the framework set out in Section V.

2. Member States may also provide a derogation in respect of Section VI.

   SECTION II

Article 25

Inadmissible applications

1. In addition to cases in which an application is not examined in accordance with Regulation (EC) No 343/2003, Member States are not required to examine whether the applicant qualifies as a refugee in accordance with Directive 2004/83/EC where an application is considered inadmissible pursuant to this Article.
2. Member States may consider an application for asylum as inadmissible pursuant to this Article if:

   (a) another Member State has granted refugee status;
   (b) a country which is not a Member State is considered as a first country of asylum for the applicant, pursuant to Article 26;
   (c) a country which is not a Member State is considered as a safe third country for the applicant, pursuant to Article 27;
   (d) the applicant is allowed to remain in the Member State concerned on some other grounds and as result of this he/she has been granted a status equivalent to the rights and benefits of the refugee status by virtue of Directive 2004/83/EC;
   (e) the applicant is allowed to remain in the territory of the Member State concerned on some other grounds which protect him/her against refoulement pending the outcome of a procedure for the determination of status pursuant to point (d);
   (f) the applicant has lodged an identical application after a final decision;
   (g) a dependant of the applicant lodges an application, after he/she has in accordance with Article 6(3) consented to have his/her case be part of an application made on his/her behalf, and there are no facts relating to the dependant's situation, which justify a separate application.

Article 26

The concept of first country of asylum
A country can be considered to be a first country of asylum for a particular applicant for asylum if:

(a) he/she has been recognised in that country as a refugee and he/she can still avail himself/herself of that protection; or

(b) he/she otherwise enjoys sufficient protection in that country, including benefiting from the principle of non-refoulement;

provided that he/she will be re-admitted to that country.
In applying the concept of first country of asylum to the particular circumstances of an applicant for asylum Member States may take into account Article 27(1).

Article 27

The safe third country concept

1. Member States may apply the safe third country concept only where the competent authorities are satisfied that a person seeking asylum will be treated in accordance with the following principles in the third country concerned:

   (a) life and liberty are not threatened on account of race, religion, nationality, membership of a particular social group or political opinion;
   (b) the principle of non-refoulement in accordance with the Geneva Convention is respected;
   (c) the prohibition of removal, in violation of the right to freedom from torture and cruel, inhuman or degrading treatment as laid down in international law, is respected; and
   (d) the possibility exists to request refugee status and, if found to be a refugee, to receive protection in accordance with the Geneva Convention.

2. The application of the safe third country concept shall be subject to rules laid down in national legislation, including:

   a. rules requiring a connection between the person seeking asylum and the third country concerned on the basis of which it would be reasonable for that person to go to that country;
   b. rules on the methodology by which the competent authorities satisfy themselves that the safe third country concept may be applied to a particular country or to a particular applicant. Such methodology shall include case-by-case consideration of the safety of the country for a particular applicant and/or national designation of countries considered to be generally safe;
   c. rules in accordance with international law, allowing an individual examination of whether the third country concerned is safe for a particular applicant which, as a minimum, shall permit the applicant to challenge the application of the safe third country concept on the grounds that he/she would be subjected to torture, cruel, inhuman or degrading treatment or punishment.

3. When implementing a decision solely based on this Article, Member States shall:

   a. inform the applicant accordingly; and
   b. provide him/her with a document informing the authorities of the third country, in the language of that country, that the application has not been examined in substance.

4. Where the third country does not permit the applicant for asylum to enter its territory, Member States shall ensure that access to a procedure is given in accordance with the basic principles and guarantees described in Chapter II.
5. Member States shall inform the Commission periodically of the countries to which this concept is applied in accordance with the provisions of this Article.

SECTION III

Article 28

Unfounded applications

1. Without prejudice to Articles 19 and 20, Member States may only consider an application for asylum as unfounded if the determining authority has established that the applicant does not qualify for refugee status pursuant to Directive 2004/83/EC.
2. In the cases mentioned in Article 23(4)(b) and in cases of unfounded applications for asylum in which any of the circumstances listed in Article 23(4)(a) and (c) to (o) apply, Member States may also consider an application as manifestly unfounded, where it is defined as such in the national legislation.

Article 29

Minimum common list of third countries regarded as safe countries of origin

1. The Council shall, acting by a qualified majority on a proposal from the Commission and after consultation of the European Parliament, adopt a minimum common list of third countries which shall be regarded by Member States as safe countries of origin in accordance with Annex II.
2. The Council may, acting by a qualified majority on a proposal from the Commission and after consultation of the European Parliament, amend the minimum common list by adding or removing third countries, in accordance with Annex II. The Commission shall examine any request made by the Council or by a Member State to submit a proposal to amend the minimum common list.
3. When making its proposal under paras 1 or 2, the Commission shall make use of information from the Member States, its own information and, where necessary, information from UNHCR, the Council of Europe and other relevant international organisations.
4. Where the Council requests the Commission to submit a proposal for removing a third country from the minimum common list, the obligation of Member States pursuant to Article 31(2) shall be suspended with regard to this third country as of the day following the Council decision requesting such a submission.
5. Where a Member State requests the Commission to submit a proposal to the Council for removing a third country from the minimum common list, that Member State shall notify the Council in writing of the request made to the Commission. The obligation of this Member State pursuant to Article 31(2) shall be suspended with regard to the third country as of the day following the notification to the Council.
6. The European Parliament shall be informed of the suspensions under paras 4 and 5.
7. The suspensions under paras 4 and 5 shall end after three months, unless the Commission makes a proposal before the end of this period, to withdraw the third country from the minimum common list. The suspensions shall in any case end where the Council rejects a proposal by the Commission to withdraw the third country from the list.
8. Upon request by the Council, the Commission shall report to the European Parliament and the Council on whether the situation of a country on the minimum common list is still in conformity with Annex II. When presenting its report, the Commission may make such recommendations or proposals as it deems appropriate.

Article 30

National designation of third countries as safe countries of origin

1. Without prejudice to Article 29, Member States may retain or introduce legislation that allows, in accordance with Annex II, for the national designation of third countries other than those appearing

on the minimum common list, as safe countries of origin for the purposes of examining applications for asylum. This may include designation of part of a country as safe where the conditions in Annex II are fulfilled in relation to that part.

2. By derogation from para 1, Member States may retain legislation in force on 1 December 2005 that allows for the national designation of third countries, other than those appearing on the minimum common list, as safe countries of origin for the purposes of examining applications for asylum where they are satisfied that persons in the third countries concerned are generally neither subject to:

   (a) persecution as defined in Article 9 of Directive 2004/83/EC; nor
   (b) torture or inhuman or degrading treatment or punishment.

3. Member States may also retain legislation in force on 1 December 2005 that allows for the national designation of part of a country as safe, or a country or part of a country as safe for a specified group of persons in that country, where the conditions in para 2 are fulfilled in relation to that part or group.
4. In assessing whether a country is a safe country of origin in accordance with paras 2 and 3, Member States shall have regard to the legal situation, the application of the law and the general political circumstances in the third country concerned.
5. The assessment of whether a country is a safe country of origin in accordance with this Article shall be based on a range of sources of information, including in particular information from other Member States, the UNHCR, the Council of Europe and other relevant international organisations.
6. Member States shall notify to the Commission the countries that are designated as safe countries of origin in accordance with this Article.

Article 31

The safe country of origin concept

1. A third country designated as a safe country of origin in accordance with either Article 29 or 30 may, after an individual examination of the application, be considered as a safe country of origin for a particular applicant for asylum only if:

   (a) he/she has the nationality of that country; or
   (b) he/she is a stateless person and was formerly habitually resident in that country; and he/she has not submitted any serious grounds for considering the country not to be a safe country of origin in his/her particular circumstances and in terms of his/her qualification as a refugee in accordance with Directive 2004/83/EC.

2. Member States shall, in accordance with para 1, consider the application for asylum as unfounded where the third country is designated as safe pursuant to Article 29.
3. Member States shall lay down in national legislation further rules and modalities for the application of the safe country of origin concept.

SECTION IV

Article 32

Subsequent application

1. Where a person who has applied for asylum in a Member State makes further representations or a subsequent application in the same Member State, that Member State may examine these further

representations or the elements of the subsequent application in the framework of the examination of the previous application or in the framework of the examination of the decision under review or appeal, insofar as the competent authorities can take into account and consider all the elements underlying the further representations or subsequent application within this framework.

2. Moreover, Member States may apply a specific procedure as referred to in para where a person makes a subsequent application for asylum:

   (a) after his/her previous application has been withdrawn or abandoned by virtue of Articles 19 or 20;
   (b) after a decision has been taken on the previous application. Member States may also decide to apply this procedure only after a final decision has been taken.

3. A subsequent application for asylum shall be subject first to a preliminary examination as to whether, after the withdrawal of the previous application or after the decision referred to in para 2(b) of this Article on this application has been reached, new elements or findings relating to the examination of whether he/she qualifies as a refugee by virtue of Directive 2004/83/EC have arisen or have been presented by the applicant.
4. If, following the preliminary examination referred to in para 3 of this Article, new elements or findings arise or are presented by the applicant which significantly add to the likelihood of the applicant qualifying as a refugee by virtue of Directive 2004/83/EC, the application shall be further examined in conformity with Chapter II.
5. Member States may, in accordance with national legislation, further examine a subsequent application where there are other reasons why a procedure has to be re-opened.
6. Member States may decide to further examine the application only if the applicant concerned was, through no fault of his/her own, incapable of asserting the situations set forth in para 3, 4 and 5 of this Article in the previous procedure, in particular by exercising his/her right to an effective remedy pursuant to Article 39.
7. The procedure referred to in this Article may also be applicable in the case of a dependant who lodges an application after he/she has, in accordance with Article 6(3), consented to have his/her case be part of an application made on his/her behalf. In this case the preliminary examination referred to in para 3 of this Article will consist of examining whether there are facts relating to the dependant's situation which justify a separate application.

Article 33

Failure to appear

Member States may retain or adopt the procedure provided for in Article 32 in the case of an application for asylum filed at a later date by an applicant who, either intentionally or owing to gross negligence, fails to go to a reception centre or appear before the competent authorities at a specified time.

Article 34

Procedural rules

1. Member States shall ensure that applicants for asylum whose application is subject to a preliminary examination pursuant to Article 32 enjoy the guarantees provided for in Article 10(1).
2. Member States may lay down in national law rules on the preliminary examination pursuant to Article 32. Those rules may, inter alia:

(a) oblige the applicant concerned to indicate facts and substantiate evidence which justify a new procedure;
(b) require submission of the new information by the applicant concerned within a time-limit after he/she obtained such information;
(c) permit the preliminary examination to be conducted on the sole basis of written submissions without a personal interview.

The conditions shall not render impossible the access of applicants for asylum to a new procedure or result in the effective annulment or severe curtailment of such access.

3. Member States shall ensure that:

(a) the applicant is informed in an appropriate manner of the outcome of the preliminary examination and, in case the application will not be further examined, of the reasons for this and the possibilities for seeking an appeal or review of the decision;
(b) if one of the situations referred to in Article 32(2) applies, the determining authority shall further examine the subsequent application in conformity with the provisions of Chapter II as soon as possible.

SECTION V

Article 35

Border procedures

1. Member States may provide for procedures, in accordance with the basic principles and guarantees of Chapter II, in order to decide at the border or transit zones of the Member State on applications made at such locations.
2. However, when procedures as set out in para 1 do not exist, Member States may maintain, subject to the provisions of this Article and in accordance with the laws or regulations in force on 1 December 2005, procedures derogating from the basic principles and guarantees described in Chapter II, in order to decide at the border or in transit zones as to whether applicants for asylum who have arrived and made an application for asylum at such locations, may enter their territory.
3. The procedures referred to in para 2 shall ensure in particular that the persons concerned:

(a) are allowed to remain at the border or transit zones of the Member State, without prejudice to Article 7;
(b) are be immediately informed of their rights and obligations, as described in Article 10(1) (a);
(c) have access, if necessary, to the services of an interpreter, as described in Article 10(1)(b);
(d) are interviewed, before the competent authority takes a decision in such procedures, in relation to their application for asylum by persons with appropriate knowledge of the relevant standards applicable in the field of asylum and refugee law, as described in Articles 12, 13 and 14;
(e) can consult a legal adviser or counsellor admitted or permitted as such under national law, as described in Article 15(1); and
(f) have a representative appointed in the case of unaccompanied minors, as described in Article 17(1), unless Article 17(2) or (3) applies.

Moreover, in case permission to enter is refused by a competent authority, this competent authority shall state the reasons in fact and in law why the application for asylum is considered as unfounded or as inadmissible.

4. Member States shall ensure that a decision in the framework of the procedures provided for in para 2 is taken within a reasonable time. When a decision has not been taken within four weeks, the applicant for asylum shall be granted entry to the territory of the Member State in order for his/her

application to be processed in accordance with the other provisions of this Directive.

5. In the event of particular types of arrivals, or arrivals involving a large number of third country nationals or stateless persons lodging applications for asylum at the border or in a transit zone, which makes it practically impossible to apply there the provisions of para 1 or the specific procedure set out in paras 2 and 3, those procedures may also be applied where and for as long as these third country nationals or stateless persons are accommodated normally at locations in proximity to the border or transit zone.

SECTION VI

Article 36

The European safe third countries concept

1. Member States may provide that no, or no full, examination of the asylum application and of the safety of the applicant in his/her particular circumstances as described in Chapter II, shall take place in cases where a competent authority has established, on the basis of the facts, that the applicant for asylum is seeking to enter or has entered illegally into its territory from a safe third country according to para 2.
2. A third country can only be considered as a safe third country for the purposes of para 1 where:

    (a) it has ratified and observes the provisions of the Geneva Convention without any geographical limitations;
    (b) it has in place an asylum procedure prescribed by law;
    (c) it has ratified the European Convention for the Protection of Human Rights and Fundamental Freedoms and observes its provisions, including the standards relating to effective remedies; and
    (d) it has been so designated by the Council in accordance with para 3.

3. The Council shall, acting by qualified majority on a proposal from the Commission and after consultation of the European Parliament, adopt or amend a common list of third countries that shall be regarded as safe third countries for the purposes of para 1.
4. The Member States concerned shall lay down in national law the modalities for implementing the provisions of para 1 and the consequences of decisions pursuant to those provisions in accordance with the principle of non-refoulement under the Geneva Convention, including providing for exceptions from the application of this Article for humanitarian or political reasons or for reasons of public international law.
5. When implementing a decision solely based on this Article, the Member States concerned shall:

    (a) inform the applicant accordingly; and
    (b) provide him/her with a document informing the authorities of the third country, in the language of that country, that the application has not been examined in substance.

6. Where the safe third country does not re-admit the applicant for asylum, Member States shall ensure that access to a procedure is given in accordance with the basic principles and guarantees described in Chapter II.
7. Member States which have designated third countries as safe countries in accordance with national legislation in force on 1 December 2005 and on the basis of the criteria in para 2(a), (b) and (c), may apply para 1 to these third countries until the Council has adopted the common list pursuant to para 3.

CHAPTER IV

PROCEDURES FOR THE WITHDRAWAL OF REFUGEE STATUS

Article 37

Withdrawal of refugee status

Member States shall ensure that an examination to withdraw the refugee status of a particular person may commence when new elements or findings arise indicating that there are reasons to reconsider the validity of his/her refugee status.

Article 38

Procedural rules

1. Member States shall ensure that, where the competent authority is considering withdrawing the refugee status of a third country national or stateless person in accordance with Article 14 of Directive 2004/83/EC, the person concerned shall enjoy the following guarantees:

   (a) to be informed in writing that the competent authority is reconsidering his or her qualification for refugee status and the reasons for such a reconsideration; and
   (b) to be given the opportunity to submit, in a personal interview in accordance with Article 10(1)(b) and Articles 12, 13 and 14 or in a written statement, reasons as to why his/her refugee status should not be withdrawn.

   In addition, Member States shall ensure that within the framework of such a procedure:

   (a) the competent authority is able to obtain precise and up-to-date information from various sources, such as, where appropriate, from the UNHCR, as to the general situation prevailing in the countries of origin of the persons concerned; and
   (b) where information on an individual case is collected for the purposes of reconsidering the refugee status, it is not obtained from the actor(s) of persecution in a manner that would result in such actor(s) being directly informed of the fact that the person concerned is a refugee whose status is under reconsideration, nor jeopardise the physical integrity of the person and his/her dependants, or the liberty and security of his/her family members still living in the country of origin.
2. Member States shall ensure that the decision of the competent authority to withdraw the refugee status is given in writing. The reasons in fact and in law shall be stated in the decision and information on how to challenge the decision shall be given in writing.
3. Once the competent authority has taken the decision to withdraw the refugee status, Article 15, para 2, Article 16, para 1 and Article 21 are equally applicable.
4. By derogation to paras 1, 2 and 3 of this Article, Member States may decide that the refugee status shall lapse by law in case of cessation in accordance with Article 11(1)(a) to (d) of Directive 2004/83/EC or if the refugee has unequivocally renounced his/her recognition as a refugee.

CHAPTER V

APPEALS PROCEDURES

Article 39

The right to an effective remedy

1. Member States shall ensure that applicants for asylum have the right to an effective remedy before a court or tribunal, against the following:

   (a) a decision taken on their application for asylum, including a decision:

      (i) to consider an application inadmissible pursuant to Article 25(2),
      (ii) taken at the border or in the transit zones of a Member State as described in Article 35(1),
      (iii) not to conduct an examination pursuant to Article 36;

   (b) a refusal to re-open the examination of an application after its discontinuation pursuant to Articles 19 and 20;
   (c) a decision not to further examine the subsequent application pursuant to Articles 32 and 34;
   (d) a decision refusing entry within the framework of the procedures provided for under Article 35(2);
   (e) a decision to withdraw of refugee status pursuant to Article 38.

2. Member States shall provide for time-limits and other necessary rules for the applicant to exercise his/her right to an effective remedy pursuant to para 1.
3. Member States shall, where appropriate, provide for rules in accordance with their international obligations dealing with:

   (a) the question of whether the remedy pursuant to para 1 shall have the effect of allowing applicants to remain in the Member State concerned pending its outcome;
   (b) the possibility of legal remedy or protective measures where the remedy pursuant to para 1 does not have the effect of allowing applicants to remain in the Member State concerned pending its outcome. Member States may also provide for an ex officio remedy; and
   (c) the grounds for challenging a decision under Article 25(2)(c) in accordance with the methodology applied under Article 27(2)(b) and (c).

4. Member States may lay down time-limits for the court or tribunal pursuant to para 1 to examine the decision of the determining authority.
5. Where an applicant has been granted a status which offers the same rights and benefits under national and Community law as the refugee status by virtue of Directive 2004/83/EC, the applicant may be considered as having an effective remedy where a court or tribunal decides that the remedy pursuant to para 1 is inadmissible or unlikely to succeed on the basis of insufficient interest on the part of the applicant in maintaining the proceedings.
6. Member States may also lay down in national legislation the conditions under which it can be assumed that an applicant has implicitly withdrawn or abandoned his/her remedy pursuant to para 1, together with the rules on the procedure to be followed.

CHAPTER VI

GENERAL AND FINAL PROVISIONS

Article 40

Challenge by public authorities
This Directive does not affect the possibility for public authorities of challenging the administrative and/ or judicial decisions as provided for in national legislation.

Article 41

Confidentiality
Member States shall ensure that authorities implementing this Directive are bound by the confidentiality principle as defined in national law, in relation to any information they obtain in the course of their work.

Article 42

Report
No later than 1 December 2009, the Commission shall report to the European Parliament and the Council on the application of this Directive in the Member States and shall propose any amendments that are necessary. Member States shall send the Commission all the information that is appropriate for drawing up this report. After presenting the report, the Commission shall report to the European Parliament and the Council on the application of this Directive in the Member States at least every two years.

Article 43

Transposition
Member States shall bring into force the laws, regulations and administrative provisions necessary to comply with this Directive by 1 December 2007. Concerning Article 15, Member States shall bring into force the laws, regulations and administrative provisions necessary to comply with this Directive by 1 December 2008. They shall forthwith inform the Commission thereof.

When Member States adopt those provisions, they shall contain a reference to this Directive or shall be accompanied by such a reference on the occasion of their official publication. The methods of making such reference shall be laid down by Member States.

Member States shall communicate to the Commission the text of the provisions of national law which they adopt in the field covered by this Directive.

Article 44

Transition
Member States shall apply the laws, regulations and administrative provisions set out in Article 43 to applications for asylum lodged after 1 December 2007 and to procedures for the withdrawal of refugee status started after 1 December 2007.

Article 45

Entry into force
This Directive shall enter into force on the 20th day following its publication in the Official Journal of the European Union.

Article 46

Addressees

This Directive is addressed to the Member States in conformity with the Treaty establishing the European Community.

Done at Brussels, 1 December 2005.
For the Council
The President
Ashton of Upholland

[1] OJ C 62, 27.2.2001, p. 231 and OJ C 291, 26.11.2002, p. 143.
[2] OJ C 77, 28.3.2002, p. 94.
[3] OJ C 193, 10.7.2001, p. 77. Opinion delivered following non-compulsory consultation.
[4] OJ L 304, 30.9.2004, p. 12.
[5] OJ L 50, 25.2.2003, p. 1.
[6] Council Framework Decision 2002/584/JHA of 13 June 2002 on the European arrest warrant and the surrender procedures between Member States (OJ L 190, 18.7.2002, p. 1).
[7] OJ L 31, 6.2.2003, p. 18.

ANNEX I

Definition of "determining authority"

When implementing the provision of this Directive, Ireland may, insofar as the provisions of section 17(1) of the Refugee Act 1996 (as amended) continue to apply, consider that:

- "determining authority" provided for in Article 2(e) of this Directive shall, insofar as the examination of whether an applicant should or, as the case may be, should not be declared to be a refugee is concerned, mean the Office of the Refugee Applications Commissioner; and
- "decisions at first instance" provided for in Article 2(e) of this Directive shall include recommendations of the Refugee Applications Commissioner as to whether an applicant should or, as the case may be, should not be declared to be a refugee.

Ireland will notify the Commission of any amendments to the provisions of section 17(1) of the Refugee Act 1996 (as amended).

ANNEX II

Designation of safe countries of origin for the purposes of Articles 29 and 30(1)

A country is considered as a safe country of origin where, on the basis of the legal situation, the application of the law within a democratic system and the general political circumstances, it can be shown that there is generally and consistently no persecution as defined in Article 9 of Directive 2004/83/EC, no torture or inhuman or degrading treatment or punishment and no threat by reason of indiscriminate violence in situations of international or internal armed conflict.

In making this assessment, account shall be taken, inter alia, of the extent to which protection is provided against persecution or mistreatment by:

(a) the relevant laws and regulations of the country and the manner in which they are applied;

(b) observance of the rights and freedoms laid down in the European Convention for the Protection of Human Rights and Fundamental Freedoms and/or the International Covenant for Civil and Political Rights and/or the Convention against Torture, in particular the rights from which derogation cannot be made under Article 15(2) of the said European Convention;
(c) respect of the non-refoulement principle according to the Geneva Convention;
(d) provision for a system of effective remedies against violations of these rights and freedoms.

ANNEX III

Definition of "applicant" or "applicant for asylum"

When implementing the provisions of this Directive Spain may, insofar as the provisions of "Ley 30/1992 de Régimen jurídico de las Administraciones Públicas y del Procedimiento Administrativo Común" of 26 November 1992 and "Ley 29/1998 reguladora de la Jurisdicción Contencioso-Administrativa" of 13 July 1998 continue to apply, consider that, for the purposes of Chapter V, the definition of "applicant" or "applicant for asylum" in Article 2(c) of this Directive shall include "recurrente" as established in the abovementioned Acts.

A "recurrente" shall be entitled to the same guarantees as an "applicant" or an "applicant for asylum" as set out in this Directive for the purposes of exercising his/her right to an effective remedy in Chapter V.

Spain will notify the Commission of any relevant amendments to the abovementioned Act.

Index

A
Access to asylum procedure, 7, 9, 11–13, 22–23, 25–26, 28–30, 34, 41, 68, 70, 100, 114, 127, 143
Access to a legal counsel, 128–129
Airports, 22–23, 28–29, 36–38, 41, 47, 89
Amnesty International, 28, 104, 126, 132
Asylum Procedures Directive, 5, 8, 26, 74, 91, 119, 145, 154

B
Biometrics, 24
Border control, 11, 22–24, 29, 34, 36, 40–41, 78–79, 94, 107–108, 137

C
Common European Asylum System, 2–3, 8, 16, 20, 33, 45, 81, 96–97, 107, 112, 135, 144, 151, 153–155
Closer cooperation, 24
Convention against Torture, 23, 25, 29, 37, 44

D
Deportation, 28–29
Dublin
- Convention, 3, 27, 36, 75, 108, 113–114
- III Proposal, 117–118, 122, 136
- II Regulation, 3, 24–27, 36, 41, 66, 111–112, 114–115, 117, 120, 126, 135–136
- System, 3–7, 8–10, 66, 75, 111–117, 120, 122, 135, 140, 155

E
ECRE, 6–7, 39, 86–87, 89, 91, 112, 135–137
Elgafaji case, 5, 18, 68, 121–122, 146, 151
EU Charter of Fundamental Rights, 8, 11, 23, 35, 87, 101–102, 106–107, 149
European Asylum Support Office, 8, 10, 17, 69, 81, 96–97, 118, 136, 146, 148, 155
Expulsion, 7, 21, 27–30, 36, 38, 56, 60, 73–75, 78, 80, 86–92, 94, 96, 107

F
Frontex, 11, 17, 23–24, 33–34, 42, 81, 96–97, 99–102, 108, 119

G
Good faith, 38–39, 48–49, 52–56, 58, 60

H
Hague Programme, 64, 83, 116 118, 120, 125, 144, 154
Harmonisation, 2, 4–5, 8, 17, 27, 67–68, 74–77, 80, 82, 109, 112, 117, 122, 135, 140–148, 151–155
Human Rights Committee, 28, 30, 32, 37, 41–42

I
Influx, 16, 152
International maritime law, 29, 32

F. A. N. J. Goudappel and H. S. Raulus (eds.), *The future of asylum in the European Union*, DOI: 10.1007/978-90-6704-802-6,

M
Minimum standards, 8, 44, 60, 65, 85, 118, 140, 151, 153–154

P
Post-departure, 45–46, 48–50, 53, 59

Q
Qualification Directive, 5–6, 8, 11, 17–18, 44–46, 48–49, 53–54, 57–63, 67–68, 84, 119–122, 140–150, 152–154

R
Reasoned Decision, 131
Reception Conditions Directive, 5, 8–9, 60, 66, 112, 117, 136, 144, 153–154
Refoulement, 2, 4, 7–8, 12–13, 22–23, 25, 29–30, 33, 35, 37–38, 40–41, 55, 60, 81, 84, 97–98, 107, 127, 132, 137, 146, 148–149, 151
Regional protection programmes, 13, 18, 70
Resettlement, 17–19, 70–71
RSD Handbook, 2, 4, 39, 45–46, 48, 126, 130, 132

S
Safe third countries, 26, 35–36, 144
Schengen Borders Code, 33–34, 36, 41, 86, 98
Stateless persons, 11, 30, 44, 51, 62, 121
Stockholm Programme, 3, 12–13, 17, 20, 62, 73, 76, 78–83, 99, 101, 106–107, 118, 141, 148, 154–155

T
Tampere Programme, 16–17, 44, 74, 79–80, 135
Third pillar, 27

U
Unauthorized entry, 22, 37
UNHCR, 2, 9–10, 17, 20, 23, 27–28, 32, 34–35, 38, 41, 46, 50, 54, 56–57, 60–61, 66–71, 76, 84, 112, 128, 135

MIX
Papier aus verantwortungsvollen Quellen
Paper from responsible sources
FSC® C105338

If you have any concerns about our products,
you can contact us on
ProductSafety@springernature.com

In case Publisher is established outside the EU,
the EU authorized representative is:
Springer Nature Customer Service Center GmbH
Europaplatz 3, 69115 Heidelberg, Germany

Printed by Libri Plureos GmbH
in Hamburg, Germany